AF739486

Migration and Development in Africa

African Migration and Diaspora

Series Editor: John A. Arthur, University of Minnesota,
Duluth and Mary Setrana, University of Ghana

Migration is transforming the socioeconomic, political, and cultural landscapes of Africa. For a growing number of Africans, migration has become the vehicle for establishing interconnections with the international community. Migration is a poverty-reduction strategy designed to empower Africans and create agencies for self-improvement and community development. Africa and Africans are aspirational actors imbued with energy, talents, and buoyed by rich cultural traditions and heritages that resonate in their migratory profiles.

The African Migration and Diaspora Series is a collection of monographs and edited volumes on contemporary transnational African migration and how these migrations are defining and transforming African societies. This series accentuates how African immigrants influence and are influenced by their host societies, including a synthesis of how migratory outcomes are played out in the migrant countries of origination. It also builds social, cultural, economic, and political platforms to provide a comprehensive understanding of the importance of migration in Africa's rising.

Recent Titles

Class Formations and Inequality Structures in Contemporary African Migration: Evidence from Ghana by John A. Arthur

Migration and Development in Africa: Trends, Challenges, and Policy Implications edited by Steve Tonah, Mary Setrana, and John A. Arthur

Migration and Development in Africa

Trends, Challenges and Policy Implications

Edited by
Steve Tonah, Mary Boatemaa Setrana, and
John A. Arthur

LEXINGTON BOOKS
Lanham • Boulder • New York • London

Published by Lexington Books
An imprint of The Rowman & Littlefield Publishing Group, Inc.
4501 Forbes Boulevard, Suite 200, Lanham, Maryland 20706
www.rowman.com

Unit A, Whitacre Mews, 26-34 Stannary Street, London SE11 4AB

Copyright © 2017 by Lexington Books

All rights reserved. No part of this book may be reproduced in any form or by any electronic or mechanical means, including information storage and retrieval systems, without written permission from the publisher, except by a reviewer who may quote passages in a review.

British Library Cataloguing in Publication Information Available

Library of Congress Cataloging-in-Publication Data Available

Names: Tonah, Steve, editor. | Setrana, Mary Boatemaa, editor. | Arthur, John A., 1958-2016, editor.
Title: Migration and development in Africa : trends, challenges, and policy implications / edited by Steve Tonah, Mary Boatemaa Setrana, and John A. Arthur.
Description: Lanham : Lexington Books, 2017. | Series: African migration and diaspora | Includes bibliographical references and index.
Identifiers: LCCN 2017026847 (print) | LCCN 2017027795 (ebook) | ISBN 9781498516846 (Electronic) | ISBN 9781498516839 (cloth : alk. paper) | ISBN 9781498516853 (pbk. : alk. paper)
Subjects: LCSH: Africa—Emigration and immigration—Economic aspects. | Europe—Emigration and immigration. | Migration, Internal—Africa. | Return migration—Africa. | Economic development—Africa. | Africa—Economic conditions.
Classification: LCC HB2121.A3 (ebook) | LCC HB2121.A3 M52 2017 (print) | DDC 304.8096—dc23
LC record available at https://lccn.loc.gov/2017026847

Printed in the United States of America

Dedicated to the Memory of
Professor John A. Arthur

Contents

Preface ix

1 Introduction 1
Steve Tonah and Mary Boatemaa Setrana

2 Political Participation Beyond National Borders: The Case of Ghanaian Political Party Branches in the Netherlands 41
Richard Kwabena Owusu Kyei and Mary Boatemaa Setrana

3 Transnational Migration among Migrants from Cameroon 57
Danielle Minteu Kadje

4 Partnering for Rural Development in Ghana: The Case of Ghanaian Hometown Associations in the United Kingdom 69
Leander Kandilige

5 Comparative Analysis of Educational Performance of Children from Migrant and Nonmigrant Households in Ghana 89
Theophilus Kwabena Abutima

6 Brain Drain or Brain Gain? The Contribution of Skilled Migrants to Development in Kenya 107
Jane Mwanji

7 The Repatriation of Destitute Nigerians in Colonial Ghana 125
Omon Merry Osiki

8 From Seasonal Migrants to Settlers: Climate Change and Permanent Migration to the Transitional Zone of Ghana 147
Peter Bilson Obour, Kwadwo Owusu, and Joseph K. Teye

9 Hindered Pathways Toward Development? West African Mobilities and European Borders in the Twenty-first Century 165
Joris Schapendonk

10 Mapping Out the Role of Labor Migrants in Ghana's Oil and Gas Economy 183
Sylvia Esther Gyan and Rabiu K. B. Asante

Index 195

About the Contributors 197

Preface

Mobility and migration are not a new phenomenon in Africa. Africans, just like people elsewhere, have always been on the move. They have moved from their places of abode to different places since the precolonial period till today. What has changed is the nature of the migration, the destinations and the motives for moving from a settlement or territory to the other.

During the precolonial period people usually moved in groups in search of better places of abode, to flee from despotic rulers, and especially, to flee from more powerful neighbors who frequently raided adjacent groups for slaves, war booty and women. The nature and direction of migration on the continent changed during the colonial period as the European colonial powers pacified many regions and introduced new forms of economic activities and infrastructural development. Trading routes changed from the inland regions toward the coastal areas as the colonial powers directed key infrastructural facilities such as rails and road networks toward the coastal towns and capitals. The postcolonial period has been characterized by increased migration resulting from increased population growth and economic activities as well as improved transportation, communication and other infrastructural facilities across the continent. These changes have affected the form and direction of migration on the African continent.

The introduction to this book presents the main trends in African migration since the last two decades. It analyzes the major migration trends, the various migration hubs across the continent and the underlying factors explaining the changing nature of migration across the continent. Besides analyzing migration from a regional and continental perspective, the introductory chapter also explores in some detail the complex relationship between migration and development. A few of the chapters in the book examine the phenomenon of migration from a national perspective by focusing on migration trends in countries such as Ghana, Cameroon, Kenya, and Nigeria. Two chapters examine the migration links between Africa and Europe with one of them focusing on the political links between Ghana and the Netherlands while the other focuses on economic exchanges between the Cameroonian diaspora in Germany and selected groups and organizations in Cameroon.

A major strength of this book is the varied disciplinary perspectives used by the authors in explaining the phenomenon of migration and development in Africa. The authors are specialists in the fields of sociology, anthropology, geography, history, philosophy and migration studies. Examining migration from so many different perspectives enriches the analysis and brings in new insights that would otherwise have been missing with the use of a single disciplinary perspective.

This book would not have been possible without the substantial initial efforts of the late Professor John A. Arthur, of the University of Minnesota, Duluth. It was Prof. Arthur who together with Dr Mary Boatemaa Setrana selected the title of the book, initiated the call for papers, reviewed and edited the first draft of papers that were submitted. Sadly, Prof. Arthur met his untimely death before the manuscript could be completed. The current editors expanded the list of contributors and completed work on the individual manuscripts.

We would like to thank the publishers, Lexington Books, for their trust and confidence. Following Prof. Arthur's passing, they threw the challenge of completing the book to the new editors. We believe we have justified the trust imposed in us by the publishers and wish to express our profound appreciation for the support and look forward to more collaboration in the future.

Steve Tonah and Mary Boatemaa Setrana
Legon, December 2015

Chapter 1

Introduction

Migration and Development in Africa: Trends, Challenges and Policy Implications

Steve Tonah and Mary Boatemaa Setrana

1.0 MOBILITY AND MIGRATION

Mobility and migration have always been an ongoing phenomenon across Africa. People have always moved as groups or individuals from their places of abode and settled at different locations for a short period or, as it often turns out, for a much longer period than intended. Indeed, mobility was part and parcel of many forms of livelihood, including pastoralism, hunters and gatherers and farmers (De Bruijn, Van Dijk and Foeken 2001, Hahn and Klute 2007). While the movement of small groups of people across short and long distances in search of a permanent abode was quite common, mass migration, involving the movement of large numbers of people from one location to the other, was less common and often a result of extraordinary circumstances such as wars among neighboring groups, internecine conflicts, environmental degradation, extreme poverty, ecological disasters, emergence of new trading routes and other economic opportunities (Akabzaa et al. 2010, Christian Aid 2007, Myers 2002).

This introductory chapter has ten sections. We begin by describing our main sources of information and data. The next section provides a brief overview of migration across Africa during the precolonial, colonial and the postindependence period. It is followed by an analysis of contemporary migration within and outside the African continent. The subsequent section explores some new migration configurations, such as irregular migration within and from the continent, human trafficking and forced migration. The next major section examines the complex relationship between migration and development. This includes an analysis of the migration-development debate, and the benefits, consequences and challenges of migration on development in Africa. In the penultimate section, we analyze the policy implications of the diverse forms of migration on the continent and make some recommendations. The final section provides a brief summary of the remaining chapters of the book.

2.0 DATA SOURCES

It is now commonplace to lament about the absence of reliable data and information on African migration. Data in the form of surveys are often not available or where available they are either not reliable or not current since many countries do not conduct such surveys regularly. Such data are also often stacked in offices in their raw form waiting to be analyzed and published. Most of the information presented in this chapter has been obtained from secondary sources, such as books, journal articles, working papers and unpublished conference and workshop papers. We have also benefited from theses, research works, survey data and academic materials from several sources, including the Centre for Migration Studies of the University of Ghana, Legon. Furthermore, this chapter has benefited from data obtained from international organizations such as the International Organization for Migration (IOM), ACP Observatory on Migration, UN Department of Social and Economic Affairs, UNHCR, and other local and international institutions. Primary and secondary data obtained from these institutions were analyzed and have been incorporated into several sections of the chapter.

3.0 MIGRATION IN PRECOLONIAL, COLONIAL AND POSTINDEPENDENCE AFRICA

3.1 Migration in the Precolonial Period

During the precolonial period, the availability of vast unoccupied lands across the African continent provided the impetus for groups of people to move from one location to another in search of better life and to colonize new areas. In many places, leaders of established chiefdoms and kingdoms could not always provide safety and security for their subjects. Flourishing kingdoms and empires such as those of the West African states of Ghana, Mali and Songhai ultimately succumbed to more powerful groups. The effect of such forceful takeovers of existing kingdoms by their more powerful neighbors was often the displacement of large sections of the population (Boahen 1966, Stride and Ifeka 1971). In other places, the demise of commercial activities and trading routes, harsh, exploitative and dictatorial leadership and fratricidal conflicts resulted in large population movements. But above all, it was the practice of slavery, particularly the infamous transatlantic slave trade, involving the raiding of weak, poorly protected and smaller groups by their more powerful neighbors and their subsequent enslavement that accounted for the mass movement of people across and beyond Africa between the sixteenth and nineteenth centuries (Miers and Kopytoff 1977, Stride and Ifeka 1971, Lovejoy 1981).

3.2 The Colonial Era

The colonial period and the subsequent partition of Africa by Western governments initially resulted in the pacification of large sections of the African continent and a partial halt to the forced displacement of people by their more powerful neighbors. The colonial masters that governed the different African states initially instituted measures to prevent people from moving illegally across the newly created national borders as part of attempts to consolidate their hold over their territories. However, the promotion of cash crops such as cocoa, coffee, tea, cotton and sisal, the exploitation of mineral resources such as gold, manganese, diamond and bauxite, and the provision of infrastructural facilities linking the production centers to the coastal ports resulted in the mass migration of labor to the main coastal towns and other centers of economic activities In West Africa, migrant labor moved from the Sahelian countries to the coffee, cocoa and groundnut plantations in Ghana, Senegal, Côte d'Ivoire and Nigeria (Adepoju 2005). Eastern and Southern Africa witnessed the displacement of the indigenous population from their lands and the occupation of such lands by immigrants from Europe and Asia, who took over such lands and established agricultural plantations and ranches. The newly established plantations and mines relied heavily on migrant labor from the region (Johnson and Altbeker 2011).

3.3 The Postindependence Era

The pattern of migration established during the colonial period has been broadly maintained across Africa in the postindependence era. Generally, the main migration pattern involves large numbers of people moving from the inland regions to the coastal towns or to the capitals and major cities. However, new forms of labor migration as well as illegal and irregular forms of migration have since emerged in the postindependence era. During this period the intensity of migration within countries and across the continent has increased considerably. This is mainly a result of urbanization and rural-urban migration. More and more Africans are leaving their settlements for the urban centers and the regional and national capitals. Rural-urban migration and the growth among the urban residents has resulted in the creation of megacities, such as Lagos, Kano, Abidjan, Cairo, Kinshasa, Johannesburg, Nairobi and Addis Ababa across Africa (Elkan 1967, Caldwell 1969, O'Connor 2007).

Intra-country and intracontinental migration still constitute the bulk of most migrations in Africa. Indeed, it is established that most migrations take place within the continent and only a small number of people move overseas. Flahaux and De Haas (2016) estimate that in 2000, African countries had on the average 2.3% of their citizens officially living abroad, down from 2.8% in 1960. Similarly, Abdellatif (2010) indicates that with a total estimated figure of 5,287,911 persons living in the OECD countries in 2000, sub-Saharan African migration to the OECD countries constitutes only a marginal phenomenon. The movement of persons within the continent has been largely facilitated by improvements in regional infrastructure and the establishment of regional organizations, such as ECOWAS, SADC, EAC and COMESA, that have promoted free movements of persons and goods across borders and given some rights of residence to persons from neighboring states (Campbell 2010).

In spite of the existence of numerous regional organizations across Africa, the phenomenon of national governments expelling migrants from their territories has become commonplace. Many African governments have carried out expulsion exercises during periods of economic decline or social upheavals. These include Ghana, Nigeria, Côte d'Ivoire, Sierra Leone, Cameroon, Gabon, Kenya, Sudan, Libya, Algeria, Morocco, Namibia, Botswana and South Africa. In such countries, migrants have been typically accused of taking away jobs from locals or are blamed for worsening societal vices, such as crime, armed robbery, support for opposition parties or rebels, or for simply being different from the indigenous populations (Zoomers and Naerssen 2006, Adepoju 2010, Campbell 2010).

In addition, the postindependence era has also seen the emergence of new forms of migrations. There have been changes in the main migration hubs since the 1960s. Old regional migration hubs have been replaced by new ones while new destinations have emerged. For example, during the 1950s and 1960s, Ghana attracted a lot of the labor migrants from neighboring West African countries, particularly from Mali, Nigeria, Niger and Burkina Faso. In the 1970s and 1980s, Côte d'Ivoire and Nigeria replaced Ghana as the preferred destinations for labor migrants in West Africa (Adepoju 2005, Vollmer, Sert and Icduygu 2015). Other new migration destinations include oil-rich Gabon and Libya for countries in Central and Northern Africa while Kenya and South Africa maintained their positions as the most attractive destinations for migrants in Eastern and Southern Africa, respectively (Johnson and Altbeker 2011, Adepoju 2010).

Furthermore, since independence, there has been a gradual increase in the proportion of Africans overseas, especially in Europe, North America, and more recently in Asia (particularly China). Initially, the migration stream from Africa to Europe followed the country of colonization: Migrants from Anglophone West African countries (especially Nigeria and Ghana) migrated predominantly to the United Kingdom while those from Francophone African countries of Senegal, Mali, Cameroon and Democratic Republic of the Congo (DRC), among others, migrated to France, and to a lesser extent, Belgium. Lusophone migrants from Angola, Mozambique, Guinea Bissau and Cape Verde migrated preferably to Portugal while residents of Southern Africa went in large numbers to the United Kingdom. Most of these migrants during the 1960s and 1970s belonged to the educated elite group. Since the 1970s there has been a change in the composition of African migrants with most of them now consisting of lowly skilled and educated persons. These migrants have also diversified their destinations to include other Western European countries, such as the Netherlands, Germany, Italy and Spain (Flahaux and De Haas 2016). North Africans from Algeria, Morocco and Tunisia moved initially to France but have also subsequently diversified their destinations to include Holland, Germany, Belgium and Italy.

It was not until the 1980s and 1990s that African migration to the United States and Canada began to pick up, almost surpassing those to the traditional European destinations (Loxley, Sackey and Khan 2015). Generally, while African migrations to Europe and North America have increased considerably since independence, there has been a decrease in European immigration to Africa, especially to Northern and Eastern Africa. However, Africa has remained an attractive destination for migrants from the Middle East, India and Lebanon since the 1960s (Akyeampong 2006).

One major consequence of over four decades of African migration to Western Europe, North America and Asia is the (re-)emergence of African diaspora settlements. There are large numbers of Nigerians, Kenyans, Senegalese, Ethiopians, South Africans, Algerians and Moroccans in many Western countries. The African diaspora in China is also growing rapidly.

Another major development since independence is the increasing feminization of migration in Africa. Large numbers of women are leaving their homes permanently either alone or with their children. Some factors accounting for the migration of women include increasing job opportunities for women in the care industry due to demographic transitions in the Global North; enhanced access to education, and loss of jobs for males as a result of national and global economic crises (Adepoju 2010). These driving forces have resulted in social changes that have significant impact on the family. Gender roles and division of labor in the traditional African family system have changed because women are leaving behind their children in the care of their husbands and extended family members. Similarly, female migration has become an important livelihood strategy for the survival of the family as remittances are transferred back home for other purposes (Adepoju 2010).

African migration since independence has shifted from the traditional migration patterns, where migrants departed and returned after a period of sojourn abroad. Through enhanced technological advancement, migrants find it cheaper to liaise with family back home (Vertovec 2009). They communicate with their families and friends, visit home often, participate in the development agenda of the home countries and also adjust to life in their host countries simultaneously (Vertovec 2009).

The next section provides an overview of the book, direction and recent trends in migration within Africa since the last decade. It also examines the key migration policies of a few African countries.

4.0 MIGRATION WITHIN THE AFRICAN CONTINENT

The volume of migration from, to and within each African country can be measured in absolute or relative terms. The former measures the total number of noncitizens or foreign-born individuals who have settled permanently in a particular area/country within a period of time, usually a year while the latter measures the proportion of migrants with respect to the total population in a given area/country within the same time period, which is usually referred to as the intensity of migration (immigration and emigration intensity).

Available data indicate that the total population of migrants in Africa remained relatively stable between 1990 and 2005 and has only surged in the last decade. The total migrant population was 15,690,623 in 1990 and 16,352,814 in 1995. This decreased to 14,800,306 in 2000, increased to 15,191,146 in 2005 and then surged to 16,840,014 in 2010 and to 20,649,557 in 2015. This clearly shows that the migrant population in Africa only increased substantially between 2010 and 2015 (see Table 1.1). In regional terms, West Africa has always had the highest population of migrants. This is followed by Eastern Africa, Southern Africa, Middle Africa and Northern Africa in that order. However, Southern Africa has witnessed the highest increases in the proportion of migrants in the last decade with the total number of migrants rising from 1,439,426 persons in 2005 to 3,435,194 in 2015, an increase of about 138%. The migrant population in Western, Eastern, Middle and Northern Africa only increased by 24%, 29%, 19% and 21%, respectively (see Table 1.1).

The population of migrants is, as expected, unequally distributed among the various countries in each of the five broad subregions in Africa. In West Africa, Côte d'Ivoire, with a total of 2,175,399 international migrants in 2015, had by far the largest number of migrants in both absolute and

Table 1.1 Total Migrant Stock at Mid-Year in Africa by Region (1990–2016)

Region in Africa	*Year*					
	1990	*1995*	*2000*	*2005*	*2010*	*2015*
Eastern	5,964,031	5,022,742	4,844,795	4,745,792	4,657,063	6,129,113
Middle	1,460,530	2,646,108	1,756,687	1,928,828	2,139,979	2,307,688
Northern	2,403,200	2,081,640	1,885,650	1,782,054	1,921,613	2,159,048
Southern	1,392,359	1,191,582	1,222,314	1,439,426	2,203,306	3,435,194
Western	4,470,503	5,410,742	5,090,860	5,295,046	5,918,053	6,618,514
SSA	14,690,319	15,324,570	13,716,539	13,951,086	15,496,764	18,993,986
Africa	15,690,623	16,352,814	14,800,306	15,191,146	16,840,014	20,649,557

Source: UN Department of Economic and Social Affairs (2015)

proportional terms. 26% of the population was international migrants in 1998 (including those born in the country) but this reduced to about 11.2% in 2010 and further down to 9.6% in 2015 mainly due to the civil strife in the country between 2002 and 2009. Nigeria, on the other hand, had only 1,199,115 international migrants in 2015 (about 0.77% of an estimated total population of 156 million) while Burkina Faso had 704,676 migrants (about 3.9% of the estimated population of 18 million). With the exception of Gambia (9.7%) all other countries in the subregion had a comparatively small number of migrants. Côte d'Ivoire therefore remains the most attractive destination in West Africa with most migrants coming from the neighboring countries of Burkina Faso, Mali and Guinea. Most of them work in the agricultural and the services sectors of the economy (UNDESA 2015, IOM 2009, IOM 2015).

In Northern Africa, Libya and Sudan with 771,146 and 503,477 persons, respectively, have the largest number of migrants in the subregion. They are followed by Egypt and Algeria with 491,643 and 242,391 persons, respectively. In 2015, most of the labor migrants in Libya were from Somalia (104,539), Iraq (68,477) and Saudi Arabia (35,474). Those in Sudan, on the other hand, were from Eritrea (159,748), South Sudan (135,558), Chad (74,518) and Ethiopia (60,734). Most of them fled to Sudan in response to conflicts, droughts and civil wars in the region. Generally, in addition to attracting migrants from neighboring African countries (mainly Sudan, Somalia and Western Sahara) Northern African countries had a sizeable number of migrants from the Middle East, mainly from Palestine, Iraq and Saudi Arabia (UNDESA 2015)

In Middle Africa, conflicts and civil wars in Rwanda, Angola, Sudan, South Sudan, Central African Republic and the DRC largely account for most of the international migrants in the region. The DRC with 545,694 persons

Table 1.2 African Countries with High Migrant-Sending Population (1995–2015)

Country	*Year and Population of Emigrants*				
	2015	*2010*	*2005*	*2000*	*1995*
Burkina Faso	1,425,661	1,363,291	1,292,475	1,220,746	1,203,875
Somalia	1,276,600	1,015,331	799,201	745,054	708,529
Congo (DRC)	1,192,697	1,042,390	943,240	470,644	448,034
Sudan	1,190,255	552,453	712,592	489,049	419,086
Mali	902,279	740,091	674,809	665,493	735,081
Côte d'Ivoire	675,031	623,391	566,860	465,706	290,523
Mozambique	628,844	595,684	540,784	549,630	727,897
South Sudan	615,130	385,700	233,443	333,894	430,929
Zimbabwe	603,246	442,484	257,572	225,464	190,903
Uganda	597,176	582,089	457,637	466,080	389,990

Source: UN Department of Economic and Social Affairs (2015)

had the largest number of international migrants in 2015. This is followed by Chad (516,968), Congo (392,996), Cameroon (381,984) and Gabon (268,384). Most migrants from the war-ravaged countries fled to the DRC, Congo, Cameroon and Gabon. Oil-rich Gabon with its relative prosperity has a high proportion of international migrants (15.6% of total population in 2015) and attracts migrants from several regions of Africa (UNDESA 2015).

In Eastern Africa, Kenya, Ethiopia, South Sudan and Uganda (with 1,084,357, 1,072,949, 824,122 and 749,471 persons, respectively) had the largest number of international migrants in the subregion in 2015. The sending countries are mainly Somalia, Sudan, South Sudan, DRC and Uganda (see Table 1.2). Most of them were fleeing conflicts and civil wars in their countries while countries such as Kenya receive both labor migrants (from Uganda and Tanzania) and refugees (from Somalia, South Sudan and Sudan). Ironically, Countries such as the DRC, Uganda, Sudan and South Sudan send and at the same time receive large numbers of refugees from neighboring countries (UNDESA 2015).

South Africa, with 3,142,511 international migrants in 2015, is the most attractive destination in Southern Africa, and indeed the entire African continent. Its immigrant population dwarfs by far those of Botswana (160,664) and Namibia (93,888). Indeed, South Africa attracts large labor migrants, refugees and illegal migrants not only from the neighboring countries of Mozambique, Lesotho, Namibia and Zimbabwe but also from the rest of Africa, Asia (China, India) and Europe (United Kingdom, Germany).

In sum, with the exception of the Maghreb countries (Morocco, Algeria and Tunisia), most migration in Africa is intra-country or intracontinental. Most poor migrants remain within their own countries and they mainly move to the urban towns; only the relatively well-to-do move to neighboring countries (Flahaux and De Haas 2016). A very small proportion of migrants move beyond the African continent, but the number of West and East Africans moving abroad has increased since the 1980s. According to Flahaux and De Haas (2016, 10), "the Maghreb is Africa's emigration region par excellence. This is mainly a result of its geographical proximity to Europe and their strong colonial and post-colonial links to France and the labour recruitment agreements these countries signed with European countries since the 1960s."

There has, however, been a decreasing trend in intracontinental migration between the 1960s and 2000s (Flahaux and De Haas 2016). This means that though still the largest in terms of migration destinations, fewer Africans are moving to other African countries. Wealthy Africans who can afford to move beyond their countries increasingly prefer to go to destinations outside the African continent. Political instability and economic decline during the 1980s and 1990s, as well as the increasing discrimination, xenophobia, expulsions and attacks on migrants have compelled many Africans to seek greener pastures outside the continent.

Table 1.3 Countries with High Population of Migrants from Africa (1995–2015)

Country	*Year*				
	2015	*2010*	*2005*	*2000*	*1995*
State of Palestine	494,396	438,877	395,021	299,868	267,526
United Kingdom	357,929	277,074	192,664	168,755	148,777
France	243,082	225,329	183,695	168,551	152,012
Syria	183,929	40,112	35,584	31,114	28,032
India	103,582	85,976	65,478	54,602	42,241
Germany	77,731	78,722	59,067	53,915	71,869
China	49,332	38,960	32,326	31,874	24,298
Saudi Arabia	56,652	50,834	44,811	38,605	30,625
United States	54,265	45,558	37,369	32,896	40,815
Italy	46,082	36,821	28,336	24,500	29,482
Yemen	32,482	29,046	25,996	22,667	19,942
Lebanon	30,443	27,054	24,238	23,554	22,597
Russia Federation	27,750	23,805	19,102	16,434	30,787
The Netherlands	26,312	20,106	13,986	12,017	15,955

Source: Author's csompilation from UN Department of Economic and Social Affairs (2015)

In spite of this, only an estimated 2.3% of African migrants were officially living outside the continent in 2000. This figure has not changed much since then. However, the proportion of Africans living in Europe and North America has been increasing (see Table 1.3). In addition to European countries with which they have colonial ties, Africans have since the 1980s also moved to new destinations in Western Europe, particularly Holland, Germany and Italy.

5.0 MIGRATION OUTSIDE THE AFRICAN CONTINENT

In this section, we present a brief description of African migration to Europe, North America, the Gulf Cooperation Countries (GCC), China and Latin America.

5.1 Migration to Europe and North America

African migration to Europe began in large numbers during the 1960s. Most of the migrants came from the Maghreb countries of Morocco, Algeria and Tunisia and their main destination was to France, the former colonial power in these countries. This period coincided with an expansion in the industrial economies of Europe with its associated high demand for labor, particularly of the unskilled type. Migrant laborers from the Maghreb countries were therefore welcome in France and other highly industrialized economies of

Europe. Most of the North Africans who went to Europe initially on a temporary basis found it difficult to return home and gradually became permanent residents of France. In the 1970s and 1980s, the destination countries for immigrants from North Africa expanded to include the Netherlands, Belgium, Germany, and much later, Italy and Spain as a result of increased demand for unskilled labor in these countries (De Haas 2008).

Emigration from sub-Saharan African countries, on the other hand, was limited to a few elite persons who went to Europe either because they were part of the local political leadership or went for purposes of trading and to study. In the early 1960s, most of the newly independent African countries sent their citizens to Western European countries to acquire higher education, skills and training required for nation building. The main destinations of migrants from sub-Saharan Africa (SSA) were France, United Kingdom, Portugal, and to a lesser extent, Italy and Spain. Some of the educated elite remained abroad upon the completion of their studies and constituted the first group of African immigrant in these Western European countries (Arthur 2014). Other African countries sent large numbers of young people to study and train in Eastern European countries (East Germany and the former Soviet Union, in particular) in the 1960s and 1970s usually on exchange programs. Some of these graduates ended up as permanent migrants in the various Eastern European countries or later on moved to Western Europe in search of jobs and economic opportunities.

Since the 1980s, largely due to the increasing poverty and the deterioration in the living conditions in most African countries but also due to authoritarian leadership, political instability, civil wars, drought and terrorism, the number of Africans leaving the continent to settle permanently abroad has increased considerably. Between 2000 and 2005 the IOM estimates that 440,000 people emigrated from Africa yearly (IOM 2008). While most North Africans prefer to migrate to Europe, the Middle East and Asia, sub-Saharan Africans tend to move to Europe, North America and China.

Besides the typical Western European destinations, sub-Saharan Africans have since the 1980s migrated in large numbers to the United States and Canada. In 1980, Nigeria, Ghana and Ethiopia with an estimated migrant population of 24,000, 8,000 and 5,000 persons, respectively, constituted nearly 58 percent of the black African population in the United States. During this period, there were very few migrants from the remaining African countries. However, by 1990, the population of black African migrants in the United States rose to 184,000 and then to 574,000 in 2000. By 2009 there were 1,081,000 black Africans in the United States with only about 42% of them coming from the three dominant migrant-sending countries of Nigeria (19%), Ethiopia (13%) and Ghana (10%). By 2009, a number of African countries, including Kenya, Somalia, Liberia, Sudan, Sierra Leone and Cameroon had joined the migration trail and began sending migrants to the United States (Capps, McCabe and Fix 2012). However, in comparison with migrants from Europe and Latin America, the proportion of African immigrants in the United States is small. By 2010 only 1.5 million Africans, that is 4% of the total of 38 million immigrants, were in the United States. Only about 100,000 Africans come to the United States yearly (Capps, McCabe and Fix 2012).

Africans in the United States are mainly legal permanent residents, naturalized US citizens or refugees. Most of them enter as students to reunite with family members already domiciled in the United States, by way of the diversity lottery visa or as displaced or stateless persons. According to Arthur (2014), African immigrants in the United States can be broadly categorized into two main groups. The first consists of the so-called "underclass" who are often poorly educated and sell African immigrant wares or work as taxi drivers, custodians and janitors or other menial jobs. The second group consists mainly of persons from the "middle class and the elite." They are highly educated or professionally trained and work as lecturers, medical doctors and health professionals, engineers and in other skilled professions (Arthur 2014).

Canada, on the other hand, has become an important destination for African immigrants only since the 1980s. There is a growing presence of Africans in that country and according to Loxley, Sackey and Khan (2015, 4) "the share of landed immigrants in Canada from Africa has more than doubled from an annual average of five per cent in the 1980s to currently over ten per cent." In 2011 many more Africans settled in Canada than those from Europe, Latin America, the Caribbean and South America. While in 2006 there were 342,325 African immigrants in Canada, by 2011 the figure had shot up to 447,135, an increase of 31% over the five-year period (Loxley, Sackey and Khan 2015). Most of the African immigrants for 2011 came from North Africa (37.4%), East Africa (32.1%) and West Africa (15.1%) with a small proportion from Central (6.5%) and Southern Africa (8.9%). At least one third of African immigrants in Canada hold a bachelor's degree, suggesting a high brain drain in Africa (Loxley, Sackey and Khan 2015).

5.2 Migration to Fast-Growing Economies

In the last decade or more, many more Africans are seeking greener pastures in fast-growing countries in Asia (mainly India and China), the Gulf Cooperation Countries (GCC) (Emirates, Saudi Arabia) and Latin America (Argentina and Brazil) because of the rapid progress made by these newly industrializing countries. Most of the African immigrants in India, Bangladesh and the GCC are from North Africa. The African migrant population in India and China has risen sharply in the last decade while the number of those moving to Brazil and Argentina is picking up quickly from low levels (Zoomers and Naerssen 2006).

The GCC, on the other hand, have turned to African countries in their quest to fill their labor shortages in sectors such as health, construction and other service-based jobs ahead of the Emirate Expo in 2020, the 2022 World Cup in Qatar and other significant development projects. Professionals and non-skilled temporary labor from Africa have recently been in high demand in the GCC, partly to replace the shortfall in recruitment from Asian countries. Health workers, mainly nurses and doctors, as well as low-skilled workers such as domestic and sex workers, construction laborers, miners, cleaners, security officers and taxi drivers are among persons regularly recruited to work in the GCC. Ghana and Nigerian doctors are in high demand in Saudi Arabia while Kenyans, Ethiopians and Somalis move regularly across the Gulf of Aden to the Middle Eastern countries (Zoomers and Naerssen 2006, Malit and Youha 2016).

A unique feature of labor migration to the GCC is that it is often contract based. Migrants are not encouraged to settle permanently and they enjoy no right of family reunification. In recent times, there have been reports of abuse and maltreatment of migrant workers, especially women in the GCC, resulting in some African countries discouraging or placing a ban on the movement of their citizens to the Gulf region (Malit and Youha 2016, Van Moppes 2006, Broekhuis 2006).

5.3 African Migration to China

According to Wyatt (2010) a small number of people of African origin were already living in Guangzhou, the capital of the Guangdong Province, in the 11th century. Similarly, Bodomo (2012) traces the earliest contact between Africans and Chinese to the travels of Admiral Zheng during the Ming Dynasty (1368–1644) to the East African coast for trading purposes in 1402. However, not much is known about these early contacts between the two peoples and specifically about such early African migrants in China.

African presence in China since the 1960s is associated with the large numbers of diplomats as well as African students, professionals and military personnel who were domiciled or trained in China during this period. Most of them, however, returned home after the completion of their duty tours or courses/training. The rise of African enclaves in Guangzhou is a new phenomenon dating back to the late 1970s following the social and economic reforms that created Special Economic Zones in the province. The city of Guangzhou and the surrounding areas are host to a number of migrants, middlemen and traders from different African countries who have moved to China as a result of the Asian financial crisis and to take advantage of the economic opportunities offered by that country (Bodomo 2010, Bodomo 2012, Haugen 2012, Lan 2014). In addition to trading, said to account for nearly 80% of the economic activities of Africans in China, many African migrants have established factories, or are working as teachers, travel guides, translators, athletes, students and artists of all categories.

There are no official statistics on the size of the African immigrant population in Guangzhou or China. Bodomo (2012) estimates the number of Africans in Guangzhou at more than 100,000 but the Chinese state media commonly report that as many as 130,000 African immigrants were registered as residents of Guangzhou alone in 2008 with another 60,000 staying in the city's hotels in 2007. This figure excludes undocumented immigrants and itinerant traders lodging in informal guesthouses (Haugen 2012). Cissé (2013, 20) claims that "this overall number remains insignificant compared to the rest of Africans present in other Chinese cities for study, work and business purpose."

The African migrant population in Guangzhou is very diverse and almost all African countries are represented. Nigerians are the most dominant group but there are also large numbers from Senegal, Mali, Guinea and Ghana. African migrants can be commonly found in two neighborhoods: the Xiaobei area where most of the French-speaking Muslims gather and the Sanyuanli area dominated by the English-speaking Christians (Lan 2014). Another area of African immigrant presence is in Dongguan, Southern China where African traders sell Chinese manufactured products to African merchants. Currently, Yiwu in Eastern China which is said to be the "warehouse" of Chinese manufactured products is slowly overtaking Guangzhou in terms of African presence in China (Bodomo 2010, Bodomo and Ma 2010, Cissé 2013). In Yiwu, there are more North African migrants (from Mauritania, Morocco, Egypt, Libya, Tunisia and Algeria), mainly persons who studied in Chinese institutions and decided to reside permanently there to be engaged in the foreign-trade business. There is, moreover, African presence also in Shanghai, Beijing, Chongqing, Tianjin and in major towns across mainland China.

A small number of Africans live in Hong Kong (about 200 persons) and Macau (about 1000 persons). Those in Hong Kong are mainly white South Africans, while Portuguese-speaking Africans from Cape Verde, Angola, Mozambique and Guinea Bissau dominate in Macau. Indeed, Bodomo (2012, 186) argues that the African community in Macau is "the most established and the most organized African community in China." Generally, the African migrant community in China is still in the early stages of community formation.

6.0 NEW MIGRATION CONFIGURATIONS

6.1 Irregular Migration

Although most migrations from Africa abroad actually proceed legally and follow the normal travelling procedures and regulations, irregular migration has also become common in recent times. Irregular migration from Africa typically occurs when migrants decide to stay beyond the period stipulated in their visas or use fake documents to travel and stay in their destinations. Contrary to common perceptions, most irregular migrants from Africa to Europe are well educated and able to afford the considerable cost of the journey to Europe. Others typically obtain visas to one country and then cross over by land into another country, usually one with a restrictive visa policy (De Haas 2008). The Pew Hispanic Centre estimates that in 2007 there were about 200,000 unauthorized black Africans residing in the United States, that is, about 21% of all black African migrants in that country (see Capps, McCabe and Fix 2012). Similarly, a BBC report in 2007 quotes a Migration Policy Institute data indicating that approximately between seven and eight million irregular migrants from Africa live in the European Union (BBC News, July 2, 2007).

The phenomenon of irregular migration has become topical since the 2000s following the increasing numbers of migrants crossing the Mediterranean Sea from Northern African countries and Turkey. Migration routes from Africa to Europe are becoming numerous, expensive and increasingly riskier. Following restrictive immigration policies adopted by many European and North American countries, several new transition zones and migration hubs have arisen between the places of origin and the destinations (Van Moppes 2006). Cities along the Saharan routes (such as Agadez, Tamanrasset, Seguedine, Arlit, Assamaka and Gatroun) and those with boat and flight connections to Europe (such as Guessan, Tangier, Tobruk and Bizerte) have become locations for persons specializing in the illegal transport of African migrants to Southern Europe (DRF 2016). Departing from coastal locations in Morocco, Algeria and Libya, African migrants hope to reach the Canary Islands, especially Fuerteventura, the Spanish enclaves of Ceuta and Melilla, Malta, Lampedusa, Sicily and coastal Italy. Following the civil war in Syria, African migrants have also joined the exodus through Turkey, Greece and the Balkan states with the hope of reaching Western and Northern Europe (DRF 2016).

Data on irregular migration across the Mediterranean Sea from North Africa to Southern Europe are uncoordinated. However, available data indicate that there is an increase in the number of West Africans attempting the risky journey by boat. For example, between January and June 2016, nearly

17% of all such arrivals in Italy were Nigerians while Côte d'Ivoire, Guinea and Senegalese nationals constituted 7%, 7% and 6%, respectively, of arrivals in that country. This was an increase of 54% for Nigerians and 42% for Senegalese when compared to the same period in 2015 (DRF 2016).

6.2 Human Trafficking

Trafficking involves the recruitment, transportation, transfer, harboring or receipt of persons by means of threat, adoption, fraud or deceit, and for payment by an intermediary (ILO 2003a). Human trafficking takes place both within and outside the African continent. Such trafficking usually involves young boys and girls as well as adult females who are enticed with promises of obtaining employment and lucrative remunerations in their destination areas only for them to end up working as child laborers on farms, fishing enterprises and other menial jobs. The girls and women often end up in brothels as sex workers. As a result of its illegal nature, it is difficult to get accurate data and information about human trafficking (ILO 2003b).

According to Sawadogo (2012), poverty, the desire of young people for emancipative adventure and negative cultural practices account for the expansion of human trafficking in West Africa. He argues that the practice of placing children outside their biological family so as to secure a good education and working opportunities and parents' ignorance of the risks involved in entrusting their children to extended family, tribesmen and religious groups contribute inexorably to the growth of transnational trafficking of persons.

The recruitment of boys and girls for menial work by false pretenses is a common phenomenon in most African countries. In West Africa, Côte d'Ivoire is the main destination for trafficked children from Mali, Burkina Faso and Togo, who work as forced labor on the country's plantations (Adepoju 2005, Troung 2006). About 330,000 children were employed on cocoa farms throughout West Africa. In Côte d'Ivoire, around 12,000 children working on cocoa farms were recruited by intermediaries and had no relations whatsoever with the owner of the farm (Onuoha 2013, IITA 2002, Sawadogo 2012). Gabon, Mauritania, Sudan and South Africa are also well-known destinations for human trafficking in Africa. Trafficked victims are engaged as sex workers and sex slaves, or work in bars, hotels and brothels, while some also work under hazardous conditions in factories, fishing communities, mines and construction sites (De Haas 2006, Onuoha 2013).

Since the 1990s, women from African countries such as Ghana, Nigeria, Cameroon and many others have been recruited to the Middle East and Europe ostensibly for the purposes of providing them with employment as housemaids and domestic servants but have invariably ended up as sex slaves in private homes or commercial sex workers or for pornography. Women from West and East Africa are regularly recruited for domestic work in Saudi Arabia, Kuwait, United Arab Emirates and Lebanon as domestic servants but end up having to offer sexual services to their employers in addition (Gikuru 2013). According to Adepoju (2010), women are trafficked from Ethiopia, Uganda, Kenya and Nigeria with promises of good jobs and are subsequently coerced into commercial sex work and pornography in Italy, Germany, Spain, France, the United Kingdom and the Netherlands. An estimated 10,000 Nigerian women are reported to be working as sex workers in Italy (De Haas 2006, NAPTIP 2009, Onuoha 2013). There are also reports of international trafficking of young women to South Africa from neighboring countries (IOM 2008, Troung 2006).

6.3 Conflicts, Refugees and Displaced Populations

Conflicts are the bane of social and economic development in Africa. The sources of these conflicts are varied, ranging from internecine wars, ethnic and communal clashes, insurgencies and terrorism, political repression and threats on political opponents, to mention only a few. There are also reports of frequent malnutrition, hunger and disease as a result of drought, failing crop harvests, and other natural and man-made disasters. The impact of these afflictions is the high and growing numbers of refugees and internally displaced persons (IDPs) on the continent. Refugees can be defined as people who have fled their country to another territory in search of safety from war, repression and other catastrophes. IDPs, on the other hand, are persons who have been forced for one reason or another to leave their place of residence to another place within the same country. According to the UNHCR (2016), SSA hosted about 4.4 million refugees, while the continent hosted 29% of the world's displaced persons in 2015. Most of the refugee population in Africa comes from Somalia, South Sudan, Central Africa Republic (CAR), Burundi and Nigeria.

Somalia has the largest refugee crisis in Africa and the third largest worldwide (UNHCR 2015b, 2016). The country has been engulfed by fratricidal conflicts since 1991. Clan and inter-ethnic fighting have resulted in the over 1.1 million Somali refugees in neighboring Ethiopia, Kenya and Djibouti while others have gone abroad. In South Sudan, since December 2013 conflict has displaced over one million people from their homes into neighboring regions of Jonglei and Upper Nile and to neighboring Ethiopia (mainly Ogaden) and Sudan. In the CAR, armed conflicts between Seleka rebels and anti-Balaka militia since March 2013 have resulted in more than 415,000 persons becoming internally displaced while over 900,978 persons have fled across the border into Cameroon, Chad, the DRC and the Republic of Congo.

In Darfur and neighboring regions of Sudan, ongoing fighting between the government and different militia groups is reported to have killed over 300,000 persons and forced thousands of persons across the border to Chad and the CAR (UNHCR 2015a, 2016).

The Great Lakes region has become synonymous with violent conflicts, killings, looting and burning of settlements, and IDPs and refugees. Rwanda, Burundi and Eastern DRC are all receiving refugees from their neighbors but they are also the source of refugees as militias and rebel groups are given security in one country and engage in cross-border raids into neighboring regions. The region has not known peace for more than three decades (Khadiagala 2006).

West Africa has its fair share of conflicts, refugees and IDPs. Although violent conflicts in Sierra Leone, Liberia and Côte d'Ivoire appear to have abated, they have flared up in other parts of the subregion. Currently, fighting between Boko Haram insurgents in North-Eastern Nigeria has engulfed countries in the Lake Chad region (Nigeria, Niger, Cameroon and Chad). Nigeria has over 2.2 million IDPs and over 200,000 refugees in neighboring countries, while the Diffa region of Niger has over 241,000 IDPs and thousands of refugees (DRF 2016, UNHCR 2016). Similarly, Mali, Niger and Chad are currently battling Tuareg rebels and Al Qaeda-backed rebel groups in the Sahel. For example, in December 2012, the National Movement for the Liberation of Azawad (NMLA) seized a large Malian territory and declared it independent of the central government. The rebels were expelled with the assistance of foreign troops sending thousands fleeing for their lives (Sawadogo 2012).

Finally, in North Africa, Egypt, Tunisia and Algeria are engaged in unending low-intensity battles with rebels and terrorist groups, while there is an ongoing war in Libya between government troops and several rebel groups and with the ensuing chaos the country has become a source and destination for refugees and migrants from Africa (ACLED 2014).

7.0 MIGRATION AND DEVELOPMENT: THE COMPLEX RELATIONSHIP

Within the migration literature, only a few scholars have highlighted the theoretical underpinnings surrounding migration and development (see De Haas 2010, Bakewell 2012, Faist 2008). Dwelling on these discussions, this section deliberates on the influence of such debates on migration and development in Africa. In recent times, the linkage between migration and development has received much attention in international and academic discourses (Bakewell 2012). However, the complex nature of this relationship has attracted a multidisciplinary approach to its study, resulting in a lack of consensus building on the direction of its impact (De Haas 2010).

Among the earlier discourses was the position of the optimists on the relationship between migration and development. This viewpoint discussed the impact of migration on development in the light of remittance inflows and return migration (De Haas 2010). They explained development as a process emanating from the movement from a less endowed area, country or continent to a more developed region, country or continent. They attributed economic growth to the movement of people from rural to urban areas or migration from a developing to a developed country (De Haas 2010). Hence, African countries were expected to boost their national economies and modernize with the experience or knowledge acquired by their citizens and remittances sent from abroad (Kindleberger 1965). Remittances sent back to the origin country were expected to improve the livelihoods of left behind families while return migration brought changes and innovation to the place of origin (Cerase 1970). Migrants' investment generated jobs and return migrants arrived with ideas, knowledge and capital which contributed to the development of African countries.

On the other hand, in the 1960s, the pessimistic view challenged the optimistic view on the positive impact of migration on development (De Haas 2010, Aggarwal, Demirgüç-Kunt and Peria 2006). Migration was seen as resulting from the underdevelopment of African countries because there was a decrease in rural production and an increase in levels of inequality (Lipton 1980). The pessimists argued that the increasing inequality in development around that period was due to migration. Many African countries were faced with the challenges of brain and brawn drain. African governments expressed concern about the migration of their skilled, educated and trained personnel abroad (Baldwin 1970).

Scholars such as Adepoju and Wiel (2010), Adepoju, Naerssen and Zoomers (2008), Oucho (2008) and Manuh (2005) writing on migration and development in Africa also highlighted similar concerns. Rural communities, they argued, lost able-bodied youth who worked on the farms to increase agricultural production which has always been the backbone of many African countries. Some studies, for example, Ratha and Mohapatra (2011), Adams (2006) and Quartey (2006), also contend that remittances to African countries are invested in unproductive activities, such as food, housing, medical bills and financing the travel expenses of other family members, resulting in high inflation. Similarly, others have also emphasized that remittances from migrants end up replacing the traditional local production since migrants import items which are mostly not produced in the country of origin (De Haas 2010).

Based on their empirical and policy evidence, the pessimists challenged the view that migration had a positive impact on development in sending communities. They conclude that investments by migrants rather weaken home country national economies, increase their dependency, strengthen the host country economies and further widen the inequality gap between the host and home countries (De Haas 2010, Ghosh 2006).

Following these discourses, De Haas (2010) argues that both the optimistic and pessimistic views are unidirectional in their line of argument on migration and development. He opines that:

> The fundamental question is . . . not whether migration has either positive or negative developmental impacts, but why migration has contributed to development in some communities and much less, or even negatively, in others (Ghosh 1992,432, Taylor 1999) and what factors explain this differentiation. Furthermore, impacts often change with the different stages of the migration process (Jones 1998, Lucas 1987). Hence, we need to better understand the geographically differentiated and socially disparate nature of migration and remittance impacts as well as how these impacts change over time. (De Haas 2007)

Indeed, migration has been an enduring part of African history, taking different shapes through the precolonial to postindependence periods. The impact of migration on African countries is diverse, with some reaping the benefits while others are not. Some of these differences have been transformed overtime while others have stayed unchanged. These have compelled international organizations, governments and civil society organizations to provide diverse suggestions to the management of migration in Africa (Bakewell 2012, Oucho 2008). International organizations and governments have realized that managing migration through strategic policies has adverse effects on the involvement of migrants and their households in the development agenda of the country (De Haas 2010). On the other hand, if migration is not managed well, there are bound to be negative consequences.

8.0 BENEFITS, CONSEQUENCES AND CHALLENGES OF MIGRATION ON DEVELOPMENT IN AFRICA

8.1 Remittances

Remittances are a crucial external source of funding in developing countries (Adam 2006). They are estimated to be three times the size of the Overseas Development Aid and second to Foreign Direct Investment in developing countries. They are an important source of foreign exchange and savings to developing countries. The World Bank (WB) estimates the world remittance inflows as exceeding $601 billion in 2015. Out of this amount developing countries received as much as US$441 billion, accounting for 10% of the

Table 1.4 Migrant Remittances to Africa in 2014

Regions	*Inflows of Migrant Remittances (Millions of US$) 2014*
Eastern Africa	4, 590.6
Middle Africa	315.3
Northern Africa	31, 339.9
Southern Africa	1, 585.1
Western Africa	25, 984.4
Total for Africa	63, 815.3

Source: UNDESA (2016)

gross domestic product (GDP) in about 25 developing countries (WB 2016). The Middle East and North Africa (MENA) region alone receives 51.7% (showing an increase from 48.8% in 2013 and 50.9% in 2014) while SSA records about 34.8% (showing a slight increase from 33.2% in 2013 to 34.5% in 2014). Nigeria (US$20.8bn) and Egypt (US$20.4bn) are among the top ten remittance-receiving countries worldwide. Compared to the statistics a decade ago, the number of recipients of international remittances in Africa has diversified, but according to Oucho (2008, 53) "even the much-touted North-to-Africa remittances benefit only a few African countries, namely those with well-established connections with destination countries in the Global North."

In 2014, the total remittance inflow to Africa was US$63,815.3 million. Northern Africa received the highest remittances with an amount of US$31,339.9 million, followed by Western Africa. Middle African countries received a minimum of about US$315.3 million (see Table 1.4). Generally, there has been a decline in remittances to Africa over the last decade. These reductions, according to the WB, are a result of several factors, including the effect of the world's economic crises in the main remittance-source countries, lower prices of crude oil, devaluation of countries' currencies due to shortage of foreign currencies, lower exchange rates in the black market which prevents migrants from using the formal channels of remittance transfers and the depreciation of the euro against the US dollar (WB 2016).

Trends in remittance flows indicate that international migrant households receive higher amounts of remittances than internal migrant households, while male migrants remit higher amounts than their female counterparts (Adepoju and Wiel 2010). Males remit US$1,446 compared to US$878 sent by female migrants (Mohapatra and Ratha 2011) while on average, African migrants send about US$1,268 a year (Bollard, McKenzie and Morten 2010). This amount is estimated to be more than the average annual per capita income of many African countries (Mohapatra and Ratha 2011).

Studies have shown that African migrants invest mainly in housing and land purchases. Remittances are also invested in health, education, businesses, farming and agricultural equipment, purchasing of land and used as a form of insurance for unforeseen circumstances in migrant households. At the household level, remittances are used for everyday expenses (ACP 2011) and have been identified to reduce the depth of poverty in developing countries. Several studies (see Adams 1991, Adams and Cuechueche 2010, and Anyanwu and Erhijakpour 2010) have supported this assertion that remittances increase household income, thereby reducing the severity of poverty. According to Adams and Page (2005), on average, a 10% increase in the share of international migrants in a country's population will lead to 2.1% decline in the share of people living on less than US$1.00 per day.

In some African countries, empirical evidence indicates that remittances have been used to improve human capital through investment in education (see chapter 5, in this book). The number of school attendees and extent of enrolment have increased due to inflows of remittances to households in the home country (Mohapatra and Ratha 2011). In other studies, there is evidence that households receiving remittances have better health outcomes because the money is used for paying medical bills and health care services and purchasing food (Mohapatra and Ratha 2011). Writing on the impact of remittances, Mohapatra and Ratha (2011) established that migrant households' vulnerability to risks such as drought, famine and accidents is cared for using remittances. Studies undertaken by Quartey (2006) and Mohapatra and Ratha (2011) have also recognized that migrant households make savings with financial institutions as a strategy to overcome difficulties in life. Remittances serve as social security in most African households due to the absence of state welfare services. In times of political or economic instability, remittances help to reduce the impact of such circumstances (Kapur 2004).

Despite these important benefits of remittances, pessimists have argued that the flow of remittances to developing countries has its negative consequences. Some authors claim that remittance inflows lead to a high rate of dependency and inequality within households in the receiving country. Able-bodied household members may refuse to work since remittances may be sent at some particular intervals (Mohapatra and Ratha 2011). Again, such negative arguments dwell on the fact that remittances breed inequalities between migrant and nonmigrant households as well as internal and international migrant households (Adams and Page 2005). While migrants receive extra income through remittances to supplement household incomes, nonmigrant households may lack such benefits. On the other hand, remittances may negatively affect local economies as migrants introduce foreign goods and people develop preference for them to the detriment of local goods (Mohapatra and Ratha 2011, De Haas 2010).

Another aspect of remittances that has received less attention in the literature is social remittances. These are transfer of knowledge, skills, ideas, values and expertise by migrants to their countries of origin (Levit 1998).

Migrants abroad acquire new skills, knowledge, norms and values which help them to function in various capacities upon return to the home country. Such attitudes and values include work ethics, values on political ideologies and participation and professional network, and skills which are useful for reintegrating into the social and economic milieu of the home country (Setrana and Tonah 2016). Some studies on the continent have shown that some African returnees are highly skilled and are endowed with skills which are useful for the development agenda of their countries (see Anarfi, Kwankye and Ahiadeke 2005, De Vreyer, Gubert and Robilliard 2009). For instance, migration has empowered and emancipated women by giving them the opportunity to play an active part in negotiating their roles, rights and responsibilities across borders as well as assimilating them into their respective destination societies (Adepoju and Wiel 2010, De Haas 2007).

8.2 Brain Drain, Brain Gain and Brain Circulation

The migration of educated persons from their countries of origin to foreign countries for better opportunities is referred to as brain drain. Oucho (2008) contends that some authors in an attempt to qualify the magnitude of the effect of the concept have used terms such as "highly skilled," "skilled," "the skilled," "professionals" and "trained or talented individuals." Reasons for these terminologies have been enlisted to include "people who have worked their way up the corporate ladder, those with their own successful businesses, those with critical role in the public sector, degree holders and/ or those with extensive experience in a given field" (Oucho 2008).

Brain drain has raised several concerns among African governments because about 40% of Africa's top professionals live abroad (UNESCO 2004). Labor migration accounts for a significant proportion of international migration (De Haas 2008). Between 1985 and 1990, Africa lost 60,000 doctors, university lecturers and engineers (UNESCO 2004). One out of every nine tertiary-educated persons born in Africa lives in OECD countries and in other countries, women with tertiary education living outside their home countries outnumber men (OECD-UNDESA 2013). Data from the Republic of Congo, Sierra Leone and Togo stress the fact that women with tertiary education living outside these countries were as high as 10% in 2010/2011 (OECD-UNDESA 2013). The Pacific Island and SSA are the leading regions with high levels of emigration of health professionals (13%), followed by Latin America, the Caribbean Islands (11%), the MENA (10%) (WHO 2006, Serour 2009). Health professionals are among workers with a high rate of emigration (Teye, Setrana and Acheampong 2014). About 30,000 nurses and midwives educated in SSA are employed in the developed countries (WHO 2006). It is estimated that about 56% of doctors and 24% of nurses trained in Ghana are working in developed countries, mainly in Europe and North America (Anarfi, Quartey and Agyei 2010). African professionals represent a loss of $184,000 to Africa (Oyowe 1996). It is therefore not surprising that many African countries have very poor development indicators, such as poor health indicators.

Some African scholars (Manuh, Asante and Djangmah 2005, Oucho 2008, Teye, Setrana and Acheampong 2014) view brain drain as the "draining" of the highly skilled by developed countries. These movements lead to a vicious cycle of poverty in many African countries since people whose education have been financed by the taxpayers' monies, or limited resources in developing countries end up migrating elsewhere. The continent loses an amount of US$4 million every year on hiring consultants and expatriates (Oduba 2000 cited in Benedict and Upkere 2012). According to Benedict and Upkere (2012) a country does lose not only the benefits associated with tapping the knowledge of these experts at the appropriate institutions but also potential taxpayers' contribution and even spend money to import expatriates to fill certain skill gaps.

On the other hand, some arguments following the optimist line of thought describe "brain drain" as a consequence of underdevelopment in African countries. The lack of equipment, high unemployment rate, poor infrastructural facilities and low wages, among others, are said to be the main reasons explaining the movement of skilled persons from the continent for better opportunities elsewhere (Lowell and Findlay 2002, Mugimu 2010). In this respect, the benefits of brain drain are gained through remittances, while the level of unemployment is reduced in the home country through the export of "excess labor" to developed countries (De Haas 2007).

Despite these divergent views, there is a general consensus in the literature, that both pull and push factors are the causes of brain drain. The push factors are the factors that drive skilled professionals to leave their country of origin. These factors include the poor educational system, poor institutional factors, inadequate human resources management, unconducive political factors and trafficking of intellectuals, among others (Benedict and Upkere 2012). On the other hand, the pull factors are those factors that attract skilled professionals to the country of destination. The pull factors include better wages, availability of infrastructure, job opportunities, better wages, similar educational systems and suitable environment, among others. In fact, governments of advanced countries are themselves instituting policies to attract the best brains from developing countries through either the diversity lottery visa or point system (Mugimu 2010). For example, in the United States there is the diversity lottery visa system while Australia and the United Kingdom recruit highly skilled professionals through the point system.

Manuh, Asante and Djangmah (2005), in theorizing about brain drain versus brain gain, identified a third perspective that suggests that brain drain benefits no country, be it the host or home country. This argument drifts away from the optimistic, deterministic explanation of brain drain. Sako (2002, 27) explains that most potential labor migrants to Western countries find themselves in low-paid jobs despite their level of education. Such downgrading and mismatching of skills accrue just a limited amount of money to the migrant thereby affecting the quantum of remittance flows to the home country.

Several attempts have been made to reverse the brain drain to a brain gain. African governments have adopted various programs and policies to engage their diaspora in the development of their countries. Increasing advancement in technology has made communication cheaper and movement easier than before, thereby encouraging "brain circulation," instead of the traditional unidirectional flow of migration and skills. Through such advancement in technology, migrants' associations (such as ethnic and hometown associations), churches and political party external branches provide diverse support to the country of origin (Setrana and Kyei 2015). Migrant associations contribute to the socioeconomic development of rural communities in the home country through the establishment of educational fund, provision of health facilities and professionals, schools and job creation, among others (Akologo 2005, Mohamoud 2010, see also chapter 4 in this book). Similar projects are implemented by African-emigrant churches abroad. These churches support their counterparts in Africa to establish schools and set up educational fund (Mensah 2009, Tonah 2007). Trust plays a critical role in the negotiation and implementation of development projects by diaspora associations in their countries of origin (Akologo 2005, Alhassan 2010).

Diaspora engagement through external branches of political parties enables African emigrants to contribute to political stability, the development of democracy and the rule of law on the continent (Setrana and Kyei 2015). Through the external party branch exchanges, brains are "gained and transferred" through the sharing of political ideas between emigrants and local residents (Setrana and Kyei 2015).

Brains are also gained and circulated through the transfer of knowledge by the diaspora to some specific sectors of Africa's development. Through programs such as the Migration for Africa's Development (MIDA), the IOM encourages skills development and transfer in the health sector in African countries (IOM 2004). Another program facilitating transfer of knowledge among the African diaspora is the TOKTEN (Transfer of Knowledge Through Expatriate Nationals), funded by the UNDP. TOKTEN encourages the transfer of knowledge by enabling experienced African emigrants to be engaged over a period in their home countries (Quartey 2006). Countries such as Ghana, Liberia and Sudan have benefited immensely from this program. In addition, some African universities are also facilitating knowledge transfer and the sharing of ideas under the Carnegie Next Generation of Academics in Africa Project. Under this program African scholars abroad spend some time teaching and doing research in selected African universities (Ratha and Mohapatra 2011).

9.0 POLICY IMPLICATIONS

This chapter has shown that with the exception of North Africans who mainly migrate out of the continent, most Africans typically move from one part of their country to the other. When they decide to leave their countries, the majority of them move to other countries within the African continent. Some of the major migration hubs on the continent currently include Côte d'Ivoire, Gabon, Kenya, Tanzania, Djibouti, Sudan and South Africa. Regional organizations such as ECOWAS, EAC, SADC and COMESA do promote the free movement of persons and goods within the continent and their respective subregions. The benefits of allowing labor, goods and capital to move freely within the continent have been widely espoused: It contributes to increased intra-African trade flows; encourages a more efficient allocation of resources by bridging the gap in excess demand in factor or goods market; contributes to the retention of skilled professionals on the continent; promotes social and cultural links and so on (cf. Shimeles 2010). There is, however, the need for policy coordination by national governments of both origin and destination countries to manage the size and composition of migrants. Most migrant-receiving countries prefer to receive professionals and persons with the required skills and training while keeping out the bulk of the untrained and low-skilled persons. The result of this is that most migrants leave their countries and enter their destination countries illegally, swelling the numbers of undocumented immigrants. Hence, there is a need for close collaboration between the main sending countries and the receiving ones on how to properly and formally organize the migration flow from one country to the other.

9.1 Illegal Migrants, Xenophobia and Expulsions

The high and rising numbers of legal and illegal migrants is putting enormous pressure on the main migrant-receiving countries. South Africa has received thousands of migrants from the Southern Africa region (mainly from Mozambique, Zimbabwe, Lesotho, Swaziland, etc.) and beyond since the early 1990s. Similarly, Côte d'Ivoire and Nigeria have also been inundated with migrants from neighboring countries. These have resulted in discriminations and attacks on migrants as well as xenophobia in the migrant-receiving countries. Many African countries have at various times expelled migrants from their territories, often at short notices. These have resulted in the seizure of properties of migrants, immense misery and suffering and even deaths as fleeing migrants rush across the borders for safety (Adepoju 2010, Campbell 2010, Crush and Pendleton 2004, Zoomers and Naerssen 2006). There is a need for a policy on how African countries should treat migrants residing in their territories and on the proper methods of expelling illegal migrants. There is also the need for a clear-cut policy on how to better promote the integration of migrants in the receiving countries and reduce the stereotyping and scapegoating of migrants by the local population.

9.2 Transcontinental Migration

Several studies have shown that transcontinental emigration from Africa has gained momentum in recent decades. Furthermore, it is mainly the wealthier individuals who move overseas. Many countries that have invested a high proportion of their resources in training their citizens have seen these professionals and skilled labor move abroad in huge numbers (Flahaux and De Haas 2016, Shimeles 2010). The cases of doctors, nurses, paramedical personnel, teachers, lecturers, engineers and other scientists who have emigrated to Europe and North America are well documented (Adepoju 2010, Arthur 2014).

There is a need for individual countries, continental organizations and multilateral institutions to put in place policies which will minimize the exodus of highly skilled professionals out of Africa and encourage them to stay in Africa. Since the main driving force is the huge wage differentials in income between the developed countries and Africa as well as the poor working conditions across Africa, there is a need for monetary and non-monetary incentives to retain highly skilled professionals on the continent.

African governments, individually and collectively, have been rather slow to offer suggestions on the ordeal that awaits irregular migrants who cross the Sahara Desert and the Mediterranean Sea in an attempt to get to Europe. Many are unsuccessful and die during the journey. It is surprising that sending and transit countries such as Senegal, Nigeria, Chad, Niger, Mali, Mauritania and Sudan seem unconcerned, while their citizens die trying to reach Europe, when there could be a better surveillance of these deadly migration routes.

9.3 Diaspora Policy

The existence of strong and vibrant ethnic and national diaspora populations abroad have to be acknowledged. Diaspora populations do serve several purposes as they are the source of much of the financial and technical support transferred yearly to Africa. Governments should work to exploit the benefits that the diaspora population offers. This will make more funds, resources and technical knowledge available to the state, communities, families and individual households.

Migrants' sojourn abroad reduces the burden of unemployment that has engulfed many African countries. Governments and regional organizations should have dialogue with the main receiving countries to treat African nationals humanely and fairly. Governments should facilitate the return of their nationals abroad, particularly the highly skilled persons. At the same time, measures should be put in place to promote linkages between Africans at home and those abroad through programs such as exchanges, sabbaticals and tourism. The haphazard and poorly organized manner in which skilled professionals are poached by foreign countries should be replaced with a well-organized and planned system whereby bilateral agreements can be formally signed between sending and receiving countries for their mutual benefits.

9.4 Asylum Seekers, Refugees and Internally Displaced Persons

Conflicts and, to a lesser extent, disasters are the main sources of Africa's huge numbers of refugees and IDPs. Many regions of Africa have not known peace for a long period due to internecine wars, civil strife and the numerous insurgencies on the continent. To reduce the specter of human suffering, poverty and deaths, policy measures aimed at tackling the root causes, and the trigger factors of such conflicts and insurgencies should be implemented. Such policies should tackle local or regional inequalities, discrimination, social exclusion, acute poverty and religious extremism which are at the root of these conflicts.

9.5 Migration Policies, Laws and Data

National, regional and continental bodies should adopt and implement the appropriate laws and policies that protect migrants, refugees and asylum seekers, stateless persons and IDPs against discrimination, unfair treatment, mass expulsions, and other malpractices such as human trafficking and migrant smuggling. Some of these laws and regulations include the African Union's Declarations on Migration, Ouagadougou Action Plan and African Charter on Human and Peoples' Rights. There are also regional regulations dealing with migration such as the ECOWAS Protocols on Migration. Countries such as Ghana, Nigeria, Kenya and South Africa have comprehensive national migration policies guiding migration decisions in their respective countries. Other countries should be encouraged to draft national migration policies. For these policies to function adequately, national, regional and international bodies should develop a comprehensive and coherent database on the composition of African migrants, remittances and their activities since there is a dearth of data and information in these areas. Most of the available data on African migration are collected from destination countries and take away the cultural context of the information provided.

9.6 Facilitating Remittance Transfers

Measures should be adopted to encourage the use of formal channels for remittance transfers. The implementation of such measures will allow institutions to capture data on migrant remittances; secondly, the security of migrants' savings would be guaranteed; thirdly, both receiving and sending countries will benefit from increased remittances since they constitute a major component of the GDP in many African countries and, finally, to help reduce the operations of "black markets" in certain African countries. National and regional bodies should open up the financial institution market for competitive engagement in transferring remittances while also making such opportunities available, accessible (especially in the rural areas) and charging cheaper fees (WB 2016).

10.0 THE CHAPTERS IN THIS BOOK

The first is this introduction. It examines the changing migration trends in Africa as well as the complex and controversial links between migration and development across Africa. It also discusses the policy implications of some of the challenges of migration.

Chapter 2 analyzes the contributions of Cameroonian migrants in Germany to development back at home, especially in the health and education sectors. Though scattered throughout Germany, the Cameroonian diaspora mainly reside in the state of North Rhein Westfalia. They are well organized along ethnic, regional, town and national lines which are registered into associations and organizations. These migrant associations contribute to the development of Cameroon through mobilizing their members to actively participate in projects and contribute financially toward them, as well as promoting trade and commercial exchanges between entrepreneurs in Cameroon and their counterparts in Germany. They also build and equip schools in Cameroon, share their technological expertise, promote the adoption of relevant technology in schools and universities in Cameroon and contribute in diverse ways toward improving the health sector in Cameroon.

The chapter concludes that Cameroonian migrants in Germany are transnational in their outlook and activities. They do not identify exclusively with either their home or host country. Instead, they build up connections with and owe allegiances to both countries; they are "*Here*" (in Germany) and "*There*" (in Cameroon). The chapter highlights the paradigm of transnational spaces in policy analysis and the contributions of the Cameroonian diaspora in Germany to social and economic development in Cameroon.

Chapter 3 investigates the transnational political practices of Ghanaian political party branches in the Netherlands as a source of social change and their contributions to the political development of Ghana. First, they trace Ghanaian migration to the Netherlands and the formation of foreign branches of Ghanaian political parties in that country within the context of transnationalism and transnational politics. The authors note that Ghanaian migrants in the Netherlands are politically active in both the Netherlands and Ghana. They participate in Dutch local and national elections and also actively participate in the political processes in Ghana. The emergence of the two main Ghanaian political party branches in the Netherlands, that is, the National Democratic Congress (NDC) and the New Patriotic Party (NPP), and their activities in both the Netherlands and Ghana are described in detail.

The author concludes that improvements in communication technologies and international travels have encouraged Ghanaian emigrants in the Netherlands to influence political activities in Ghana through the formation of external party branches abroad, active involvement in political campaigns and voting in national elections, and making financial and material contributions to political parties. These political activities of Ghanaians in the Netherlands promote good governance, consolidate democracy and contribute to the socioeconomic development of Ghana.

Chapter 4 assesses the types of partnerships that are formed between two Ghanaian hometown associations in the United Kingdom (the Kwahuman Association and the Kassena-Nankana Development League) and their local communities in Ghana. It examines how the interpersonal relations that connect migrants, former migrants and nonmigrants in origin and destination areas through enduring links of kinship, friendship and shared community of origin help realize development prospects at the subnational level.

The chapter concludes that the size of hometown associations sometimes determines the number and type of local partners they are able to collaborate with, and suggests that the prevailing sociocultural conditions within origin communities equally impinge on these decisions. Furthermore, the author takes issue with Amartya Sen's conceptualization of development, describing it as normative and prescriptive in nature and failing to address the underlying questions of how this is achieved in practice and by whom. He also discusses development discourses spearheaded by international development agencies such as the IMF and the WB, describing them as being unidirectional and focusing mainly on the potential benefits of brain gain and migrants' remittances home.

In the author's view, the focus on state-diaspora relations as prime drivers of development de-emphasizes the role of local partners as well as institutions in realizing and sustaining migrant-funded development initiatives.

Chapter 5 compares the academic performance of children who remain at home when their parents migrate with children from nonmigrant parents in six basic schools in Accra and Sunyani. The findings show that there is no significant difference in the academic performance of children from migrant households and those from nonmigrant households. Hence, parental migration in the Ghanaian context is not detrimental to the academic performance of children left behind. This is due to the availability of extended family members or kin relatives to care for children in the absence of their biological parents. The author recommends that policies regarding the welfare of children in Ghana should be fashioned toward promoting traditional Ghanaian family values such as the close collaboration among the extended family and communal responsibility and support for children.

Chapter 6 examines the issues of the "brain drain" of highly skilled professionals from Kenya to the United Kingdom, the United States, Canada and Ghana. While in the 1960s and 1970s, the emigration of skilled professionals was considered a loss to the countries of origin, in recent times, some scholars have challenged the "brain drain" argument and indicated that migrants who go abroad are of benefit to their home countries through remittances, skills and technology transfer, trade and investment, among others. These scholars have proposed the idea of "brain gain" whereby sending countries are said to obtain immense benefits from their citizens who migrate abroad or "brain circulation" in the case of migrants who remain transnational and contribute to both the sending and receiving countries.

Upon an examination of the Kenyan situation, the author concludes that highly skilled professionals were more likely to participate in development-oriented transnational activities like remittance transfers, investment and return-visits, than migrants with low levels of education. This contributes to the development of their communities of origin and the Kenyan state. The chapter further concludes that though most Kenyan migrants in the four countries were employed, many were not working in jobs that matched their training, and some were doing jobs that were beneath their qualifications. These findings raise valid "brain waste" concerns.

Chapter 7 examines the plight of the Nigerian immigrant community in colonial Ghana. The Gold Coast's thriving economy and social life attracted many Nigerians and other West Africans to that country during the colonial period. Despite its attractions, life in the Gold Coast was unbearable for poor migrants and the destitute. The colonial authorities therefore resorted to repatriating extremely poor and destitute migrants to their countries of origin so as to cut down on the number of "undesirable immigrants" in Ghana.

Based on a reconstruction of archival materials, the chapter analyzes the causes, course and consequences of the problems of destitution and repatriation as they affected Nigerians in colonial Ghana. It also discusses the strategies adopted by the various stakeholders to ensure smooth repatriation exercises. The author points out that the colonial policy of repatriating "undesirable immigrants" merely used them as scapegoats for the problems of the colony and concludes that the repatriation of destitute Nigerians and others served the interests of the colonial authorities in particular and that of the Ghanaian society at large.

Chapter 8 examines the changing labor migration pattern from the northern savannah areas to the forest-transition zone in central Ghana. The authors argue that with the advent of climate change and increased climate variability characterized by severe weather conditions, prolonged drought and reduced crop yields, many seasonal migrants are moving with their families to settle permanently in more suitable farming areas in the country. The transitional zone offers migrant farmers from northwestern Ghana quite a number of advantages: Crop yields are better and farmers can crop a larger variety of crops; earnings from non-farming activities are higher; and because the migrants live far from home, members of their extended family do not make much demands on them. Ironically, while migrant farmers from the Upper West region are moving in droves to the Brong Ahafo region, the indigenous population of the area is deserting the rural settlements for the urban centers. The authors recommend that migrant farmers be assisted to overcome the challenges confronting them in their new destinations such as the difficulty in acquiring large farm lands, lack of access to credit facilities and shortage of farm labor.

Chapter 9 criticizes the widely held view in the transnational migration literature that migrants are part of both their destination countries and their countries of origin. They are therefore seen as being both "here" and "there." The author argues that such arguments do not capture the often bumpy journeys that many African migrants undertake, the hardships they go through, and the investments they make before they reach the ideal social status of a trans-migrant. Furthermore, in his view, the transnational lens reduces migrants' life-worlds to a simple "here-there" phenomenon, as if migrants connect to only two places, the country of origin and the destination. To elaborate on the diverse pathways to development, this chapter focuses on migration trajectories from West Africa to Europe using a number of ethnographic case study materials. With these qualitative insights, the author argues that transnational spaces are full of spatial frictions (e.g., physical immobility, secrecy) that we tend to overlook with the transnational frameworks. Instead of transnational engagements, he advocates for a more critical approach that considers mobility itself as development.

Finally, Chapter 10 examines the role of labor migrants in Ghana's offshore oil and gas industry as well as the contributions of migrants to the provision of auxiliary services in the Sekondi-Takoradi metropolis. They analyze the skills and expertise that labor migrants bring to the oil industry, the process of getting employment on the rig as well as the impact of their employment on the oil and gas industry in Ghana. The study revealed that there are two groups of labor migrants working on the rig. The first group consists mainly of expatriates and a few Ghanaians working in high-end jobs on the rig, while the second group consists of Ghanaians working in low-end jobs. The authors conclude that workers in the low-end jobs were able to improve their living conditions but risk losing their jobs. Therefore to ensure job security for labor migrants, there is a need to come out with clear policies outlining rules and regulations governing working on the oil rigs. Furthermore, labor migrants, whether from Ghana or abroad, have an important role to play in the emerging oil industry in Ghana.

REFERENCES

Abdellatif, Ben Hadj. 2010. "African Skilled Labour Migration: Dimensions and Impact," in *International Migration Within, To and From Africa in a Globalised World*, edited by Aderanti Adepoju, 97–118. Accra: Sub-Saharan Publishers.

ACP. 2011. *Migration, Remittances and Development in Africa: The Case of Lusophone Countries.* Brussels-Belgium: ACP.

Adams, Richard. Jr. 1991. *The Effects of International Remittances on Poverty, Inequality and Development in Rural Egypt.* Research Report 86. Washington: International Food Policy Research Institute.

Adams, Richard. 2006. *Remittances and Poverty in Ghana.* Policy Research Working Paper 3838, Washington, DC: World Bank.

Adams, Richard Jr, and John Page. 2005. "Do International Migration and Remittances Reduce Poverty in Developing Countries?" *World Development* 33(10): 1645–1669.

Adams, Richard H, and Alfredo Cuecuecha. 2010. "Remittances, Household Expenditure and Investment in Guatemala." *World Development* 38(11): 1626–1641.

Adepoju, Aderanti. 2005. "Patterns of Migration in West Africa," in *At Home in the World? International Migration and Development in Contemporary Ghana and West Africa,* edited by Takyiwah Manuh, 24–54. Accra: Sub-Saharan Publishers.

Adepoju, Aderanti. 2010. *International Migration within, to and from Africa in a Globalised World.* Accra, Ghana: Sub-Saharan Publishers.

Adepoju, Aderanti, Ton Van Naerssen, and Annelies Zoomers, eds. 2008. *International Migration and National Development in Sub-Saharan Africa: Viewpoints and Policy Initiatives in the Countries of Origin.* Leiden: Koninklijke Brill NV.

Adepoju, Aderanti, and Arie van der Wiel. 2010. *Seeking Greener Pastures Abroad: A Migration Profile of Nigeria.* Ibadan: Safari Books Limited Sub-Saharan Publishers.

Aggarwal, Reena, Asli Demirgüç-Kunt, and Maria Soledad Martinez Peria. 2006. "Do Workers' Remittances Promote Financial Development?" *Policy Research Working paper* 3957, Washington, DC: World Bank.

Akabzaa, Thomas, Alex Asiedu, Agnes Budu, Peter Quartey, and Sarah Akuoni. 2010. *Migration and Economic Development in Ghana*. Accra: Woeli Publishing Services.

Akologo, Zan S. 2005. "The Role of Diaspora-Based Organisations in Socioeconomic Development at the Local Level in Ghana," in *At Home in the World? International Migration and Development in Contemporary Ghana and West Africa,* edited by Takyiwaa Manuh, 335–350. Accra: Sub-Saharan Publishers.

Alhassan, Osman. 2010. "The Case of Ghana," in *Building Institutional Cooperation Between the Diaspora and Homeland Governments in Africa: The Cases of Ghana, Nigeria, Germany, USA and the UK*, edited by Ali. Mohamoud, 41–42. The Hague: African Diaspora Policy Centre.

Akyeampong, K. E. 2006. "Race, Identity and Citizenship in Black Africa: The Case of the Lebanese in Ghana." Africa 76(3): 297–323.

Anarfi, John K, Stephen Kwankye, and Clement Ahiadeke. 2005. "Migration, Return and Impact in Ghana: A Comparative Study of Skilled and Unskilled Transnational Migrants," in *At Home in the World? International Migration and Development in Contemporary Ghana and West Africa*, edited by Takyiwaa Manuh, 204–226. Accra: Sub-Saharan Publishers.

Anarfi, John, Peter Quartey, and John Agyei. 2010. "Key Determinants of Migration among Health Professionals in Ghana". Brighton, UK: Development Research Centre on Migration, Globalization & Poverty. Accessed June 15, 2015. http://www.migrationdrc.org/publications/research.../Quartey_et_al_Health_workers.pdf.

Anyanwu, John C, and Andrew E.O. Erhijakpour. 2010. "Do International Remittances Affect Poverty in Africa?" *African Development Review* 22: 51–91.

Armed Conflict Location and Event Data Project (ACLED). 2014. Regional Report: North Africa. Accessed February 20, 2015. http://www.acleddata.com/wp-content/uploads/2014/04/ACLED-Regional-Report-North-Africa-April-2014.pdf.

Arthur, John. 2014. *Class Formations and Inequality Structures in Contemporary African Migration*. London: Lexington Books

Bakewell, Oliver. 2012. "Introduction," in *Migration and Development,* edited by Oliver Bakewell, xiii–xxiii. Cheltenham: Edward Elgar.

Baldwin, George B. 1970. "Brain Drain or Overflow". *Foreign Affairs* 48(2): 358–372.

Benedict, Olumide H, and Wilfred Isioma Ukpere. 2012. "Brain Drain and African Development: Any Possible Gain from the Drain?" *African Journal of Business Management* 6(7): 2421–2428.

Boahen, Adu A. 1966. *Topics in West African History*. London: Longman.

Bodomo, Adams. 2012. *Africans in China: A Socio-Cultural Study and its Implications on Africa-China Relations*. New York, NY: Cambria Press.

Bodomo, Adams. 2010. "The African Trading Community in Guangzhou: An Emerging Bridge for Africa-China Relations." *China Quarterly* 203: 693–707.

Bodomo, Adams, and Grace Ma. 2010. "From Guangzhou to Yiwu: Emerging Facets of the African Diaspora in China." *International Journal of African Renaissance - Multi-Inter and Transdisciplinarity* 5(2): 283–289.

Bollard, Albert, David McKenzie, and Melanie Morten. 2010. "The Remitting Patterns of African Migrants in the OECD." *Journal of African Economies* 19(5): 605–634.

Broekhuis, Annelet. 2006. "International Migration and Development in Burkina Faso. Viewpoints and Policy Initiatives." *Working Papers Migration and Development Series*. Report No. 7. Nijmegen.

Caldwell, John C. 1969. *African Rural-Urban Migration: The Movement to Ghana's Towns*. New York, NY: Columbia University Press.

Campbell, Eugene K. 2010. "Irregular Migration within and to the Republic of South Africa and from the African Continent to the European Union: Tapping Latent Energy of the Youth," in *International Migration Within,To and From Africa in a Globalised World,* edited by Aderanti Adepoju, 169–207. Accra: Sub-Saharan Publishers.

Capps, Randy, Kristen McCabe, and Michael Fix. 2012. "Diverse Streams: Black African Migration to the United States." *Migration Policy Institute*: Washington DC, USA.

Cerase, Francesco. 1970. "Nostalgia or Disenchantment: Considerations on Return Migration," in *The Italian Experience in the United States*, edited by S. M. Tomasi and M. H. Engel, 217–239. New York, NY: Centre for Migration Studies.

Christian Aid. 2007. *Human Tide: The Real Migration Crisis—A Christian Aid Report* London: Christian Aid.

Cissé, Dauda. 2013. "South-South Migration and Sino-African Traders: A Comparative Study of Chinese in Senegal and Africans in China." *African Review of Economics and Finance* 3(1): 17–28.

Crush, Jonathan, and Wade Pendleton. 2004. *Regionalizing Xenophobia? Citizen Attitudes to Immigration and Refugee Policy in Southern Africa.* SAMP Migration Policy Series 30, Cape Town: Idasa.

Danish Refugee Council (DRF). 2001. *Mixed Migration in West Africa.* Copenhagen, 2016.

De Bruijn, Maryan, Rijk Van Dijk, and D. Foeken. 2001. *Mobile Africa: Changing Patterns of Movement in Africa and Beyond.* Leiden: Brill.

De Haas, Hein. 2006. "International Migration and Development in Nigeria." *Working papers Migration and Development Series.* Report No. 6. Nijmegen.

De Haas, Hein. 2007. *Remittances, Migration and Social Development: A Conceptual Review of Literature.* Social Policy and Development Programme Papers No. 34. Geneva: UNRISD.

De Haas, Hein. 2008. "North-Africa Migration Systems: Evolution, Transformations and Development Linkages," in *Migration and Development: Perspectives from the South,* edited by Stephen Castles and Raul Delgado Wise. Geneva: International Organization for Migration.

De Haas, Hein. 2010. "Migration and Development: A Theoretical Perspective." *International Migration Review* 44(1): 1–38.

Philippe, Flore Gubbert, and Anne-Sophie Robilliard.2009. *"Return Migrants in Western Africa: Characteristics and Labour Market Performance."* Document de Travail No 2009–06, Paris: DIAL.

Elkan, Walter. 1967. "Circular Migration and the Growth of Towns in East Africa." *International Labour Review* 96(6): 581–589.

Faist, Thomas. 2008. "Migrants as Transnational Development Agents: An Inquiry into the Newest Round of the Migration–Development Nexus." *Population, Space, Place* 14: 21–42. doi:10.1002/psp.471.

Flahaux, Marie-Laurence, and Hein De Haas. 2016. "African Migration: Trends, Patterns, Drivers." *Comparative Migration Studies* 4(1). doi 10.1186/s40878–015–0015–6.

Ghosh, Bimal. 2006. *Remittances and Development: Myths, Rhetoric and Realities.* Geneva: International Organization for Migration.

Ghosh, Bimal. 1992. "Migration-Development Linkages: Some Specific Issues and Practical Policy Measures." *International Migration* 30(3): 423–456.

Gikuru, Caroline M. 2013. "The Plight of Kenyan Domestic Workers in Gulf Countries." MA thesis., College of Arts and Sciences, University of San Francisco." Accessed June 15, 2016. http://repository.usfa.edu/cgi/viewcontent.cgi?article=1104&context=thes

Hahn, Peter H, and Georg Klute, eds. 2007. *Cultures of Migration. African Perspectives.* Berlin: Lit Verlag.

Haugen, Ø. Heidi. 2012. "Nigerians in China: A Second State of Immobility." *International Migration* 50(2): 65–80.

International Labour Organisation (ILO). 2003a. "ILO Report on Child Trafficking in West and Central Africa." Accessed September 3, 2016. http://www.ilo.org/global/about-the-ilo/press-and…/index.htm.

International Labour Organization (ILO). 2003b. *Trafficking in Human Beings: New Approaches to Combating the Problem.* Geneva: ILO.

International Organisation for Migration (IOM). 2004. *Migration and Development: Current Policy Challenges.* Geneva: IOM/Migration Policy and Research Department.

International Organisation for Migration (IOM). 2008. "Human Trafficking in Eastern Africa: Research Assessment and Baseline Information in Tanzania, Kenya, Uganda and Burundi." Accessed July 23, 2016. http://www.eac.int/migration/index.php?option=com_docman.

International Organisation for Migration (IOM). 2009. Migration en Côte d'Ivoire. Profile National 2009. Accessed June 15, 2016. http://www.iom.int.

International Organisation for Migration(IOM). 2016. "2015 Global Migration Trends: Factsheet" Geneva: IOM/IOMs Global Migration Data Analysis Centre.

Johnson, Sandy, and Antony Altbeker. 2011. *South Africa's Migration Policies. A Regional Perspective.* Centre for Development and Enterprise, Johannesburg, South Africa and Enterprise, Johannesburg, South Africa. Accessed September 15, 2016. http://www.cde.org.za

Jones, R. C. "Introduction: The Renewed Role of Remittances in the New World Order." *Economic Geography* 74(1) (1998).

Kapur, Devesh. 2004. "Remittances: The New Development Mantra?" G-24 Discussion Papers No. 24, Paper presented at the G-24 Discussion Series, New York and Geneva, United Nations, April 2004.

Khadiagala, Gilbert M. eds. 2006. *Security Dynamics in Africa's Great Lakes Region*. Boulder: Lynne Reinner.

Kindleberger, Charles. P. 1965. *Europe's Postwar Growth: The Role of Labor Supply*. New York, NY: Oxford University Press.

Lan, Shanshan. 2014. "State Regulation of Undocumented African Migrants in China: A Multi-Scalar Analysis." *Journal of Asian and African Studies* 1–16. Accessed September 3, 2016. http:// Jas.sagepub.com.

Levitt, Peggy. 1998. "Social Remittances: Migration Driven Local-Level Forms of Cultural Diffusion." *International Migration Review* 32(4): 926–948.

Lucas, Robert E. B. 1987. "Emigration to South-Africa's Mines." *The American Economic Review* 77(3): 313–330

Lovejoy, E. Paul. ed. 1981. *The Ideology of Slavery in Africa*. Beverly Hills: Sage Publications.

Lowell, Lindsay B, and Allan Findlay. 2002. *Migration of Highly Skilled Persons from Developing Countries: Impact and Policy Responses*. Geneva: IMB-ILO/DfID.

Loxley, John, Harry A. Sackey, and Syeed Khan. 2015. "African Immigrants in Canada: A Profile of Human Capital, Income and Remittance Behaviour." *Canadian Journal of Development Studies* 36(1): 3–23.

Malit, Frolian, and Ali Al Youha. 2016. "Kenyan Migration to the Gulf Countries: Balancing Economic Interests and Worker Protection." Migration Policy Institute. Accessed August 31, 2016. http://migration policy.org/article/Kenyan-migration-gulf-countries.

Manuh, Takyiwaa, ed. 2005. *At Home in the World? International Migration and Development in Contemporary Ghana and West Africa*. Accra: Sub-Saharan Publishers.

Manuh, Takyiwaa, Richard Asante, and Jerome Djangmah. 2005. "The Brain Drain in the Higher Education Sector in Ghana," in *At Home In The World? International Migration and Development in Contemporary Ghana and West Africa*, edited by Takyiwaa Manuh, 250–276. Accra: Sub-Saharan Africa Press.

Mensah, Joseph. 2009. "Doing Religion" Overseas: The Characteristics and Functions of Ghanaian Immigrants Churches in Toronto, Canada." *Human Rights and the Social Science* 4: 21–44.

Miers, Suzanne, and Igor Kopytoff, ed. 1977. *Slavery in Africa: Historical and Anthropological Perspectives*. Madison, Wisconsin: The University of Wisconsin Press.

Mohamoud, Awil. 2010. *Building Institutional Cooperation Between the Diaspora and Homeland Governments in Africa: The Cases of Ghana, Nigeria, Germany, USA and the UK*. The Hague: African Diaspora Policy Centre.

Mohapatra Sanket, and Dilip Ratha. 2011. "Remittance Markets in Africa." *World Development*: 3–59.

Myers, Norman. 2002. "Environmental Refugees: A Growing Phenomenon of the 21st Century." *Biological Sciences* 357 (1420): 609–613.

Mugimu, Christopher B. 2010. "Brain Drain to Brain Gain: What are the Implications for Higher Education in Africa." *Comparative & International Higher Education* 2: 37–42.

National Agency for the Prohibition of Trafficking in Persons and Other Related Matters (NAPTIP)/UNICEF. 2009. "Nigeria: Country Response on Trafficking in Persons Especially Children and Women 2002–2007." Accessed June 26, 2016. http://www.unicef.org/nigeria/ng_ publi-cations_countryresponse.pdf.

O'Connor, Anthony. 2007. *The African City*. London: Routledge.

OECD-UNDESA. 2013. *World Migration in Figures*. http://www.oecd.org/els/mig/World-Migration-in-Figures.pdf.

Onuoha, Browne. 2013. "Human Trafficking in Africa: The Role of Universities in Teaching and Research." *Journal of Social Science* 34(1): 61–74.

Oucho, John. 2008. "African Brain Drain and Gain, Diaspora and Remittances: More Rhetoric than Action," in *International Migration and National Development in Sub-Saharan Africa Viewpoints and Policy Initiatives in the Countries of Origin*, edited by Aderanti Adepoju, Ton van Naerssen and Annelies Zoomers 49–66. Leiden: Brill.

Oyowe, Augustine. 1996. "Brain Drain: Colossal Loss of Investment for Developing Countries." *The Courier* ACP-EU, No. 159, (September-October): 59–60.

Quartey, Peter. 2006. *The Impact of Migrant Remittances on Household Welfare in Ghana. Research Paper 158*. Nairobi: African Economic Research Consortium.

Ratha, Dilip, Sanket Mohapatra, C. Ozden, S. Plaza, W. Shaw, and A. Shimeles. 2011. "Leveraging Migration for Africa: Remittances, Skills, and Investments". Washington DC: The International Bank for Reconstruction and Development/The World Bank. Accessed February 20, 2016. http://www.worldbank.org

Sako, Soumana. 2002. "Brain Drain and Africa's Development: A Reflection." *African Issues* 30(1): 25–30.

Sawadogo, Relwende W. 2012. "The Challenges of Transnational Human Trafficking in West Africa." *African Studies Quarterly* 13, no. 1&2: 95–115.

Serour, Gamal I. 2009. "Healthcare Workers and the Brain Drain." *International Journal of Gynecology and Obsteric* 106(2): 175–8.

Setrana Mary B, and Justice Richard Kyei Owusu. 2015. "L'engagement Politique de la Diaspora Ghanéenne aux Pays-Bas." *Afrique contemporaine* 4(256): 91–101.

Setrana, Mary B, and Steve Tonah. 2016. "Do Transnational Links Matter? Labour Market Participation of Ghanaian Return Migrants." *Journal of Development Studies* 52(4): 549–560. doi 10.1080/00220388.2015.1126255.

Shimeles, Abebe. 2010. "Migration Patterns, Trends and Policy Issues in Africa. African Development Bank, Working paper series No. 119, Tunis, December 2010. Accessed June 15, 2016. http://www.afdb.org.

Stride, G. T, and Caroline Ifeka. 1971. *Peoples and Empires of West Africa. West Africa in History 1000–1800*. Edingburgh: Nelson.

Taylor Edward. 1999. "The New Economics of Labour Migration and the Role of Remittances in the Migration Process." *International Migration* 37(1): 63–88.

Teye, Joseph K, Mary Botemaa Setrana, and Agyeiwaa Abigail Acheampong. 2014. "Migration of Health Professionals from Ghana. Trends, Drivers and Emerging

Issues". In *Ghana: Social, Economic and Political Issues,* edited by Roscoe, Coleen, 253–274, New York: Nova Science.

Tonah, Steve. 2007. "Ghanaians Abroad and Their Ties Home. Cultural and Religious Dimensions of Transnational Migration." Working Paper No. 25. Bielefeld: Center on Migration, Citizenship and Development (COMCAD).

Troung, Thanh-Dam. 2006. "Poverty, Gender and Human Trafficking in Sub-Saharan Africa: Rethinking Best Practices in Migration Management." UNESCO Project to Fight Human Trafficking in Africa, Paris, France. Accessed April 28, 2016. http://www.unesco.org/shs/humantrafficking.

UNESCO. 2004. "From Brain Drain: Well-Educated Migrants Worldwide are not Only a Source of Revenue but Potential Key Actors" *Education for Today*: 18. Accessed June 15, 2015. http://www.unesco.org/education/education_today/brain.pdf.

United Nations High Commission for Refugees (UNHCR). 2016. *Global Trends 2015a*. UN: Geneva.

United Nations High Commission for Refugees (UNHCR). 2016. "Resettlement Fact-sheet 2015b." Accessed October 15, 2016. http:// www.unhcr.org/524c31a09.html.

United Nations High Commission for Refugees (UNHCR). 2015. "Global Trends, Forced Displacement in 2015." Accessed June 15, 2016. http://reliefweb.int/report/world/unhcr-global-trends-forced-displacement-2015.

United Nations Department of Economic and Social Affairs (UNDESA). 2015. "Trends in International Migration Stock: Migrants by Destination and Origin 2015." Accessed July 15, 2015. UN database, POP/DB/MIG/Stock/Rev 2015.

Van Moppes, David. 2006. "The African Migration Movement: Routes to Europe." Working Papers Migration and Development Series, Report No. 5. Nijmegen.

Vertovec, Steven. 2009. *Transnationalism*. London: Routledge.

Vollmer, A. Bastian, Deniz S. Sert, and Ahmet Icduygu. 2015. "EU Migration Legacies—Perspectives from Sending Countries." *Migration and Development* 4, Vol. 2: 232–237.

World Bank. 2016. *Migration and Remittances Factbook 2016*. Washington, DC: World Bank.

World Health Report. 2006. *Working Together for Health*. Geneva: World Health Organization.

Zoomers, Annelies, and Ton. van Naerssen. 2006. "International Migration and National Development in Sub-Saharan Africa. Viewpoints and Policy Initiatives in the Countries of Origin." Migration and Development Research Group, Radboud University, Nijmegen, the Netherlands.

Chapter 2

Political Participation Beyond National Borders

The Case of Ghanaian Political Party Branches in the Netherlands

Richard Kwabena Owusu Kyei and
Mary Boatemaa Setrana

1.0 INTRODUCTION: CHANGING ROLE OF IMMIGRANTS

Previously in the migration literature, immigrants were to assimilate into the host society and abandon their original cultural heritage or maintain their ethnic identities with the view of returning to their country of origin sooner or later which sometimes becomes a myth of return (Martiniello 2005). Immigrants were tagged as belonging to the host country or to the country of origin. However, over the last few decades, migration scholars have acknowledged that contemporary immigrants and their predecessors maintain different forms of ties with their home countries and at the same time incorporate into the host countries (Levitt and Jaworsky 2007, Portes, Guarnizio and Landholt 1999, Vertovec 1999).

Studies in the United States on transnationalism have shown that immigrants who engage in transnational practices are those who have lived in the host country for a long period of time, are well educated and are involved in the local politics of the host country (Guarnizio, Portes and Haller, 2003,1239, Portes, Escobar and Radford 2007,276). Similar studies in the Netherlands also showed that immigrants from different social classes engage in transnational practices and they do not have any negative effect on their integration in the host country (Mugge 2010, Snel, Engbersen and Leerkes 2006). However, a comparative study across some European countries has revealed that immigrants with robust transnational practices are not well integrated into the host society (Koopmans et al. 2005, 142). Morawska argued that it is difficult for a person to be incorporated into the local politics of the host country and at the same time be active in the politics of the country of origin (Morawska

2003, 161–65). Other scholars have, however, countered this argument saying that they could exist simultaneously (Pantoja 2005, Levitt 2007).

Transnational scholars have recognized that Ghanaian emigrants have double commitments as they incorporate into the life of their countries of residence and simultaneously influence the lives of families, friends and communities in Ghana (Mazzucato 2005). Much of their economic activities have been acknowledged through individual remittances and Home Town Associations (HTA) (Mazzucato, Kabki, and Smith 2006, Mohan 2006,Nijenhuis and Zoomer 2012). Yet, there is a lacuna in the literature on the systematic study of transnational political practices of Ghanaians abroad and the effect they have on the politics in Ghana. Political parties are crucial and fundamental in ensuring stable and participatory democracy which provides favorable environment for socioeconomic development of the nation-state (Huntington 1993,Manning 2005). After three short-lived republics due to military coup d'états in the first two decades after independence, Ghana's Fourth Republic which began in 1992 has existed over two decades (Fridy 2007, Lindberg and Morrison 2005, Morrison 2004). The institutionalization of political parties is fundamental in the longevity of participatory democracy and sustainable development and this work examines the contribution of Ghanaians abroad to the growth of political parties in Ghana.

The purpose of this study is to investigate transnational political practices of Ghanaian political party branches abroad as a source of social change and a contributive factor to the political development of Ghana. This chapter examines Ghanaian emigrants' participation in political decision-making in the home country. Through the transnational political activities of Ghanaians abroad, the chapter highlights the role they play in Ghana's political development. It explores the formation and activities of Ghanaian political party branches in the Netherlands and that of their members toward politics in Ghana. Political party branch in the diaspora also referred to as "external branch" is defined here as any group of immigrants that come together in the host country to share the vision and mission of any political party in the home country and are recognized by the political party's headquarters in the country of origin. There are two transnational actors in this work, namely the individual members of political party branches and the political party branches in the diaspora as organizations or collective actors. The individual actors here are, namely, political party members and political party sympathizers. A political party member is any person who is a card bearing member of a political party and a political party sympathizer is any person who shares the vision and mission of a political party but he or she is not registered in a political party.

This work used mainly qualitative research methods and so the findings are not representative and cannot be generalized; however, this is compensated through the rich and in-depth description of the fieldwork. Moreover, this work breaks the ground for future studies. Data for this study were drawn from various sources including census. Data from the Dutch Statistical Office were used to ascertain the demographic profile of Ghanaians in the Netherlands. Interviews and participant observation were used in collecting data among members of the external branches of Ghanaian political parties in Amsterdam between March and October 2014. Fifty members were engaged for this study. The decision of using these two parties is justified by the results of the national presidential elections in Ghana since the beginning of the Fourth Republic in 1992 which show that the New Patriotic Party (NPP) and the National Democratic Congress (NDC) have always obtained about 98 percent of the total vote cast (Electoral Commission of Ghana, 2013).

This chapter achieves its objectives by, first, highlighting Ghanaian migration to the Netherlands and second, discussing transnationalism and transnational politics. Consequently, we discuss the formation and transnational political activities of Ghanaian emigrants toward homeland politics and development and ends with a concluding remark.

2.0 GHANAIAN MIGRATION TO THE NETHERLANDS

Since the end of the Second World War, the Netherlands like Germany and France experienced increased number of immigrants from within and outside the European continent and so the Netherlands was transformed into an immigration country (Scholten and Holzhacker 2009). The three main categories of immigrants were from former Dutch colonies, labor immigrants and refugees from Second and Third World countries (Driessen and Dekkers 1997, 301). When the "fellow Dutchmen" repatriated from the Dutch East Indies as a result of the decolonization arrived in the Netherlands, there was a public policy to assimilate them into the Dutch society so they were dispersed throughout the country and within a decade they had assimilated into the Dutch society (Verwey-Jonker 1971, Scholten and Holzhacker 2009). Subsequently, large immigrant groups came from Dutch kingdoms such as Surinam and the Dutch Antilles and Mediterranean countries such as Italy, Greece, Morocco and Turkey (Rijkschroeff et al. 2005). The immigrants from Morocco and Turkey were referred to as "guest workers" because of the agreement between these countries and the Dutch government to recruit workers for Dutch factories in the 1960s. The Dutch government perceived the guest workers and the subsequent immigrants from former colonies as temporary immigrants who were to return to their countries of origin after some time (Crul and Vermeulen 2003). They were not identified as immigrants and the Netherlands did not perceive itself as an immigration country

(Scholten and Holzhacker 2009). The government policy aimed at the preservation of the immigrants' culture and so immigrant children were provided with the resources to study in their own language. Immigrants did not have to assimilate into the Dutch society because this could disrupt their plans of returning to their home country.

Ghanaians in the Netherlands are relatively new as an ethnic minority group compared to the Turkish, Moroccans, Antilleans and Surinamese. Mass Ghanaian migration to the Netherlands started sporadically in the 1970s and early 1980s either as political asylum seekers or as labor migrants. Around this time, the Netherlands suffered a shortage of manual labor in their factories and service sector but the government did not want to enter into a guest worker agreement with any country. Asylum seekers and labor migrants like Ghanaians entered the Netherlands with little restrictions and got absorbed into the Dutch manufacturing and service sectors where unskilled labor was needed (Van Dijk 2002).

Mass movement of Ghanaians to the Netherlands began from the late 1980s and most of them settled in the Bijlmer district of Amsterdam and to a lesser extent in The Hague. Ghanaians in Amsterdam became well known in the Netherlands after a plane crash in some buildings in the southeast of Amsterdam in September 1992 which claimed many Ghanaian lives while others got injured (Dietz et al.2011, Knipscheer et al. 2000). Ghanaians in the Netherlands are from different ethnic groups in Ghana but most of them are Akans and they consist of Asantes, Kwahus and Fantes (Setrana and Kyei 2015). Ghanaians are visible in the Netherlands through their churches, shops (food, clothing), media (television and radio broadcasting) and magazines. In 2000, the number of Ghanaians living in the Netherlands according to the Dutch government's official data were 15,610 but as of 2014, the total Ghanaian population in the Netherlands had moved up to 22,556 (Statistics Netherlands 2014). More than half of Ghanaians live in Amsterdam and according to the Amsterdam Bureau for Research and Statistics, Ghanaian immigrants in Amsterdam were about 3,608 in 1994 but as of 2013, the number had increased to about 11,602 which make Ghanaians the fourth largest ethnic minority group in Amsterdam after the Moroccans, Turkish and Surinamese (Statistics Netherlands 2014).

In spite of the medium and high level of education of Ghanaians in the Netherlands, they are employed in semiskilled and unskilled jobs mainly due to low proficiency in the Dutch language (Kyei and Smoczynski 2016), discrimination in the labor market (Choenni 2002) and the cumbersome process of recognizing foreign diplomas by the Dutch government. Such discrimination and restrictive measures heightened the engagement of Ghanaian immigrants in the economic and political development of their homeland (Anarfi, Awusabo-Asare and Nsowah-Nuamah 2000, Tonah 2007).

3.0 TRANSNATIONALISM AND TRANSNATIONAL POLITICS

Transnationalism is defined as the "processes by which immigrants forge and sustain multi-stranded social relations that link together their societies of origin and settlement" (Basch, Schiller and Szanton Blanc 1994, 7). Appadurai (1991) argues that immigrants have "deterritorialized" the nation-state through their constant interaction with people around the world and are not confined to those within the nation-state. This is possible due to the broader phenomenon of globalization and the advancement of communication technologies such as the internet, mobile phones, the low cost of traveling and the easy access to international travels that have compressed the distance between time and space (Giddens 1990, Portes 2001, Portes, Guarnizio and Landolt 1999, Vertovec 2004). Transnational scholars do not claim that transnationalism leads to the weakening of the loyalty of citizens to the nation-state rather the nation-state assumes new functions while relinquishing others (Goldring 2002). Moreover, transnational migrants' political claims are restrained or enhanced by states and so nation-states shape transnational practices (Koopmans and Statham 2010).

Transnational activities can be grouped into different spheres: economic, sociocultural and political activities and they take place either in the sending or in the receiving country (Al-Ali, Black and Koser 2001,618–626, Portes 2001,187, Portes, Guarnizo and Landholt 1999, 222). Even though theoretically it is possible to differentiate between transnational economic, social-cultural and political activities, in practice they do overlap (Van Amersfoort 2001, Martiniello and Bousetta 2008, Martiniello and LaFleur 2008). For the purpose of this chapter, transnational political activity is the focus of discussion. Transnational political activity is defined within the framework of Østergaard-Nielsen's and Vertovec's definitions. Østergaard-Nielsen describes transnational political activities in the area of homeland politics which refers to immigrants' engagement in homeland political activism in the host country with regard to issues concerning the country of origin and they may include expatriate voting, electoral campaigns and running for political office in the home country (Guarnizio, Portes & Haller 2003, Østergaard-Nielsen 2003). Immigrants may also put pressure on the receiving country to implement foreign policies that affect the home country positively (Mahler 2000). Vertovec (2004) also describes transnational electoral participation as membership in a political party in the country of origin, monetary contributions to these parties and active involvement in political campaigns in the polity of origin. In addition, Schiller and Fouron describe "trans-border citizens" as those immigrants who participate formally in the daily life and political practices and debates of two or more nation-states, claiming rights from and responsibilities to more than one government (Schiller and Fouron 1998, Soysal 1994, Yuval-Davis 1999).

The chapter adopts the theory of transnationalism in discussing the possibility of living beyond the boundaries of the host nation-state and contributing to the political life of the home country. Transnational politics is possible because of the system of governance that allows competitive elections and multiparty system of government. Although Ghanaian immigrants are away from Ghana, some exercise their fundamental citizenship rights in ensuring political stability and growth of their home country without neglecting life in the host country. Since Schiller, Basch and Blanc-Szanton (1992) introduced the concept of transnationalism into ethnic and migration studies there have been various discussions on the transnational practices of immigrants. Yet, studies have not explored the impact of transnational political participation of Ghanaian emigrants in Ghana's political processes (for exceptions, see van Hear, Pieke and Vertovec 2004, Owusu 2003).

4.0 EVOLVING TRAJECTORIES OF THE EXTERNAL POLITICAL PARTY BRANCHES

The 1992 constitution of the Fourth Republic re-introduced Ghana to the practice of liberal democracy which provided the avenue for the election of the president through the ballot box. The multiparty system of governance allows Ghanaians to express their freedom of membership or association to any political party of their choice. Unlike the first three republics that were short-lived, the Fourth Republic has experienced political stability as it has existed for over two decades. For these reasons, many Ghanaian elites who emigrated to seek political asylum and benefits started showing interest and trooping back into the country. Some immigrants organized themselves into various ethnic and political groups to contribute to the politics and development of the country. Political party branches were also established to promote and defend the liberal democratic governance that had begun through their participation in public discourse. As a result of these developments, some Ghanaian immigrants in the Netherlands saw the need to contribute to the politics of the home country through the formation of the NPP.

In 1998, some Ghanaians living in Amsterdam, who were not content with the policies and governance of the NDC, decided to mobilize Ghanaians in the Netherlands to support the NPP, which was the main opposition party in Ghana at that time. They felt the need to contribute to the stability of the fragile democratic governance in Ghana through the extension of the membership of the NPP to Ghanaians living in the Netherlands. The NPP branch in Holland began with ten members who nominated an interim chairman and secretary to lead the party. In the beginning, meetings were held in the homes of some of the members but after one year, the numbers increased beyond fifty due to effective propagation of the NPP message among Ghanaians. The numbers increased beyond one hundred and substantive executives were elected according to the NPP constitution.

Interestingly, on the other hand, some sympathizers of the NDC party began to mobilize Ghanaian immigrants in the Netherlands only when the NDC went into opposition for some period. In 2005, a group of Ghanaians living in the Netherlands started advocating for NDC on Ghanaian radio stations in Amsterdam such as *Recogin* and *Akasanoma*, and with time some people were attracted to their course of action and so the numbers increased and they started meeting in Friends' homes once every month. In 2007, the group decided to actually form an NDC branch in the Netherlands and continued in a vibrant manner to recruit members to their branch especially through the media. The numbers grew very fast to about sixty and they could no longer meet in the homes of members so they rented a hall for their meetings. The dynamism in the formation of these political parties is vital in the sense that they were formed at the loss of political power or in times of opposition. The external branch parties may enhance the implementation of sound policies and good governance through constructive criticism of the government in power.

5.0 DEMOCRATIC DEVELOPMENT AND DEMANDING FOR THEIR RIGHTS

The transnational politics of NPP and NDC external branches have the tendency of strengthening the norms of the nation-state instead of weakening it. In order for the external branches to function as extensions of the mother party, there was a need for an endorsement and inauguration in accordance with the constitution of the mother parties in Ghana. As a result, the NPP and NDC headquarters in the home country were informed about the newly established diaspora branches in the Netherlands. In 1999, a year after the formation of the NPP external branch, new executives were elected to the various positions according to the NPP constitution in Ghana. The National Executive Council in Ghana sent a delegation to help with the inauguration of the new executives. Similarly, the NDC external branch in 2007 was officially inaugurated in Amsterdam by the national executives (and among them were the National Chairman, the National Women's Organizer and the Director of International Relations) of the party in Ghana.

Apart from the formal recognition, the external branches sort for the right of inclusion in the decision-making process of the mother party in Ghana. As at 2006, no NPP external branch had the right to vote in the internal elections of the mother party in Ghana. The external party demanded recognition as a constituency with the right to vote in the election of national executives and the party's flag-bearer. Their argument was that, "they could not send their monies without attaching their voices" (key informant interview, The Netherlands, March 2014). Thus, they could not remit money to support the running of the political party without having the right to express their democratic and civic rights. Through negotiations and dialogue, each external branch of the NPP was given one vote in the 2007 national elections of NPP executives. In the 2010 national elections; each external branch was fully recognized as a constituency of the NPP with the right to vote. Since then, the NPP in the Netherlands has had twelve votes just like any constituency in Ghana for the election of the flag-bearer. Similarly, the executives of the external branches of the NDC have the right to vote and to be voted for in the election of NDC national executives and flag-bearer.

6.0 INVOLVEMENT IN HOST COUNTRY POLITICAL PARTIES

The external branches help align their political ideologies beyond the home country. Political ideas are shared and negotiated between home and host countries which could improve or hinder best practices. The external branches of the NPP and NDC in the Netherlands are affiliated with the host country political parties based on their practicing ideologies. As a liberal democratic party, the NPP is aligned to the Dutch People's Party for Freedom and Democracy (VVD). While the NDC, as a social democratic party, associates with the Dutch Labour Party (PVDA). The external party branches and their mother party in Ghana benefit from these associations in terms of finances, materials and expertise to build their political parties. They strengthen their relations also by attending various political ceremonies, for example during the inauguration of the NDC Amsterdam branch, the secretary of the International Relations Office of the PVDA attended the function. Additionally, the VVD contributed to the payment of rent for the NPP branch in Holland in the early years of its formation. In the 2000 presidential election, the flag-bearer of the NPP, John Agyekum Kufuor, was invited to a fundraising ceremony organized by the NPP branch in the Netherlands in 1999 and also to hold bilateral talks with the leaders of VVD. Mr. Kufuor attended the program together with some leading members of the party from Ghana.

7.0 FINANCIAL CONTRIBUTION OF PARTY MEMBERS

In as much as Ghanaian immigrants remit for community and family reasons, they also contribute financially to the running of both the external branches and mother political parties in the host and home countries, respectively. The external branches finance their activities through the payment of monthly dues, fundraising and individual voluntary contribution. Political party branches in the diaspora are expected by the mother party in Ghana to send money to support the running of internal elections, national elections and other activities of the party. Political party leaders from Ghana solicit for funds from Ghanaians in the diaspora. During such occasions, the preparation and the invitation of these leaders are solely done by the members of the external political party branches. Fundraising activities are organized by the external branches in their various countries to raise money and resources to help the homeland parties finance their activities. Our study reiterates previous research findings on remittances but it deviates by the discovery that Ghanaians abroad do not remit financially only for family reasons but also for the sustenance of Ghanaian political growth. One of the key informants narrated that:

> In 2000 when president Kufuor came here as flag-bearer, we raised funds for his political campaign. We sent four Toyota vehicles to Ghana and in the run-off elections, the party in Ghana pleaded for more money and we did an ad hoc appeal for funds. We stood in the market places and at vantage points here in Amsterdam and solicited for money and we had enough money which we sent home [about 30,000,000 old Ghana Cedis (US$10,000)]. In 2008 when Nana Akuffo Addo was elected flag-bearer of the party he also came here and we did raise funds to support him. In the 2012 elections, the Netherlands branch of the NPP was the second external branch to have donated the highest amount of money to support the national elections after the external branch in the United States of America. (Akwete, Amsterdam, September 10, 2014)

Particularly, during an election year, various items ranging from bicycles to mobile phones are remitted to facilitate the political campaign. Some individual members of the external branches donate in cash and kind to sponsor activities of the party even outside electoral periods. A key informant said,

> Some of our members provided photocopy machines, printers and other valuable items which were donated to the regional office in Ashanti region following their official request for these items. These items were shipped to Ghana with our own resources. On behalf of the other members in the Netherlands, I presented the items to the chairman and some executives of the party in the regional office in Ghana and they were very grateful. (Black Star Radio, RAZO Amsterdam, September 28, 2014)

8.0 CAMPAIGNING THROUGH RETURN VISITS AND COMMUNICATION

We found that through cross-border movements, some of the respondents exercise their political rights by voting in national elections and internal party elections. Some also travel home to campaign for their political parties during elections. More than half of the participants (26) visit Ghana once a year while thirteen of them visit once in every two years for reasons including political concerns. External party branch executives advise and educate their members to plan their visit to Ghana to coincide with political activities. The diaspora campaign team which usually comprises joint leading executive members of various external party branches in Europe and the United States, travel to Ghana during elections as a way of paying allegiance to the presidential candidate to either retain or gain power. In fact, almost all members admitted campaigning among their friends and relatives in Ghana to vote for their political parties. Almost all members of the external branches in the Netherlands discuss politics with more than five Ghanaians in Ghana and in the diaspora in a month.

Additionally, Ghanaians in the diaspora are actively involved in the crusade for democracy because many of the members of external branches in the Netherlands emigrated from Ghana due to political persecution and political mismanagement. The two external party branches educate Ghanaian immigrants through Ghanaian radio and television stations on the socioeconomic and political situation back home. Both parties do this with the intention of making their political parties more attractive and invite new members to join them. These forms of practice instill in Ghanaian emigrants the sense of competitive elections for the selection of the leaders of the country. These programs also aid Ghanaian emigrants to express their views on or contribute to homeland political discussions. The external branches also resort to social media to discuss their political agenda and programs. Some members of the political party branches interact on the different information technology applications such as WhatsApp, Twitter and Telegram. Apart from promoting good democratic governance, it is also a medium by which institutions are strengthened in the home country.

9.0 CONCLUSION

This chapter has explored the emergence, activities and contribution of Ghanaian emigrants to Ghana's politics through transnational political practices. We discovered that external branches of political parties were set up to hold the ruling government in the home country accountable and to strengthen the chances of their respective parties to win power in the next elections. Ghana's return to democratic rule in 1992 enforced the right to freedom of speech and association without intimidation or fear of threat. This motivated Ghanaians abroad to engage in homeland politics through the formation and membership of external political party branches in the host country. The advancement of communication technologies such as the internet and mobile phones, the low cost of traveling and the easy access to international travels have encouraged Ghanaian emigrants to influence political activities at home through voting, monetary contributions to the political parties and active involvement in political campaigns in the country of origin.

In consonance with claims by transnational scholars (see Goldring 2002), the formation of external party branches strengthen the loyalty of Ghanaian emigrants to the nation's political stability and the development of the country's young democracy. Through membership in political party branches abroad, Ghanaian emigrants exercise their democratic rights through participation and representation in homeland political parties. These activities have ripple effects on the socioeconomic development of the home country. Brains are gained and transferred through the sharing of political ideas between migrants and nonmigrants. Remittances in cash and kind are transferred and used for different purposes, including the smooth running of campaigns, elections and for purposes of sensitization. These activities are the means of promoting good governance, which have ripple effects on the development of a developing country such as Ghana.

In addition, the existence of external branches has moved Ghana's politics beyond its borders and significantly acknowledged the inclusion of Ghanaians in the diaspora in its local politics. These developments led to the passing of the Representation of People Act (Act 699) in February 2007, that recognizes the right of Ghanaians in the diaspora to vote. Unfortunately Act 699 has not been implemented and Ghanaian immigrants who want to vote in national elections have to travel home to exercise their democratic rights. Ghanaian political parties have, however, improved their internal electoral laws to ease the burden of traveling to the home country to elect national executives and the flag-bearer since they allow proxy voting.

We recommend that political parties move beyond the right of participation of external branches in their internal elections and provide a quota for their representation in the national executive councils. Neither the NDC nor the NPP has any member of the external branches in the national executive position. The strengthening of Ghana's democracy moves beyond the national borders and one cannot ignore this important and ever-growing reality of transnational political practice of Ghanaian emigrants and the immense contribution of the external branches of the political parties.

REFERENCES

Al-Ali, Nadje, Richard Black, and Khalid Koser. 2001. "Refugees and Transnationalism: The Experience of Bosnians and Eritreans in Europe." *Journal of Ethnic and Migration Studies* 27(4) : 615–634.

Anarfi, John, Kofi Awusabo-Asare, and Nicholas Nsowah-Nuamah. 2000. "Push and Pull Factors of International Migration. Country Report: Ghana." *Eurostat Working Papers 2000/E, 10.*

Appadurai, Arjun. 1991. "Global Ethnoscapes: Notes and Queries for a Transnational Anthropology," in *Recapturing Anthropology: Working in the Present*, edited by Richard G.Fox, 191–210. Santa Fe: School of American Research Press.

Basch, Linda, Nina Glick Schiller, and Christina Blanc Szanton. 1994. *Nations Unbound, Transnational Projects, Postcolonial Predicaments, and Deterritorialized Nation-States*. Langhorne, PA: Gordon and Breach.

Choenni, Chan. 2002. Ghanezen in Nederland, een profiel, Den Haag: Ministerie van Binnenlandse Zaken en Koninkrijksrelaties. Directie Coiirdinatie Integratiebeleid Minderheden. Accessed September 22, 2016. http://mighealth.net/nl/images/3/34/Ghan.pdf.

Crul, Maurice, and Hans Vermeulen. 2003. "The Second Generation in Europe." *International Migration Review* 37(4): 965–986.

Dietz, Ton, Valentina Mazzucato, Mirjam Kabki, and Lothar Smith. 2011. "Ghanaians in Amsterdam, Their Good Work Back Home and the Importance of Reciprocity." *Journal of Global Initiatives: Policy, Pedagogy, Perspective* 6(1): 132–143.

Driessen, Geert, and Hetty Dekkers. 1997. "Educational Opportunities in the Netherlands: policy, Students' Performance and Issues." *International Review of Education* 43(4): 299–315.

Electoral Commission of Ghana (EC). 2013. "Electoral Commission of Ghana 2012." Accessed January 11, 2014. *http://www.ec.gov.gh/page.php?page=529&section=49&typ=1.*

Fridy, Kevin. 2007. "The Elephant, Umbrella, and Quarrelling Cocks: Disaggregating Partisanship in Ghana's fourth Republic." *African Affairs* 106(423) : 281–305.

Giddens Anthony. 1990. *The Consequences of Modernity*. Cambridge: Polity Press.

Goldring, Luin. 2002. "The Mexican State and Transmigrant Organizations: Negotiating the Boundaries of Membership and Participation." *Latin American Research Review* 37(3): 55–99.

Guarnizo, Luis Eduardo, Alejandro Portes, and William Haller. 2003. "Assimilation and Transnationalism: Determinants of Transnational Political Action Among Contemporary Migrants." *American Journal of Sociology* 108(6): 1211–1248.

Huntington, Samuel, P. 1993. "The Clash of Civilizations?" *Foreign Affairs* 72(3): 22–49.

Knipscheer, Jeroen W, Eleonore E. M. De Jong, J. Kleber Rolf, and Ekow Lamptey. 2000. "Ghanaian Migrants in the Netherlands: General Health, Acculturative Stress and Utilization of Mental Health Care." *Journal of Community Psychology* 28(4): 459–476.

Koopmans, Ruud, and Paul Statham, eds. 2010. *The Making of a European Public Sphere: Media Discourse and Political Contention*. Cambridge: Cambridge University Press.

Koopmans, Ruud, Paul Statham, Marco Giugni, and Florence Passy. 2005. *Contested Citizenship: Immigration and Cultural Diversity in Europe.* Minneapolis: University of Minnesota Press.

Kyei, Justice R, Kwabena Owusu, and Rafal Smoczynski. 2016. "Building Bridges or Bonds: The Case of Ghanaian Second Generation Migrants in Ghanaian Churches in Amsterdam." *Antropological Research and Studies* 6: 13–24. Accessed September 22, 2016. http://www.journalstudiesanthropology.ro/en/no-6–2016/r46/.

Levitt, Peggy. 2007. *God Needs No Passport: Immigrants and the Changing American Religious Landscape.* New York: New Press.

Levitt, Peggy, and Nadya B. Jaworsky. 2007. "Transnational Migration Studies: Past Developments and Future Trends." *Annual Review Sociology* 33(1):129–156.

Lindberg, Staffan I, and K. C. Morrison Minion . 2005. "Exploring Voter Alignments in Africa: Core and Swing Voters in Ghana." *The Journal of Modern African Studies* 43(4): 565–586.

Mahler, J. Sarah. 2000. "Constructing International Relations: The Role of Transnational Migrants and Other Non–State Actors." *Identities Global Studies in Culture and Power* 7(2): 197–232.

Manning, Carrie. 2005. "Assessing African Party Systems After the Third Wave." *Party Politics* 11(6): 707–727.

Martiniello, Marco. 2005. *Political Participation, Mobilisation and Representation of Immigrants and Their Offspring in Europe.* Willy Brandt Series of Working Papers in International Migration and Ethnic Relations, School of International Migration and Ethnic Relations, Malmö University, Malmö.

Martiniello, Marco, and Bousetta Hassan. 2008. "Les Pratiques Transnationales des Immigrés Chinois et Marocains de Belgique', *Revue Européenne des Migrations Internationales* 24(2): 45–66.

Martiniello, Marco, and Jean-Michel Lafleur. 2008. "Towards a Transatlantic Dialogue in the Study of Immigrant Political Transnationalism." *Ethnic and Racial Studies* 31(4): 645–663.

Mazzucato, Valentina. 2005. *The Study of Transnational Migration: Reflections on a Simultaneous Matched-Sample Methodology.* Paper commissioned by the Social Science Research Council, New York City, presented on November 19, 2005.

Mazzucato, Valentina, Mirjam Kabki, and Lothar Smith. 2006. "Transnational Migration and the Economy of Funerals: Changing Practices in Ghana." *Development and Change* 37(5): 1047–1072.

Mohan, Giles. 2006. "Embedded Cosmopolitanism and the Politics of Obligation: The Ghanaian Diaspora and Development." *Environment and Planning A* 38(5): 867–883.

Morawska, Ewa. 2001. "Structuring Migration: The Case of Polish Income-Seeking Travelers to the West." *Theory and Society* 30(1): 47–80.

———. 2003. "Immigrant Transnationalism and Assimilation: A Variety of Combination and the Analytic Strategy it Suggests," in *Toward Assimilation and Citizenship. Immigrants in Liberal Nation-States*, edited by Christian Joppke and Ewa Morawska, 133–176. Basingstoke: Palgrave – Macmillan.

Morrison, Minion K. C. 2004. "Political Parties in Ghana Through Four Republics: A Path to Democratic Consolidation". *Comparative Politics* 36(4): 421–442.

Mugge, Liza. 2010. *Beyond Dutch Borders: Transnational Politics Among Colonial Migrants, Guest Workers and the Second Generation.* Amsterdam: Amsterdam University Press/IMISCOE.

NDC Germany. 2012. "NDC Diaspora Campaign Team Arrives in Ghana." Accessed August 10, 2014. http://www.modernghana.com/news/429339/1/ndc-diaspora-campaign-team-arrives-in-ghana.html.

Nijenhuis, Gery, and Annelies Zoomer. 2012. *Transnational Activities of Immigrant Organizations in the Netherlands: Do Ghanaian, Moroccan and Surinamese Diaspora Organizations Enhance Development?* Woodrow Wilson School of Public and International Affairs No. 1414. Center for Migration and Development,. Princeton University.

Østergaard Nielsen, Eva. 2003. "The Politics of Migrants' Transnational Political Practices." *International Migration Review* 37(3): 760–786.

Owusu, Thomas Yaw. 2003. "Transnationalism Among African Immigrants in North America: The Case of Ghanaians in Canada." *Journal of International Migration and Integration/Revue de l'integration et de la Migration Internationale* 4(3): 395–413.

Pantoja, Adrian. 2005. "Transnational Ties and Immigrant Political Incorporation: The Case of Dominicans in Washington Heights, New York." *International Migration* 43(4): 123–146.

Portes, Alejandro. 2001. "Introduction: The Debates and Significance of Immigrant Transnationalism". *Global Networks* 1(3): 181–194.

Portes, Alejandro, Cristina Escobar, and Alexandria Walton Radford. 2007. "Immigrant Transnational Organizations and Development: A Comparative Study." *International Migration Review* 41(1): 242–281.

Portes, Alejandro, Luis E. Guarnizo, and Patricia Landolt. 1999. "The Study of Transnationalism: Pitfalls and Promise of an Emergent Research Field." *Ethnic and Racial Studies* 22(2): 217–237.

Prempeh, Kwame. 2014. "NPP Diaspora Community." Accessed August 20, 2014. http://www.ghanaweb.com/GhanaHomePage/diaspora/artikel.php?ID=305873.

Rijkschroeff, Rally, Geert ten Dam, Jan Willem Duyvendak, Marjan de Gruijter, and Trees Pels. 2005. "Educational Policies on Migrants and Minorities in the Netherlands: Success or Failure?" *Journal of Education Policy* 20(4): 417–435.

Schiller, Nina G, and Eugene Fouron Georges. 1998. "Transnational Lives and National Identities." In *Transnationalism from Below*, edited by M. P. Smith and L. E. Guarnizo, 130–164. New Brunswick: Transaction Publishers.

Schiller, Nina G, Linda Basch, and Cristina Blanc Szanton. 1992. "Transnationalism: a new analytic framework for Understanding Migration." *Annals of the New York Academy of Sciences* 645(1): 1–24.

Scholten, Peter, and Ronald Holzhacker. "Bonding, Bridging and Ethnic Minorities in the Netherlands: Changing Discourses in a Changing Nation." *Nations and Nationalism* 15(1): 81–100.

Setrana, Mary B, and Justice Richard Kwabena Owusu Kyei. 2015. "L'engagement Politique de la Diaspora Ghanéenne aux Pays-Bas." *Afrique Contemporaine* 256(4): 91–101. Accessed September 22, 2016. http://www.cairn.info/resume.php?ID_ARTICLE=AFCO_256_0091.

Snel, Erik, Godfried Engbersen, and Arjen Leerkes.2006." Transnational Involvement and Social Integration." *Global Networks* 6(3): 285–308.

Soysal, Yasemin Nuhoglu. 1994. *Limits of Citizenship: Migrants and Postnational Membership in Europe*. Chicago: University of Chicago Press.

Statistics Netherlands. 2014. "Population; Sex, Origin and Generation, 1 January." Accessed February 22, 2014. *http://statline.cbs.nl/StatWeb/publication/?DM=SLEN&PA=37325ENG&D1=0&D2=a&D3=0&D4=0&D5=0,85&D6=11–17&LA=EN&HDR=G2,G3,G4,T&STB=G1,G5&VW=T.*

Tonah, Steve. 2007. *Ghanaians Abroad and Their Ties Home: Cultural and Religious Dimensions of Transnational Migration*. Working Paper, Center for Interdisciplinary Research, Bielefeld, Germany: COMCAD.

Van Amersfoort, Hans. 2001. "*Moderne Diasporas, Transnationalisme en Sociale Cohesie*." Amsterdam: Institute for Migration & Ethnic Studies (IMES).

Van Dijk, Rijk. 2002. "Ghanaian Churches in the Netherlands Religion Mediating a Tense Relationship," in *Merchants, Missionaries & Migrants: 300 years of Dutch-Ghanaian Relations,* edited by W. M. J. van Kessel, 89–97. Amsterdam: KIT Publishers.

Van Hear, Nicholas, Frank Pieke, and Steven Vertovec. 2004. *The Contribution of UK-based Diasporas to Development and Poverty Reduction*. COMPAS (Centre on Migration, Policy and Society), University of Oxford.

Vertovec, Steven. 1999. "Conceiving and Researching Transnationalism." *Ethnic and Racial Studies* 22(2): 447–462.

———. 2004."Migrant Transnationalism and Modes of Transformation." *International Migration Review* 38(3): 970–1001.

Verwey-Jonker, H. 1971. *Allochtonen in Nederland*. The Hague: Staatsuitgeverij.

Yuval-Davis, Nira. 1999. "The 'Multi-Layered Citizen." *International Feminist Journal of Politics* 1(1): 119–136. doi: 10.1080/146167499360068.

Chapter 3

Transnational Migration Among Migrants from Cameroon

Danielle Minteu Kadje

Transnational development has various impacts on local development, social and spatial relations. This chapter analyzes the case of migrants from Cameroon living in Germany and their contribution to development, especially in the health and educational sectors[1]. These migrants take part progressively in development practices, particularly in social, economic and political activities, as well as flows and exchanges. Development practices in Cameroon aim at reducing the grinding impacts of global poverty and defining the pathways to enhance well-being for the under-resourced and socially excluded.

Cameroon is peculiar because of its high emigration rate. It is not easy to obtain a comprehensive data and undertake a demographic analysis of Cameroonian migrants in Germany; 14,414 Cameroonians were officially registered in Germany for the years 1980–2006 by the German Statistical Office and the Bundesamt für Migration und Flüchtlinge (BAMF), the government institution responsible for documenting foreign migrants and refugees (Schmelz 2007). Emigration from Cameroon to Germany consists primarily of educational migration with migrants from Yaoundé, Douala and Western Cameroon being overrepresented. Based on fieldwork in Cameroon and Germany[2]and drawing upon my doctoral research work, this chapter is an analysis of the impact of transnational migration to Germany on the transformation of rural and urban regions in Cameroon.

The approach was a mixed method, involving both qualitative and quantitative research. We conducted semistructured interviews with representatives of Cameroonian associations in Germany such as *Challenge Camerounais C.C* Munich and *ARCH* Hamburg and also collected data from associations, such as *Deutsch-Kamerunische Brücke* (German-Cameroonian Bridge in Hesse), *Generation Tiers-Monde* (Baden-Würtemberg and Bavaria), *Pro New Tech* or *Ident Africa* (North-Rhine Westphalia), *AfricAvenir* (Berlin-Douala),

African Development Initiative, NEPAD Germany (Hesse) and *Africa Positive* (North-Rhine Westphalia). Data from professional associations, such as *Camfomedics* (medical associations), *VK II* (a Cameroonian association of IT specialists and engineers in Germany which is divided into different engineering and computing areas for a multidisciplinary development through the exchange and sharing of information and expertise[3]), were also collected following the same guidelines used above. Additional information and statistics from researchers, professionals from the private sector, medical specialists, development experts, government agencies and organizations (such as the *Bundesamtfür Migration und Flüchtlinge, Deutscher Akademischer Austauschdienst, Deutsche Gesellschaftfür Internationale Zusammenarbeit*, Centre for International Migration, World University Service, the German Statistical Office, the Cameroonian Embassy in Germany, OECD, the WB, and the North-South Council of Europe) are integrated into the analysis. Furthermore, available literature on Cameroonian migrants and diaspora was also incorporated into the analysis.

This chapter focuses and analyzes primarily on how migrants who are organized in associations cooperate with NGOs and local authorities in Cameroon and Germany in order to support developmental projects in Cameroon. The chapter argues that transnational development challenges traditional roles and norms of the state. Further, Cameroonian migrants do not belong exclusively to either home or host country, they build up connections with and owe allegiances to both: they are '*Here*' (Germany) and '*There*' (Cameroon). The chapter highlights the paradigm of transnational spaces in policy analysis. It focuses essentially on development and migration and can be viewed as a new approach to poverty reduction [4]in Cameroon.

1.0 TRANSNATIONALISM: A THEORETICAL FRAMEWORK

The theoretical interest of this approach is that it allows us to use transnational perspectives, which highlight the sustained connections between emigrants and their countries of origin. A transnational perspective challenges the rigid notion of emigration and return. Instead it focuses on the processes that take place within the transnational social field that is shared by migrants and nonmigrants (Carling 2005). Daniel Bach has argued that trans-state networks "instil and stimulate specific patterns of regionalization," "(whereby) the dynamics of networking usually associated with transnational interactions coalesce with a capacity to instrumentalize interstate relations and state policies through the treatment of public office as opportunities for private interactions" (Bach 2003,23).

For Basch, Glick-Schiller and Blanc-Szanton (1992) transnationalism means "the process by which immigrants forge and sustain multi-stranded social relations that link together their societies of origin and settlement." Actually, the literature on migration and development takes the transnational perspective also into account. According to a UN definition, "The term 'migrant' in article 1.1 (a) should be understood as covering all cases where the decision to migrate is taken freely by the individual concerned, for reasons of 'personal convenience' and without intervention of an external compelling factor.[5]"

However, the complex interaction between varying perceptions of *push* and *pull* factors, individual decision-making processes and the different migration destinations make it very difficult to create a unified theory of migration. It seems that factors such as perceptions of the situation in the receiving countries, as well as the policies and legislation that enable or complicate movement, play a very important role in shaping migration streams. A number of attempts have been made to capture and explain the different motivations and processes related to the decision to migrate. Many scientists emphasized the fact that until the 1970s most influential theories were those proffered by neoclassical theorists who viewed individual migration decisions as resulting from *push-pull* factors. The concept of transnationalism emerged in the late 1980s (Basch, Glick-Schiller and Blanc-Szanton 1992). Prior to that date, migration was viewed as a unilateral movement, but international migration brings new forms of migration based on cross-national and transnational networks. Complex and multidirectional migration increased, though not steadily, but it was linked to certain stages of one's private or working life (Lenz et al. 2002). The main consensus among the theorists of transnationalism is perhaps the notion of transnationalism as a process focused on the developments that take place within the transnational social field that is shared by migrants and nonmigrants (Carling 2005). However, the dimension of migration and transnationalism in relation to devising policies and strategies to promote development is only beginning to be researched and understood.

Most of the literature regarding transnationalism goes well beyond conventional borders of nation-states. It is mainly framed within the study of international migration, and the units of analysis assume a relatively obvious duality regarding behavior: duality in the daily life of the individual or the family; duality of the relationship between organizations that deal with immigrants' issues and the host and home countries. Additionally, economic, cultural, political and social activities are recognized as spaces that are built by their protagonists, mainly immigrants, and that these spaces cross geographic borders in an endless array of forms. However, the dimension of migration and transnationalism in relation to devising policies and strategies to promote development is only beginning to be researched and understood.

2.0 CAMEROONIAN ASSOCIATIONS IN GERMANY: 'HERE' AND 'THERE'

Hein de Haas (2008, 12) explicitly stated that it is important to have a more dynamic and realistic view of migration-development interconnections.[6] For him, in order to achieve a more dynamic and realistic view of migration-development interconnections, it is useful to draw on the spatiotemporal theoretical perspectives developed by Zelinsky (1971), Skeldon (1997) and de Haas (2008, 12). Orozco (2005), on the other hand, argues that four factors contribute to fostering a certain level of transnational engagement with the homeland. By a case study on Latinos and their links to their homelands, he indicates how the following four factors enable the formation of a group into a diaspora:

a. The level of community, and particularly elite and activist-consciousness about the need or desire to maintain a link with the homeland
b. The homeland's perceptions of emigrants
c. The outreach policies by governments in the homeland
d. The existence of relationships between source and destination countries

Orozco explicitly stated that the implications of these dynamics are reflected in an impact on the home country at various levels, particularly at micro and macro levels; these dynamics create 'distant proximities' (Rosenau 2003). The implications of these dynamics coincide with the development and the improvement of the quality of life for the family and they have an impact on the national economy.

Andréa Schmelz (2007, 21–22) argues that the amount of and frequency of money transfers depend on the purpose of a given project and its objective. The lack of reliable data makes it impossible to determine the total amount of money transferred by Cameroonians living in Germany to Cameroon. Remittances mainly take place through international money transfer services such as *Western Union* or *Money Gram.*[7] Cameroonian migrants in Germany send remittances to family and close friends in Cameroon for their education, health care and during births, marriages and funerals. It is important to stress that migrants contribute to the development of their countries collectively through associations and through nonprofit and/or business activities. As regards nonprofit activities, contributions aim at improving the infrastructure in Cameroonian schools and universities[8]and health institutions.

Cameroonian associations in Germany became more visible and they are embedded in a deep sense of village and community solidarity, they have traditionally contributed to the development of their home community through transfer of funds and they have been doing this in a more innovative and organized manner. These associations collect and channel migrants' funds and use them to finance, wholly or in part, a variety of productive projects in their home communities. These associations cooperate with NGOs in the execution of their projects, in order to benefit from their expertise, skills and knowledge. These associations are close to civil societies which aim at filling the gap created by the inability of the state to provide such services. Cameroonians in Germany do not belong exclusively to either home or host country; they have connections with and owe allegiances to both: they are '*Here*' (Germany) and '*There*'[9](Cameroon). The contribution from this diaspora to "home" is largely in the form of financial remittances and diversity of transfer activities in the fields of sciences, business, culture and education. There are many Cameroonian associations in Germany. The most important among them are

a. Associations of students or alumni (people who have attended schools and universities in Germany or Cameroon).
b. Professional associations such as *Camfomedics,* founded in 1994.

Table 3.1 Geographic Distribution of Migrants in Germany with Cameroonian Citizenship as at December 31, 2006

State	*Number of Cameroonians*	*% of Cameroonians*
Baden-Württemberg	2,432	16.9
Bavaria	898	6.2
Berlin	1,414	9.8
Brandenburg	746	5.2
Bremen	353	2.4
Hamburg	514	3.6
Hesse	1,360	9.4
Mecklenburg-Western Pomerania	17	0.1
Lower Saxony	1,116	7.7
North-Rhine Westphalia	3,893	27.0
Rhineland-Palatinate	913	6.3
Saarland	215	1.5
Saxony	153	1.1
Saxony-Anhalt	167	1.2
Schleswig-Holstein	121	0.8
Thuringia	99	0.7
Total	14,414	100.0

Source: Andrea Schmelz (2007, 10).

c. Development associations which focus on development policy such as *Deutsch-Kamerunische Brücke* (German-Cameroonian Bridge in Hessen), *Generation Tiers-Monde* (Baden-Württemberg/Bavaria), *Pro New Tech* or *IdentAfrica* (North-Rhine Westphalia), *AfricaAvenir* (Berlin-Douala), *African Development Initiative, NEPAD Germany* (Hessen) and *Africa Positive* (North-Rhine Westphalia).
d. Regional associations such as *Challenge Camerounais CC* founded in 1991. This association does not focus on any particular region, city or ethnic group in Cameroon but it plays an important role in this community based in Germany.

3.0 COMMUNITY BENEFITS AND BUSINESS ACTIVITIES

Cameroonians in Germany are engaged in nonprofit activities and business activities in their home country. They contribute to the support of social infrastructure particularly in:

a. Education: One of the priorities of members of the Cameroonian diaspora in Germany is to build schools and equip them; apart from this, they contribute through the donations of writing materials, schoolbooks and the payment of pupils' school fees. They are also involved in sharing their technological expertise with graduate students and academics, in addition to designing and implementing projects which aim at connecting Cameroonian and African Universities. The mission of the VKII association consists in fostering widespread support for the adoption of technology by achieving the following: channeling the talents of Cameroonian engineers and computer scientists; providing a forum for the definition of standards, the resolution of issues relating to implementation, the development and delivery of education and training programs and the development of strategies and tactics for the continued expansion of their philosophy of using technology to achieve efficient progress; ensuring that standards, policies and regulations for different fields are thoughtfully developed and implemented by serving as the primary catalyst for the identification, communication and resolution of obstacles growth of these fields; informing and educating VKII members and other stakeholders about the benefits and strategies for successfully implementing technological strategies; planning and implementation of development-oriented projects; technology and knowledge transfer.
b. Health: The Cameroonian association *Camfomedics* was founded by Cameroonian medical, pharmacy and dentistry students on May 7, 1994, in Tubingen, Germany. The name *Camfomedics* is a shortened form of "*Deutsch-Kamerunisches Forum für die Medizinischen und Paramedizinischen Wissenschaften e.V.*" (German-Cameroonian Forum for Medical

and Paramedical Sciences). This association is a diaspora initiative for the promotion of a sustainable health policy which should promote the integration and reintegration of Cameroonian and German medical students. Equipped with knowledge about the reality of life in Cameroon, experiences abroad, special skills in medical science, as well as a strong will, the association's main activities and aims are focused on training and further education, health projects in Cameroon, integration and reintegration of experts, global partnership and exchanges with other disciplines. This association has many projects in Cameroon such as *PINK* (*Praktikum in Kamerun*), a special forum for students and graduates for questions and answers about doing an internship in Cameroon. This work group has a portal about the possibility of an internship, clinical traineeship and practical year for medical students and nursing careers in Cameroon. The goal is to make it possible and to make it easier for both Cameroonian and German students to do their internships in Cameroon); *iMED* (Improving Medical Education and Health Care Delivery through Diaspora Engagement). The largest crisis of the health system in Cameroon is the lack of specialist staff. The focus of the program is to train Cameroonian doctors in the use of simple, modern, "minimally invasive" diagnostic and therapeutic instruments, such as sonography, sonographically controlled puncture, electrocardiography and endoscopy. Specialist doctors in the diaspora are obligated to work or teach for at least two weeks every twenty-four months within the scope of the project in Cameroon and conclude a volunteer contract; *eHealth*, the pilot project, serves to improve the work processes in hospitals in Cameroon by electronic means. It also makes possible a new communication platform among doctors worldwide.

c. Business activities: As regards business activities, it was not easy to get qualitative or quantitative data, since we are dealing with a young and highly educated migrant group and it may be assumed that business activities will increase in future (Schmelz 2007, 22). However, associations such as *Challenge Camerounais* and *Deutsch-kamerunische Brücke* through business forums promote business activities between German and Cameroonian companies.

The Business and Social Forum (BSF) within the framework of *Challenge Camerounais* makes a significant contribution to the development of the Cameroonian diaspora as well as to the social and economic development of Cameroon. The BSF provides a platform for exchange between actors in the business, academic and social as well as political environments in Germany and Cameroon to set up an edifying impetus to forge or intensify profitable partnerships.[10]

Figure 3.1 shows the interaction between Cameroonian associations in Germany and their recipients in Cameroon; it highlights the fact that several

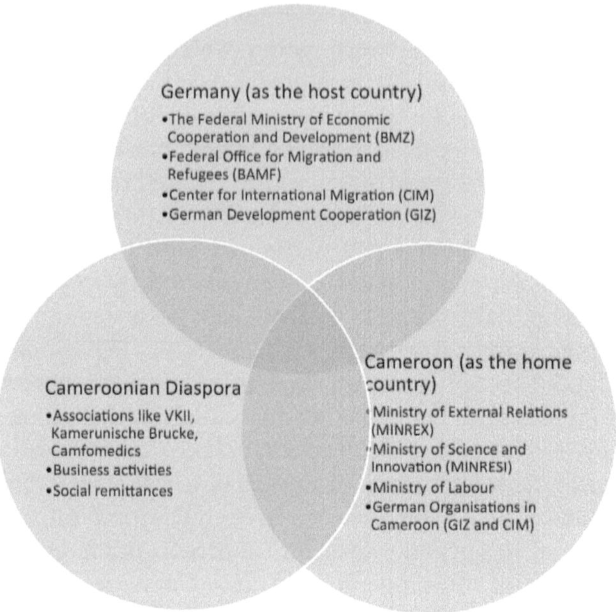

Figure 3.1 Transnational migration and development in Cameroon and Germany. Created by the author.

actors are involved in this dynamics, in both origin and destination countries. The actors are in an interdependent relationship. On the side of Germany, we notice that the level of decentralization in Germany is high and there are many initiatives at the regional level in the area of migration and development and one should mention regional initiatives such as the *Fachstelle Migration und Entwicklung* in North-Rhine Westphalia. The decentralized system in Germany offers possibilities for participation at all levels of decision-making and opens up new avenues of action under the government policy of development cooperation. A process of cooperation involving public authorities, migrant associations, NGOs and the private sector emphasizes local development and the role of local authorities. In other words, these associations stress the importance of involving institutions in both the North and South so that they are all jointly engaged in development practices in Cameroon.

4.0 CONCLUSION

Hein de Haas (2005) argues that specific policies can enhance the development potential of migration by facilitating and encouraging remittance transfers and investments; for this author, the key to more coherent migration and development policies seems to lie in encouraging circular migration through a far more liberal approach toward labor migration of both the low and highly skilled for which a real demand exists. It is important to keep in mind that a state outreach policy on diaspora must be in place. Orozco (2005, 44) argues that to realize this goal, five key elements must be accounted:

> First, state outreach policy towards the diaspora must officially recognize its communities living abroad. Second, state must establish a communication mechanism between themselves and organized diaspora groups. Third, both state and diasporic groups must develop a joint agenda that addresses issues of common concern. Fourth, the diasporic community must be allowed a substantial presence and possible influence in the nation-state. Fifth, states must invest tangible resources, both materials and human, to implement outreach efforts [. . .] The end goal of this strategy is twofold: confidence building and incorporation of citizens.

In this chapter, it has been shown that transnational migration between Cameroon and Germany can enhance the vital contribution of the Cameroonian diaspora in Germany to Cameroon, as a receiving country. This work highlights Cameroonian migrants who build up connections with and owe allegiances to both countries: they are '*Here*' (Germany) and '*There*' (Cameroon).

NOTES

1. In the frame of this research, we are relying on a concept of development which emphasizes on the human dimensions of development. In this sense, the basic purpose of development is to enlarge people's choices. The goals of development are operationalized in the Millennium Development Goals (MDGs), which among others also include the areas of health and education. Current dialogues on a post-2015 development include also goals in the area of health and education.

2. Fieldwork was conducted in Cameroon (Yaoundé and Douala) between July 1 and September 1, 2009 and September 1, 2011–September 15, 2014. Fieldwork in Germany (Kassel and Frankfurt/Main) was conducted between November 2008 and May 2009.

3. The main goal of VKII is to promote research activities.

4. Despite the renewed interests of International Financial Institutions (including the World Bank, the IMF) orientation to poverty reduction, many theorists such as Doug Porter and David Craig argue that the evaluative literature raises a number of key issues around the outcome deriving from this orientation. These include low rates of growth in high reform countries, unevenness in integration, high adjustment costs and political fallout, and the rise of concerns about long-term path dependence of growth and inequalities. See David, Craig and Porter Doug, 2003, "Poverty Reduction Strategy Papers: A New Convergence," *World Development*, Vol.31, N°1, p.53–69, 2003.

5. Measures to improve the situation and ensure the human rights and dignity of all migrant workers 1998. Report of the working group of intergovernmental experts on the human rights of migrants submitted in accordance with Commission on Human Rights resolution 1997/15. This broader definition indicates that migrants do not refer to refugees, displaced or others forced or compelled to leave their homes. Migrants are people who make choices about when to leave and where to go, even though these choices are sometimes extremely constrained.

6. For Hein de Haas (2008), in order to achieve a more dynamic and realistic view of migration-development interconnections, it seems useful to draw on the spatiotemporal theoretical perspectives developed by Zelinsky (1971) and Skeldon (1997).

7. Western Union now operates worldwide. It has more than 640 agent locations in Cameroon for people who want to send and receive money worldwide. MoneyGram is the second largest provider of money transfers in the world. The company operates in more than 200 countries with a global network of about 347,000 agent offices.

8. The "Cameroonian Association of Engineers and Computer Scientists" mostly known as VKII was founded in 2000 in Frankfurt. Today, the association brings together the highest number of Cameroonian students and professionals in Europe. The association is recognized in Germany as a nonprofit, nonpolitical and civil organization. It was built up from the grassroots to relieve the difficulties that students, alumni as well as technicians encounter in their various professions. Furthermore, the association promotes excellence within the community.Among its main goals, the VKII identifies and assigns technically oriented professionals to tackle serious and urgent problems faced in various fields of technology both in Cameroon and abroad. In order to establish a genuine link for the transfer of technologies, the association has set a board of experts which deals with institutions such as universities, factories and vocational training schools. The VKII has organized yearly symposiums since 2006 whereby many associate institutions as well as students and professionals across the world are invited. The VKII has its representatives in almost all German technical universities as well as in various industries in Europe. www.vkii.org

9. 'Here' and 'There' echoes the common French expression "Ici" et "Là-bas" to explain this transnational dynamism.

10. *Challenge Camerounais* has become one of the largest global gatherings in recent years of the African diaspora. The objective of this event, which was devoted mainly to sports in the beginning in 1992, has been supplemented over the years by cultural aspects due to the growing interest and increasing crowd turnout. The BSF was initiated in 2006, when the CC was held in Bremen. The creation of this event finally paved the way for the Challenge to incorporate the important socioeconomic component into its program.

REFERENCES

Adams, Ralph H. 1991. "The Economic Uses and Impact of International Remittances in Rural Egypt." *Economic Development and Cultural Change* 39: 695–722.

Agunias, Dovelyn R. 2006. *Remittances and Development: Trends, Impacts, and Policy Options*. Migration Policy Institute, Washington D.C.

Appleyard, Reginald. 1989. "Migration and Development: Myths and Reality." *International Migration Review* 23: 486–99.

Bach, Daniel. 2016. *Regionalism in Africa: Genealogies, Institutions and Trans-state Networks*. London: Routledge.

Carling, Jorgen. 2005. "Gender Dimensions of International Migration." Global Commission on International Migration, Geneva.

Commission on Human Rights. Fifty-fourth session, Intergovernmental working group of experts on the human rights of migrants. http://www.unesco.org/new/en/social-and-human-sciences/themes/international-migration/glossary/migrant/

David, Craig, and Doug Porter. 2003. "Poverty Reduction Strategy Papers : A New Convergence." *World Development* 31(1):53–69.

Daum, Christophe. 1998. *Les Associations de Maliens en France* (*Migrations, Développement et Citoyenneté*). Paris : Karthala.

De Haan, Arjan, Karen Brock, Grace Carswell, Ngolo Coulibaly, Haileyesus Seba, and Kazi Ali Toufique, 2000. *Migration and Livelihoods: Case Studies in Bangladesh, Ethiopia and Mali*. Brighton: Institute of Development Studies, University of Brighton, Sussex.

De Haas, Hein. 2005. "International Migration, Remittances and Development: Myths and Facts." *Third World Quarterly* 26: 1269–84.

De Haas, Hein. 2008. *Migration and Development. A Theoretical Perspective*. Oxford: International Migration Institute, University of Oxford.

Economic Commission for Africa (ECA) 2006. *International Migration and Development: Implications for Africa*. Addis Ababa: Economic Commission for Africa (ECA).

Glick-Schiller Nina, Linda Basch, and Christine Blanc-Szanton. 1992. "Transnationalism: A New Analytic Framework for Understanding Migration" in *Towards a Transnational Perspective on Migration. Race, Class, Ethnicity and Nationalism Reconsidered*, edited by Nina Glick-Schiller, Linda Basch, and Christine Blanc-Szanton. New York: New York Academy of Sciences.

Glick-Schiller, Nina, Linda Basch, and Christine Szanton. 1994. *NationsUnbound. Transnational Projects, Postcolonial Predicaments, and Deterritorialized Nations-States*. Amsterdam: Gordon and Breach.

Geddes, Andrew. 2000. *Immigration and European Integration*. Manchester: Manchester University Press.

Grillo, Ralph, and Bruno Riccio. 2004. "Translocal Development, Italy-Senegal." *Population, Space and Place* 10: 99–111.

Kritz, Mary M, Lin Lean Lim, and Hania Zlotnik, eds. 1992. *International Migration System: A Global Approach*. Oxford: Clarendon Press.

Lacroix, Thomas. 2005. *Les Réseaux Marocains du Développement: Géographie du Transnational et Politiques du Territorial*. Paris : Presses de Sciences Po.

Lenz, Ilze. 2003. "Globalization, Gender and Work: Perspectives on Global Regulation." *Review of Policy Research* 20(1): 21–43.

Manchuelle, Francois. 1997. *Willing Migrants. Soninké Labor Diaspora, 1948–1960*. Athens, Ohio : Ohio University Press.

Minteu-Kadje, Danielle. 2009. "De l'Action Publique Internationale du Codéveloppement France-Mali, in Nouveau dans Outres Anciennes." *Polis* 16: 1–2.

Minteu-Kadje, Danielle. 2014. "Penser le Codeveloppement, la Dynamique Franco-Malienne." *Sens Public* 12: 1–6. http://www.sens-public.org/spip.php?article1124

Orozco, Manuel. 2005. *Diasporas, Development and Transnational Integration: Ghanaians in the U.S., U.K. and Germany*. International through the U.S. Agency for International Development. Washington DC: Report commissioned by citizen.

Rosenau, James. 2003. *Distant Proximities: Dynamics Beyond Globalization*. Princeton: Princeton University Press.

Rostow, Walt W. 1960. *The Stages of Economic Growth*. London: Cambridge University Press.

Schmelz, Andrea. 2007. The Cameroonian Diaspora in Germany. Its Contribution to Development in Cameroon. Accessed June 16, 2015. http://www.migration4development.org/sites/m4d.emakina-eu.net/files/ the_Cameroonian _Diaspora_in_Germany.pdf

Skeldon, Ronald. 1997. *Migration and Development: A Global Perspective*. London: Longman.

Schwenken, Helen. 2005. "The Challenges of Framing Women Migrants Rights in the European Union." *Revue Européenne des Migrations Internationales* 21, 1.

Zelinski, Wilbur. 1971. "The Hypothesis of the Mobility Transition." *Geographical Review* 61, 219–49.

Chapter 4

Partnering for Rural Development in Ghana

The Case of Ghanaian Hometown Associations in the United Kingdom

Leander Kandilige

1.0 INTRODUCTION: THE EMERGENCE OF HOMETOWN ASSOCIATIONS

Globalization has intensified since the 1990s and increasing flows of people, capital and services have marked this trend. Out of the prevailing dynamics, the volume of international migration has significantly risen from 154 million in 1990 to about 244 million in 2015 (UNDESA 2016). These flows have encompassed emigration and immigration resulting in either temporary or permanent changes in locations of abode, skilled and unskilled labor migrations as well as voluntary and involuntary movements, among others.

As migrant communities grow in mass over time and space, there is a natural tendency for some participating individuals to associate with people of similar kinship, religious, sociocultural and sometimes professional backgrounds. These mostly personal decisions are rooted in subjective interpretations by migrants of the propinquity of self-identifying factors or parameters such as race, religion, ethnicity, nationality, social class, professional grouping and language. If the affinity among migrants from the same country or region of origin is judged to be strong, they tend to form what Mercer, Page and Evans (2009) describe as home associations. This conceptualization, they argue, is preferred to the popular reference to such groups as "hometown" associations (Kandilige 2012, Mazzucato and Kabki 2009, Caglar 2006, Webner 2002). As Mercer, Page and Evans (2009) explain, in the African context "hometown" does not necessarily coincide with or refer to a town but may rather refer to a district, region or even country. While maintaining the term "hometown" association in this chapter, I am using it in its broader sense as espoused by Mercer, Page and Evans (2009).

The purpose of this chapter is to assess the types of partnerships that are formed between two Ghanaian hometown associations in the United Kingdom (Kwahuman Association and the Kassena-Nankana Development League (KNDL)) and their local communities in the country of origin for the purposes of rural development. This is relevant because it contributes toward bridging a gap in migration research on Ghana. Literature on the Ghanaian diaspora, described as a "neo-diaspora" (Koser, Al-Ali, Black 2001), is gradually gaining momentum. However, in spite of the fact that research has been conducted on the relationship between the size of hometowns in Ghana and their ability to access development funding from foreign-based hometown associations (Mazzucato and Kabki 2009) or the types, characteristics, themes and activities of Ghanaian hometown associations in the Netherlands (Ong'ayo 2014), very little research has been conducted on the institutions, agencies, groups or individuals that actually serve as partners with these foreign-based hometown associations for development purposes.

Empirical migration research on Ghana, over the past decade, has examined the role of the family in migration decision-making (Tiemoko 2004); the impact of expenditure by migrants on social obligations such as funerals (Mazzucato, Kabki and Smith 2006); how identities and obligations operate within spaces of transnational communities and how these influence development (Mohan 2006); migration trends and the likely relationship between socioeconomic inequalities and violence (Langer 2007); Ghana's migration policies and the composition of migrant populations (Quartey 2009); the need for reverse remittances to be included in remittance calculations (Mazzucato 2010); and how transnational migrant arrangements affect left-behind children and families (Mazzucato and Schans 2011), among others. However, we do not know of a study that conducted an interregional comparison of Ghanaian hometown associations, especially with particular focus on their choice of local development partners and how this is ultimately tied together by the concept of trust (often taken for granted in migration and development discourses). This missing link in the migration literature on Ghana is the research problem that this chapter seeks to address.

It must be stated that hometown associations, as vessels of socialization and identity formation in host communities, have a long history in Ghana. It is commonplace for migrant communities from rural areas in Ghana to set up hometown associations in urban centers. The purpose of such associations is not dissimilar to those of diaspora communities—to support the self-help activities of members, in the first instance, and then contribute to hometown development with time. Foreign-based hometown associations can, therefore, be seen somewhat as a natural extension of urban-based hometown associations in the origin country.

The case study research methodology was adopted to guide this study. The context and processes involved in the activities of the selected hometown associations were analyzed, which enabled a measurement of their peculiarities as well as similarities. This kind of research strategy has firm roots even in classic studies in other social science disciplines (Burgess 1983, Cavendish 1982, Sassen 2006). The main methodology adopted for this study is a comparative approach (Mitchell 1987, 31–33). The main orientation of this approach is the use of almost identical methods to study two contrasting cases. The study adopted mixed methods, which, among others, allow for the triangulation of results and complementarity of techniques (Bryman 2012). The data for this chapter are from a bigger project[1] carried out over fifteen months. The chapter is based primarily on the narratives of respondents from the two hometown associations and their development partners in Ghana.

This study is distinctive in the sense that it was conducted in both the origin and destination communities in order to construct a comprehensive perspective rather than the lopsided approach often adopted by most migration researchers. The first stage of the study was carried out in the Greater London area (especially the boroughs of Southwark, Lambeth, Newham, Hackney, Haringey, Lewisham, Croydon and Brent). The main reason for the choice of these boroughs is that most Ghanaian migrants are based there (COMPAS 2004). The second phase was conducted in the Upper East Region and Eastern Region of Ghana. The Upper East Region of Ghana, located in the north of Ghana, is one of the poorest in the country and accounts for very few migrants, whereas the Eastern Region, located in the south-eastern part of the country, is much richer and accounts for one of the largest sources of Ghanaian migrants outside of the African continent (Kandilige 2012). The differences in economic affluence, migration prevalence and geographical location are important because they provide apt comparative parameters. The selection of respondents from these two regions was actualized by tracing leads from migrants belonging to the two selected hometown associations to their home regions in Ghana. Migrant associations provided information on their contacts and partners in the origin communities and they were interviewed for more information on the nature of their collaborations with migrants. In-depth interviews were conducted among local chiefs, District Chief Executives (local government officials), community development leaders, executive members of local hometown associations and local advocates. In order to gauge the perception of the beneficiary communities, 364 questionnaires were administered among heads of migrant households (246 in Kwahu and 118 in the Upper East Region). Of these, 66 percent were male and 34 percent were female.

2.0 BACKGROUND ON GHANAIAN MIGRATION TO THE UNITED KINGDOM

The composition of Ghanaian emigrants over the years has changed from mostly students in the 1960s and 1970s (Peil 1995) to a wider cohort from different socioeconomic backgrounds. Ghanaians increasingly relied upon migration as a critical livelihood strategy in the 1980s and 1990s (Wong 2013, Akyeampong 2000). These movements were triggered by unfavorable economic conditions in the country and strict conditionalities imposed by the WB and the IMF (Anarfi and Kwankye 2003). Since the 1990s, destination countries for Ghanaian emigrants have extended beyond the African continent to the Americas (Arthur 2008) and Europe (Mazzucato 2011, Vasta and Kandilige 2010). The majority of Ghanaian emigrants to Europe reside in the United Kingdom (Kandilige 2012). They are especially concentrated in the boroughs of Southwark, Lambeth, Newham, Hackney, Haringey, Lewisham, Croydon and Brent, with much smaller populations outside London in Birmingham, Milton Keynes and Manchester (COMPAS 2004).

Ghana's Ministry of Foreign Affairs recorded 46,046 registered Ghanaian immigrants in the United Kingdom and an estimated 300,000 to 500,000 in total, in 2008. In the same year, the UK Labor Force Survey also reported 43,246 male and 42,024 female Ghanaian immigrants (85,270 in total) living in the United Kingdom. According to the UK 2001 Census, the number of Ghanaians legally residing in the United Kingdom almost doubled from 32,000 in 1991 to about 56,000 by 2001. These figures do not, however, include irregular migrants and this has the potential to almost double the overall numbers. It is important to note that these figures were recorded at a period when Ghana started to experience steady economic development and a stable democracy. This is, nonetheless, consistent with the "J-curve or inverted U-curve" effect of development on emigration (de Haas 2005) or the "migration hump" (Olesen 2002, Martin and Taylor 1996). These metaphors refer to the initial steep rise in emigration as sending communities or countries develop and the gradual decrease in levels of emigration as development is sustained over a period of time.

Ghanaians in the United Kingdom comprise both forced and voluntary or economic migrants. The majority of Ghanaian forced migrants departed the country in the late 1970s and early 1980s during the military regime under Flight Lieutenant Jerry John Rawlings. Ghanaian migrant associations formed around that period were understandably active in the political process back home (in Ghana) and closely aligned themselves with opposition forces in the country. A prime example is the Ghana Welfare Association, which was founded in London in the late 1970s to help new arrivals process asylum applications and to cater for the general welfare of political refugees. Such activist groups are credited with essentially bankrolling the then opposition New Patriotic Party (NPP) into power in 2000 and again in 2004 (Mohan 2006, 878). The economic migrants emigrated to the United Kingdom in response to an unprecedented economic downturn, fiscal mismanagement and a feeble civil service system in the 1970s and 1980s. As economic crisis in the country intensified, many Ghanaians left the country leading one commentator to classify labor as "Ghana's other export" after cocoa and gold (Gagakuma 1984). This trend, however, continued through the 1990s and 2000s, even though Ghana was on a positive road to economic recovery (Addison 2004).

Since the late 1990s, the economy of Ghana has been noticeably liberalized especially in the telecommunication and financial sectors. This has created career and entrepreneurial opportunities for Ghanaian students and young professionals who had previously emigrated (Wong 2013). With the discovery of oil in 2007 and the establishment of related industries, a considerable number of Ghanaian emigrants have returned home from European countries (especially the United Kingdom) to fill job opportunities that have been created. These returned migrants constitute an important piece in the Ghanaian emigrant network tapestry.

Rather than abject poverty, the quest for economic and social resources, combined with intrinsic global inequalities in income and development, has driven Ghanaian international migration to countries such as the United Kingdom. Since international migration is characterized by a substantial amount of costs and risks, it is important to note that Ghanaian migrants are not typically from the poorest households in the country (de Haas 2005, Skeldon 1997).

3.0 CROSSBORDER PARTNERSHIPS: A THEORETICAL FRAMEWORK

This chapter is guided by two main theories—the network theory and Amartya Sen's conceptualization of human development. Within the network theory, networks are perceived as "sets of interpersonal ties that connect migrants, former migrants, and nonmigrants in origin and destination areas through bonds of kinship, friendship, and shared community of origin" (Massey et al. 1993, 448). The network theory helps explain perpetuating effects on migration prevalence and the potential size of hometown associations as well as the development partners they tend to collaborate with in executing rural development projects. Settled migrants tend to serve as what Böcker (1994) refers to as "bridgeheads" with the capacity to reduce risks and the material and psychological costs of subsequent migration.

Similarly, Massey (1998) notes that a social structure is created as the number of network connections in an origin area reaches a critical level. Participants in such network connections draw upon the ensuing social capital for the purpose of accessing employment, accommodation and services abroad. Local members of such networks also accrue social capital that is sometimes channeled toward socioeconomic and human development. These social structures further facilitate migration prevalence and form the basis for the formation of hometown associations abroad. Such associations are mainly set up to cater for the needs of migrants in host countries (Kandilige 2012, Mercer, Page and Evans 2009). As hometown associations become well established, their members then pursue development projects in their home communities in the origin country (Mazzucato and Kabki 2009). The types of partnerships they initiate and sustain over time in the origin country are informed by existing affinities on account of kinship relations or shared community of origin. This theory, therefore, helps explain the relative size of the migrant community from Kwahu compared to that from the Kassena-Nankana districts and the inclusion of migrants from less-privileged backgrounds as established networks reduce the financial and psychological costs of migration.

However, it must be noted that the network theory is not foolproof. Whereas it is essential in helping explain the perpetuating nature of migration once it commences, the theory does not give sufficient indication of the external, structural factors and internal processes that counteract the tendencies that lead to increasing migration through networks (de Haas 2008). It also minimizes the extent to which legal and physical barriers tend to influence the magnitude and nature of migration in spite of the effects of networks. Lastly, while migrants could be "bridgeheads" (Böcker 1994), they could equally be restrictive "gatekeepers" being hesitant or unwilling to assist prospective migrants. Nonetheless, this theory provides a framework for the nexus among migrants, former migrants and nonmigrants to be analyzed, as migrants attempt to participate in rural development from their country of destination.

De Haas (2009, 5) aptly notes that development not only is a complex multidimensional concept, but can also be assessed at different levels of analysis and has different meanings within different normative, cultural and historical contexts. This observation is important as it acknowledges the wide spectrum (scale) within which the concept of development could be examined—rural, urban, national, regional and international levels, for instance. Various scholars have ascribed different meanings to the concept of development. Mabogunje (1989), for example, discusses four main ways in which development is conceptualized—development as economic growth (*rising incomes and production levels*); development as modernization (*Westernization*); development as redistributive justice (*from richest to the poorest*) and development as socioeconomic transformation (*perceived transition from capitalism to socialism*). Classical development economists such as Rostow (1960) and Lewis (1955) measure development by economic growth, especially the increase in market activities.

This chapter, however, adopts Amartya Sen's (1999) conceptualization of development as the process of enhancing human capability—the ability of human beings to lead lives they have reason to value and to improve the substantive choices they have (de Haas 2009). In line with this, Amartya Sen defines human development as the process of expanding the substantive freedoms that people enjoy. These include the opportunity to live long and healthy lives, access to good accommodation, being well-clothed, having access and right to basic education, enjoying the freedom of employment choice, having the freedom of association and assembly and the ability to participate in public debate without fear of retribution (de Haas 2009). Hometown associations' interventions are, therefore, analyzed through the prism of enhancing human capability. This is preferred to the other conceptualizations of development because it provides a broader, more inclusive and agency-focused interpretation of development.

4.0 BACKGROUND ON THE TWO GHANAIAN HOMETOWN ASSOCIATIONS IN THE UNITED KINGDOM

Ghanaians have migrated to the United Kingdom under both the temporary and permanent migration categories over several decades (Anarfi et al. 2003, Quartey 2009). Even though it is difficult to gauge the exact numbers of Ghanaian migrants in the United Kingdom at any given time due to uncertainties around the quantum of migrants who are living there informally or in irregular/illegal capacities, the UNDP (2013) estimates that there were 81,917 Ghanaians residing in the United Kingdom legally. Ghanaians abroad operationalize their identities and obligations within the spaces of transnational communities and these have effects on development prospects in origin communities (Mohan 2006). Migrant collectives such as hometown associations find expression within these spaces. These ethnic-based groups serve largely as support networks for migrants in destination countries but also provide a platform for long-distance involvement of migrants in rural development in their communities of origin (Castles, de Haas and Miller 2014, Kandilige 2012, Mercer, Page and Evans 2009). The Kwahuman Association and the KNDL are two such ethnic-based migrant associations.

The Kwahuman Association (UK) represents an area in the Eastern Region of Ghana that is endowed in natural resources, forest reserves and has favorable weather conditions for agricultural production as well as human habitation. It has near homogeneous cultural belief systems and practices and it is free from ethnic conflicts. It had fifteen percent poverty rate in 2005/6 (Ghana Statistical Service 2007).

This hometown association was set up in the 1960s by a group of academics and health professionals who had migrated to the United Kingdom to pursue higher education and to take advantage of the comparatively higher wages in the health sector (Author's fieldwork 2010). In line with the principles of migrant selectivity and the concept of chain migration, the membership of this hometown association now includes migrants who are not necessarily from wealthy backgrounds. According to the respondents, the cost of migration has reduced with time, as more and more migrants from the same community settled in the United Kingdom (Author's fieldwork 2010). Members include migrants, some of whom are not proficient in the English language. Such migrants are usually employed by their kin or brethren to work in Ghanaian restaurants and shops set up by mostly pioneer migrants. It has a paid-up membership of over 500 migrants. General meetings are routinely hosted, every other month, with at least 100 migrants in attendance. The association is managed by an elected executive board and has a written constitution (Author's fieldwork 2010).

The KNDL consists of members who hail from the Upper East Region of Ghana. The area is arid, a savannah zone, with very harsh weather conditions and it is one of the poorest regions in the country. It has disparate cultural belief systems and practices and it experiences periodic ethnic conflicts, especially in the Bawku municipal area. The region had a poverty rate of 70 percent in 2005/6 (Ghana Statistical Service 2007). The KNDL was set up in the late 1990s (Author's fieldwork 2010). This is consistent with their late entry into the migration system between Ghana and the United Kingdom. The KNDL has thirty-five registered members, with fifteen being active. Most of the members are middle-class professionals and students who migrated to the United Kingdom mostly for higher education (Author's fieldwork 2010). Because of the academic and privileged background of these "pioneer" migrants, they are rather fluent in the English language. They tend to be engaged in professional roles on the UK job market, with a few being either unemployed or underemployed. In spite of its size, the KNDL is also managed by an elected executive board and has a written constitution (Author's fieldwork 2010).

5.0 DISCUSSION OF RESEARCH RESULTS AND FINDINGS

5.1 Local Presence: Partnering for Development

The transnational social space is said to be bridged by multiple physical, social, economic, political, technological, epistemic and cultural networks (Basch, Glick Schiller and Szanton-Blanc 1994, Vertovec 1999, Castles, de Haas and Miller 2014). These networks are facilitated by contemporary developments in the areas of technology, communications and transportation. As a result, international migrants are able to maintain a virtual presence in origin countries and also exchange information with networks in origin communities with unprecedented immediacy. The study found that the most popular modes of engagement are through the use of mobile phone communications and periodic return visits.

The main partners that help the two hometown associations traverse the complex mace of factors involved in the negotiation, supervision and delivery of development projects in Ghana include traditional chiefs and their councils of elders, community development committees, urban-based hometown associations and the political elites. However, the multiplicity of partners sometimes leads to duplication of effort and disjointed implementation of projects.

The chieftaincy institution is legally enshrined into the constitution of Ghana. Articles 270 (Sections 1 and 2a and b)[2], 275[3] and 276 (Section 1)[4] of the 1992 Constitution of the Republic of Ghana all firmly set out the legal recognition and authority of the chieftaincy institution, the high standards expected of candidates and their nonparticipation in active party politics. As a result, when devoid of social conflicts, this institution is regarded as a reliable, stable and neutral partner in development.

The stability and symbolism attached to the traditional system of government in Ghana has inspired a greater role for chiefs and their councils of elders in the initiation and implementation of development projects. The effectiveness of their role is, however, predicated on the absence of social conflicts. The chiefs in the areas represented by the Kwahuman Association reported cordial relations and sharing of ideas with migrants:

> Any time they [migrants] want to come they give us prior notice and Nana [the chief] and his elders also prepare and then meet them. They sometimes invite Nana and his elders to visit especially Holland and the USA. They pay for all their travel expenses so that Nana and his elders will go over to brief them on what is going on, on the ground. They then fundraise and send the money to support whatever projects they agree on. (Key Informant, Eastern Region, Ghana, May 6, 2010)

The region represented by KNDL, however, has been characterized by a number of chronic chieftaincy disputes, especially between the Kusasi and Mamprusi people in the Bawku districts (ODI and CEPA 2005). The Upper East Region comprises a multitude of languages and cultures, which have created ethnic rivalries and mutual suspicions among different ethnic groups (Langer 2007). These differences were alluded to by migrants as bottlenecks in their engagement with the traditional system of government. Migrants reported that these challenges encouraged a restriction of development initiatives to their immediate ethnic groups. Development partners, therefore, tend to be urban-based hometown associations mostly in the capital city (Accra), returnees and the political elites.

However, tensions or rivalries do also exist among communities in the Eastern Region, even though to a lesser extent. As Mohan (2006) notes, Kwahu migrants perceive a sense of "civil virtue" (Barkan, McNulty and Ayeni 1991) in which a well-developed town impacts on their personal investments and also regard an underdeveloped town as a "disgrace" and an "embarrassment." This suggests competition among migrants from different towns and the prioritization of their immediate community (village or town) over the general development of their region.

The main difference in the forms of tensions between the two communities is that whereas inter-town development disparities in the Eastern Region tend to provoke a competitive drive in migrants to raise the development standards in their immediate town in order to gain the "respect" of their colleagues from different towns, such disparities in the Upper East Region engender ethnic rivalries (Author's fieldwork 2010). Another difference is that while migrants from Eastern Region are able to accommodate town-level competition and yet organize collectively at a regional level, those from the Upper East Region organize only at the town level.

In-depth interviews and participant-observation activities revealed that migrants from the Upper East Region tend to rather rely heavily on urban-based hometown associations, returnees and political officials in the negotiation and implementation of development projects. The main collective remittances by the KNDL so far have included donations of used hospital equipment and benches to their district hospital, insecticide-treated mosquito nets to pregnant women and children, and computers to local schools. These projects have all been negotiated with and overseen by urban-based hometown associations in Ghana, returnees and political officials.

This trend of relying on political officials, in particular, has proven to be fraught with a lot of challenges. The first challenge is around continuity. Elected officials in Ghana serve four-year terms. This short period, in development terms, is only viable for the negotiation and delivery of short-term projects such as the donation of in-kind collective remittances to communities. Beyond these, it is very difficult to guarantee the kind of continuity that is required to see through medium-to-long-term projects such as the construction of schools, hospitals, accommodation for medical staff or the promotion of investments. This serves as a curtailment of the human capabilities that could have been expanded through such migrant-funded development projects.

Secondly, there is a challenge around neutrality. Elected officials invariably have vested interests in most of what they do. As a result, some projects are negotiated on behalf of the community for short-term political expediency rather than for the long-term benefit of the community. These difficulties also affect the negotiation and implementation of projects that are funded by hometown associations.

Thirdly, there is a problem of ownership. Unlike chiefs who tend to negotiate projects in consultation with their council of elders and community development committee members, and whose positions tend to be permanent, which makes the final projects more representative of the needs of the community and enhances the sense of ownership, political elites divide constituents along political party lines. Inherent divisions invariably make such projects being associated with one political party or the other.

The role of urban-based hometown associations and local community groups in the planning and execution of projects is also significant. As a 34-year-old male key informant and member of Kwahuman Association in the UK notes, there are enduring relations between foreign-based hometown associations and those based locally.

> The local association, they have so many local associations we communicate with them, we communicate with the town planning, we communicate with all those associations and the elders and so on, they are all eager that oh that is a good project and that we should bring it for them (*sic*). (Key Informant, UK, May 7, 2010)

In addition to what could be referred to as "opportunistic projects," where hometown associations accumulate whatever they can access and then send them to their counterparts in the country of origin, other projects are initiated through detailed discussions with urban-based hometown associations in Ghana. The gap between what gets sent and what is needed sometimes leads to minor complaints by local communities of dumping, even though such in-kind donations are sent in good faith. An example of targeted and appropriate in-kind collective remittance is portrayed in the sentiments of one of the chiefs:

> They use to send clinic or hospital equipment especially beds, mattresses, wardrobes and other materials that are being used at the hospital. The other day they brought some one or two containers full of hospital equipment alone (*sic*). . . . They brought incubators, bicycles for people with cardiovascular problems and so on and they are all at the clinic now. (Key Informant, Eastern Region, Ghana, May 7, 2010)

On the other hand, another foreign-based hometown association sent equipment that was judged to be inappropriate and "opportunistic." The key informant from the Abetifi Development Committee describes the arbitrary nature of this donation thus:

> The equipment they brought was so sophisticated that we couldn't even use it at our clinic over there so we had to bring it back to Korlebu, Accra [national

capital]. You see, at Abetifi we don't have a hospital. We are now planning to build one so there are some of the things when they are sent to us, we in turn donate them to other hospitals in other places. (Key Informant, Eastern Region, Ghana, May 7, 2010)

There are also differences in perceptions between hometown associations and local recipients about the real value of collective remittances. There is a perception by some urban-based hometown associations that their colleagues (migrants abroad) do not fully appreciate the contribution they are making toward development locally. Migrants are also accused of overestimating the development potential of their cash collective remittances. These sentiments are shared between local association leaders in both regions. For instance, Ada (chairman of an urban-based hometown association for the Upper East Region, Ghana, June 4, 2010) remarks that "so they [migrants] should not feel that if they send £100 that it is so much money."

His caution is reiterated by experiences recounted by a community development leader in Kwahu, Eastern Region.

I think they brought in 2000 dollars. At that time it will be about 16 million Cedis. When you hear 16 Million Cedis it sounds big but when it goes to the ground it can't do much (*sic*). So sometimes that is the problem we have with them [migrants] because they find it difficult to understand why they bring in the money and they don't see what it has been used for. . . . Also we were also having our different projects going on so we will not be able to raise so much to do what they had wanted to do (*sic*). (Key Informant, Eastern Region, Ghana, May 8, 2010)

Beyond the occasional disagreements between hometown associations and their urban-based colleagues in Ghana, they mostly work collaboratively to deliver projects for the benefit of their home communities. One area of broad agreement is the field of advocacy. Both parties team up to campaign against unfavorable political decisions as well as seek publicity against inherent socioeconomic disparities in Ghana, on the international scene. A good example of this collaboration is the lodging of a formal complaint by a hometown association representing migrants from the municipal area of the Upper East Region of Ghana (BONABOTO) at the offices of the UK Department for International Development (DFID) in Ghana and the corresponding mass demonstrations against disparities in access to education between the northern and southern regions of Ghana organized by BONABOTO, UK, and petitions to both the British prime minister and his deputy and the Department for International Development during a visit to the United Kingdom in 2008 by the Ghanaian president.

Other development partners of the Kwahuman Association include grassroots groups that operate along gender, age, business and professional lines.

These include groups such as the "Men's League," the "*Adonti* Ladies," the "Youth League," the "Akwatia Youngsters" and "Abetifi *Mma*," among others. These groups collaborate mainly with migrants in the United Kingdom in particular, European and North American countries in order to execute development projects for the benefit of their community. As a subchief of Abetifi, Kwahu explains:

> They pick their different projects. They only inform Nana [the chief] and his elders that there is this thing that they want to do and he gives them permission and they do it. Another time they call Nana that they want to inaugurate it once it is finished and he does it for them. (Key Informant, Eastern Region, Ghana, May 13, 2010)

There are no equivalent partners of this kind for the members of the KNDL. This could be attributed to their numbers, the size of their networks or the heterogeneity that characterizes their cultural set up. Close collaborations are also established between hometown associations and individual philanthropists in the United Kingdom for the purpose of enhancing rural development in Ghana. A typical example is Kwahuman Association's affiliation with Mr. Humphrey Barclay's "Friends of Kwahu-Tafo" charity in the United Kingdom to support the provision of furniture and equipment, the construction of school buildings, stocking of libraries with books, funding of sporting activities and literary competitions for the youth of the town, among others. Their ethnic group has a tradition whereby prominent and` wealthy people (Ghanaians) are installed as what is known as "Nkosuohene," meaning "development chief," in recognition of their support to a local community (Langer 2007, Kuada and Chachah 1999). This typical Ghanaian, *Akan* cultural practice has, however, been commandeered by progressive chiefs to include financial and development support from wealthy African American and Western benefactors. Mr. Barclay is one such chief (with the 'stool' name Kwadwo Ameyaw Gyeabuor Yiadom I).

From the preceding discussions, it is clear that the characteristics and number of local development partners that hometown associations tend to collaborate with, to some extent, are associated with the migration prevalence, size of the foreign-based hometown association and, most importantly, the nature of the sociocultural structures of the origin community they represent.

6.0 THE CONCEPT OF TRUST AMONG PARTNERS

Trust is fundamental in the negotiation and implementation of development projects that are funded by foreign-based hometown associations.

Both hometown associations routinely hold their Ghanaian-based partners accountable for cash as well as in-kind remittances that are sent toward rural development. Beyond this, members of the local communities also tend to hold their traditional and political representatives responsible for the timely and honest execution of migrant-funded projects. The emerging literature on foreign-based hometown associations highlights, to some extent, the role of trust among all actors involved (Mercer, Page and Evans 2009, Mazzucato and Kabki 2009, Werbner 2002). As Mazzucato and Kabki (2009) note, trust is demanded by recipient communities of their local leaders; hometown associations' leadership demands trust from local leaders especially on their ability to manage funds responsibly and to execute projects, and hometown associations are also keen to prevent local leaders making political capital out of migrant-funded projects.

The monitoring of these projects by migrants sometimes takes the form of a firm request for a public acknowledgement of their contributions in the local media. Public awareness of such contributions tends to limit the likelihood of embezzlement. In addition, this requirement is driven partly by the desire to extract social capital and recognition from such "altruistic" gestures. Migrants' families left behind also derive respect among their peers in recognition for projects that are funded by their migrant relatives. Migrants themselves enjoy opportunities for memorialization upon return as funded projects are usually adorned with plaques bearing details of the foreign-based hometown associations.

Trust is maintained among all parties through a sense of obligation. As Lyon (2000, 665) notes, the sources of obligations are located in "reputations, sanctions and moral norms." These suggest that sanctions, whether actual or threatened, are central in the toolkit of Ghanaian migrants in the United Kingdom for the continuous delivery of their development obligations (Goldberg 1998, van der Geest 1998).

As part of obliging all parties to be truthful and accountable for their actions, migrants insist on the legitimacy and representativeness of the leadership of development partners as well as their adherence to democratic principles as conditions for receipt of collective remittances. A female executive committee member of KNDL cites an example:

> I demanded certain guarantees from them because I needed to make sure that the election of people onto that committee was fair and that whatever they did they had a constitution that guided them as to, you know, what they wanted to work on, and I wasn't really impressed with the fact that they were just hand picking people to sit on it. So I decided to kind of step back for now but I think when I go back I would like to see what they doing because I've worked in this kind of area for many years here in the UK so I am fairly aware of what can go wrong if you don't get the group or groups set up properly with the right representation. You could cause lots of problems. (Key Informant, KNDL, UK, April 20, 2010)

Equally, a 61-year-old female fundraiser for the Kwahuman Association states that:

> The reason I haven't continued to collect it [funds] is, you know, when you collect this fundraising these people [British] they want an evidence to see that you haven't spent the money. So initially I sent £500 so now I'm waiting for them even to send me a picture that we've done foundation, we've done this. Every time I'm phoning I don't get any word from them (*sic*). (Key Informant, Kwahuman Association, UK, April 17, 2010)

Beyond suspicion of possible wrongdoing, there are instances of actual evidence of hometown associations being let down by their local partners. As a key informant from the Kwahuman Association laments, a migrant-funded supermarket project had to be canceled due to the embezzlement of funds by local partners:

> Yes, that was a good plan to build a big roof supermarket. We thought of doing this project will cost, you know, millions of Cedis and we don't have money to build this outright. So it is going to be stages, you know, project which is stage 1, stage 2, stage 3, stage 4 and then the whole thing will be completed (*sic*). So we started with stage 1 which according to them [local partners] the government had given them about 350 million Cedis so we donated 170 million Cedis which, you know, will come to half a billion to start the project. They were rushing us and so on. Our people ordered me to go and present to them the 170 million Cedis, which was the equivalent of about £10,000 at that time. The money is gone astray (*sic*). (Key Informant, Kwahuman Association, UK, April 18, 2010)

Accounts like these have engendered a feeling of frustration on the part of some migrants. One person remarked:

> You can't help Ghanaians. That's one thing you just cannot. Honestly they take too much advantage and they think we don't know what goes on, we do. Even though we've been away from the country for a long time, we still know what goes on. (Key Informant, Kwahuman Association, UK, April 18, 2010)

Similar expressions of doubt and mistrust characterize some individual remittances. A member of the KNDL used her personal experience to explain the point that lack of trust inhibits the initiation and implementation of development projects. She explains further:

That is the difficult side of it. As I said, you send them money and they embezzle it so it is difficult for us people living over here to put up houses because your own brother or sister or best friend that you trust to do something for you will clean you out. (Key Informant, KNDL, UK, April 23, 2010)

The importance of trust in the negotiation and implementation of local development projects cannot therefore be underestimated regardless of the size of the foreign-based hometown association. These perspectives on the concept of trust are borne out especially by the network theory, which predicates outcomes of relationships on trust. It emphasizes the fact that functional relationships among migrants, former migrants and nonmigrants allow for migrants to serve as "bridgeheads" while dysfunctional (situations of mistrust) lead to migrants rather becoming restrictive "gatekeepers."

7.0 CONCLUSION

The significance of the role of nationals abroad to the development process in their countries of origin is in no doubt even though the processes and stakeholders in the execution of development initiatives vary in time and space. This chapter has highlighted the nature, structure and effectiveness of partnerships that have been established between two Ghanaian hometown associations and their networks of former migrants and nonmigrants. While the study finds that the size of hometown associations sometimes determines the number and type of local partners they are able to collaborate with, it also suggests that the prevailing sociocultural conditions within origin communities equally impinge on these decisions.

Secondly, the chapter suggests that development conceptualized as a means of increasing the substantive capabilities that people have reason to enjoy (Sen 1999, UNDP 2009) is to some extent normative and prescriptive in nature and fails to address the underlying questions of how this is achieved in practice and by whom. In addition, development discourses spearheaded by international development agencies (such as the IMF, UNDP and the WB) and Western countries have focused, in a unidirectional fashion, on the potential volume of remittances and "brain gain" from migrants of developing countries that could bolster socioeconomic development in origin countries (Castle, de Haas and Miller 2014, UNDP 2009, Gibson and Mackenzie 2011). This apparent obsession with how to maximize remittance receipts is conceptualized within a framework of origin state-diaspora relations as prime drivers of development. However, such lopsided analysis de-emphasizes the role of local partners as well as institutions in realizing and sustaining migrant-funded development initiatives. Within the Ghanaian context, traditional leaders, for instance, are found to be stable, reliable and mostly neutral partners in the negotiation and execution of migrant-funded projects. This implies a critical role for some non-statutory institutions as partners in the process of delivering development. As a result, Western prescriptions of development models, without adequate understanding of the types and hierarchy of local stakeholders, would invariably result in ineffective implementation of projects and a reduction in their impact on human capabilities. This does not, however, preclude a role for state actors, including that of the political elites. They have the ability to use political power and networks as leverage for securing concessions such as waivers of import duties on charitable donations and acquisition of licenses and permits on behalf of migrants. Nonetheless, inherent challenges around neutrality, continuity and a sense of ownership are highlighted by this research as potentially detrimental.

Finally, networks yield positive social capital when there is mutual trust among all partners. Mistrust, as a result of actual or perceived attempts by any actor in the network to defraud, extract undue political capital or obtain undeserved memorialization, serves as a disconnect in the development loop.

NOTES

1. This project was among members of the Ghanaian diaspora in the United Kingdom and heads of migrant households in Ghana, community leaders and Ghanaian political elites, the Bank of Ghana, Ghana Statistical Service and the Department of National Archives. The UK component of the bigger study comprised of interviews with 20 key informants, a survey of 120 Ghanaian migrants, participant-observation activities and library research. The Ghana component involved a survey of 346 heads of migrant households, interviews with 20 key informants (community leaders and political elites), data from the Bank of Ghana, Ghana Statistical Service and the Department of National Archives.
2. 270 (1) The institution of chieftaincy, together with its traditional councils as established by customary law and usage, is hereby guaranteed. (2) The parliament shall have no power to enact any law, which—(a) confers on any person or authority the right to accord or withdraw recognition to or from a chief for any purpose whatsoever; or (b) in any way detracts or derogates from the honor and dignity of the institution of chieftaincy.
3. A person shall not be qualified as a chief if he has been convicted for high treason, treason, high crime or for an offence involving the security of the state, fraud, dishonesty or moral turpitude.
4. 276 (1) A chief shall not take part in active party politics; and any chief wishing to do so and seeking election to Parliament shall abdicate his stool or skin.

REFERENCES

Addison, Ernest K. Y. 2004. The Macroeconomic Impact of Remittances. Paper at Conference on Migration and Development in Ghana, La Palm Royal Beach Hotel, Accra, Ghana. September 14–16, 2004."

Akyeampong, Emmanuel. 2000. "Africans in the Diaspora: The Diaspora in Africa." *African Affairs* 99, 395:183–215.

Anarfi, John, Stephen Kwankye, Ofosu-Mensah Ababio, and Richmond Tiemoko. 2003. *Migration from and to Ghana: A Background Paper*. University of Sussex: DRC on Migration, Globalisation and Poverty.

Barkan, Joel D, Michael L. McNulty, and M. A. O. Ayeni. 1991. "'Hometown' Voluntary Associations, Local Development, and the Emergence of Civil society in Western Nigeria." *The Journal of Modern African Studies* 29, 03: 457–80.

Basch, Linda, Nina Glick Schiller, and Christina Szanton-Blanc. 1994. *Nations Unbound: Transnational Projects, Postcolonial Predicaments, and Deterritorialized Nation-States*. Langhorne, PA: Gordon & Breach.

Böcker, Anita. 1994. "Migration Networks: Turkish Migration to Western Europe," in *Courses of International Migration*, edited by Bob van der Erf and Liesbeth Heering, Luxembourg: Netherlands Interdisciplinary Demographic Institute.

Bryman, Alan. 2012. *Social Research Methods*. 4th Edition, Oxford: Oxford University Press.

Burgess, Robert G. 1983. *Inside Comprehensive Education: A Study of Bishop McGregor School*. London: Methuen.

Caglar, Ayse. 2006. "Hometown associations, the rescaling of state spatiality and migrant grassroots transnationalism." *Global Networks* 6, 1: 1–22.

Castles, Stephen, Hein de Haas, and Mark J. Miller. 2014. *The Age of Migration: International Population Movements on the Modern world*. Houndmills Basingstoke: Palgrave Macmillan.

Cavendish, Ruth. 1982. *Women on the Line*. London: Routledge & Kegan Paul.

COMPAS Report Team. 2004. *The Contribution of UK-Based Diasporas to Development and Poverty Reduction*. Oxford: ERSC Centre on Migration, Policy and Society (COMPAS).

De Haas, Hein. 2005. "International Migration, Remittances and Development: Myths and Facts." *Third World Quarterly* 26, 8:1269–84.

De Haas, Hein. 2008. *Migration and Development: A Theoretical Perspective*. Working Paper No. 9. Oxford: International Migration Institute (IMI), University of Oxford.

De Haas, Hein. 2009. *Mobility and Human Development. Human Development Research Paper* UNDP: Human Development Reports.

Gagakuma, Setorwu. 1984. "Labour: Ghana's Other Export." *New African* 196, 42.

Ghana Statistical Service. 2007. *Pattern and Trends of Poverty in Ghana 1991–2006*. Accra: Ghana Statistical Service.

Gibson, John, and David McKenzie. 2011. "Eight Questions About Brain Drain." *The Journal of Economic Perspectives* 25, 3:107–28.

Kandilige, Leander. 2012. *Transnationalism and the Ghanaian Diaspora in the UK: Regional Inequalities and the Developmental Effects of Remittances at the Subnational Level*. DPhil. Thesis, University of Oxford.

Kapur, Devesh. 2010. *Diaspora, Development, and Democracy: The Domestic Impact of International Migration from India*. Princeton: Princeton University Press.

Kleist, Nauja. 2008. "Mobilising 'the Diaspora': Somali Transnational Political Engagement." *Journal of Ethnic and Migration Studies* 34, 2: 307–23.

Koser, Khalid, Nadje Al-Ali, and Richard Black. 2001. "Refugees and Transnationalism: The Experience of Bosnian and Eritreans in Europe." *Journal of Ethnic and Migration Studies* 27, 4: 615–34.

Kuada, John, and Yao Chachah. 1999. *Ghana: Understanding the People and Their Culture*. Accra: Woeli Publishing Services.

Langer, Arnim. 2007. *When Do Horizontal Inequalities Lead to Conflict? Lessons From a Comparative Study of Ghana and Côte d'Ivoire*. CRISE Annual Report, 8. Horizontal Inequalities and Conflict: Understanding Group Violence in Multiethnic Societies.

Lyon, Fergus. 2000. "Trust, networks and norms: the creation of social capital in agricultural economies in Ghana." *World Development* 28, 4: 663–81.

Mabogunje, Akin. 1989. *The Development Process*. London and Boston: Hutchinson.

Martin, Philip. L, and J. Edward Taylor. 1996. "The Anatomy of a Migration Hump," in *Development Strategy, Employment, and Migration: Insights from Models*, edited by J. E. Taylor, 43–62, Paris: OECD Development Centre.

Massey, Douglas S, Joaquin Arango, Graeme Hugo, Ali Kouaouci, Adela Pellegrino, and J. Edward Taylor. 1993. " Theories of International Migration: A Review and Appraisal." *Population and Development Review* 431–66.

Massey, Douglas S, and Emilio A. Parrado. 1998. "International Migration and Business Formation in Mexico." *Social Science Quarterly* 1–20.

Mazzucato, Valentina. 2011. "Reverse Remittances in the Migration–Development Nexus: Two-Way Flows Between Ghana and the Netherlands." *Population, Space and Place* 17, 5: 454–68.

Mazzucato, Valentina, and Djamila Schans. 2011. Transnational Families and the Well-Being of Children: Conceptual and Methodological Challenges. *Journal of Marriage and Family* 73, 4: 704–12.

Mazzucato, Valentina, and Mirjam Kabki. 2009. "Small is Beautiful: The Micro-Politics of Transnational Relationships Between Ghanaian Hometown Associations and Communities Back Home." *Global Networks* 9, 2: 227–51.

Mazzucato, Valentina, Mirjam Kabki, and Lothar Smith. 2006. "Transnational Migration and the Economy of Funerals: Changing Practices in Ghana." *Development and Change* 37, 5: 1047–72.

Mercer, Claire, Ben Page, and Martin Evans. 2009. "Unsettling Connections: Transnational Networks, Development and African Home Associations." *Global Networks* 9, 2: 141–61.

Mitchell, James C. 1987. *Cities, Society, and Social Perception: A Central African Perspective*. Oxford: Oxford University Press.

Mohan, Giles. 2006. "Embedded Cosmopolitanism and the Politics of Obligation: the Ghanaian Diaspora and development." *Environment and Planning A*. 38, 5: 867–83.

Oversees Development Institute (ODI) and Centre for Policy Analysis (CEPA). 2005. *Economic Growth in Northern Ghana*. Revised report for DFID. Accra. Ghana.

Olesen, Henrik. 2002. "Migration, Return, and Development: An Institutional Perspective." *International Migration* 40, 5: 125–50.

Ong'ayo, Anthony O. 2014. *How Can the EU and Member States Foster Development Through Diaspora Organisations? The Case of Ghanaian Diaspora Organisations in the Netherlands*. Discussion Paper No. 162. European Centre for Development Policy Management (ECDPM).

Peil, Margaret. 1995. "Ghanaians Abroad." *African affairs* 94, 376: 345–67.

Quartey, Peter. 2009. *Migration in Ghana: A Country Profile 2009*. Geneva: IOM.
Sassen, Saskia. 2006. *Territory, Authority Rights: From Medieval to Global Assemblages*. Princeton NJ: Princeton University Press.
Skeldon, Ronald. 1997. *Migration and Development: A Global Perspective*. Harlow, Essex: Addison Wesley Longman.
Tiemoko, Richard. 2004. "Migration, Return and Socio-Economic Change in West Africa: The Role of the Family." *Population Space and Place* 10, 2: 155–74.
UNDESA. 2016. "Monitoring Global Population Trends." United Nations Department of Economic and Social Affairs, Population Division.
United Nations Development Programme (UNDP). 2009. *Overcoming Barriers: Human Mobility and Development. Human Development Report 2009*. New York: United Nations Development Programme.
United Nations Development Programme (UNDP). 2013. "Trends in International Migrant Stock: Migrants by Destination and Origin, The 2013 Revision." Population Division, United Nations Department of Economic and Social Affairs, New York.
Van Der Geest, Sjaak. 1998. "Yebisa wo Fie: Growing Old and Building a House in the Akan Culture of Ghana." *Journal of Cross-Cultural Gerontology* 13, 4: 333–59.
Vasta, Ellie, and Leander Kandilige. 2010. "'London the Leveller': Ghanaian Work Strategies and Community Solidarity." *Journal of Ethnic and Migration Studies* 36, 4: 581–98.
Vertovec, Steven. 1999. "Conceiving and Researching Transnationalism." *Ethnic and Racial Studies* 22, 2: 447–62.
Werbner, Pnina. 2002. *Imagined Diasporas Among Manchester Muslims*. Santa Fe, NM: SAR Press.
Wong, Madeleine. 2013. "Navigating Return: The Gendered Geographies of Skilled Return Migration to Ghana." *Global Networks* 14, 4: 438–57.

Chapter 5

Comparative Analysis of Educational Performance of Children from Migrant and Nonmigrant Households in Ghana

Theophilus Kwabena Abutima

1.0 THE DESIRE TO MIGRATE

International migration flows have increased over the past decades. More people than ever are living outside their country of birth. The total population of international migrants globally stands at 232 million people as at 2013 compared with 175 million in 2000 and 154 million in 1990 (UNDESA 2013). Current estimates reveal that developed countries are home to 136 million international migrants compared to 96 million in the developing countries, and most of these international migrants are labor migrants aged 20–64 years (UNDESA 2013). Other estimates also posit that the number of people of African descent who live outside the continent of Africa is close to 140 million and most of them are in the Western Hemisphere (Shinn 2008). The Organization for Economic Co-operation and Development (OECD) countries are home to a significant number of Ghanaian immigrants (Manuh 2006). Likewise, there may be a similar number of Ghanaian immigrants in other countries including African countries. This phenomenon tends to be attributed to current trends of globalization and the progressive increase in uneven global economic development (GCIM 2005). This phenomenon has encouraged many people, particularly labor migrants from developing countries to cross borders in search of better job opportunities and livelihoods in relatively developed countries. For most people on the African continent, migrating to Europe is a dream they would like to realize at all costs. The opportunity to work in the rich West usually results in wealth for the entire family (*Cortenraad* 2009). Consequently, many of these men and women are parents who have left their children in the home country under the care of extended family members, friends or neighbors (Yeoh and Lam 2007, 120).

It must be noted that parents play very crucial roles in the nurturing, development and the future outcome of children in every aspect of their lives (Hakim 2003). They have the responsibility of meeting the social, economic, psychological, educational and health care needs of children (Asima 2010). However, most parents are not able to migrate with their children due to either family reasons or the immigration policies at the destination or a combination of these factors and are therefore left in the care of family members, friends, neighbors and other acquaintances back home. Little emphasis has, however, been placed on the effect of parental absence on these left-behind children, especially in Africa and Ghana in particular. The few studies in this area present conflicting evidence about the impact of migration on the educational performance of children left behind. This chapter therefore attempts a comparative analysis of the educational outcomes of children who have been left behind by international migrant parent(s) and children who live with both parents in Ghana to ascertain the impact of migration on children's educational performance in the Ghanaian context.

The study used was conducted in selected public and private schools in Accra in the Greater Accra Region and Sunyani in the Brong Ahafo Region. Using mixed-methods research approach, the study focused on children of international migrants between the ages of twelve and seventeen years who have been left behind in Ghana. Also, children of nonmigrant parents were added to the study sample and used as a control group to measure the educational outcome of children of migrant parents. In all, a total of 213 children which comprised 116 children of migrant parents and 97 children of nonmigrant parents were purposively sampled from eight Junior High Schools in Accra and Sunyani for the study. In-depth interviews were conducted with some children of migrant parents, teachers and caregivers. The languages for the interviews were English and Twi (the dominant local language in Ghana). Pseudonyms were also used to represent everyone in this study. All the interviews were audio-recorded alongside field notes. The recorded interviews were later transcribed and analyzed.

2.0 PARENTING AND FAMILY STRUCTURE

Biological parents play various roles in the nurturance of children. Most of these roles are gendered, with mothers often performing primary parenting roles that need daily attention while fathers play breadwinning roles (Downey 1998, 878–893). Thus, the involvement and influence of the father and mother are very crucial in every facet of a child's development and children may not be able to take absolute advantage of their full potential in life without comprehensive support of their parents. In these contemporary societies where extended families are being transformed, coupled with a growing emphasis on the nuclear family structure (Nukunya 2003), the responsibility for fathers and mothers to satisfy the needs of children without the support of other family members has also increased (Fritsch and Burkhead 1981). Studies by Wang and Wu (2003, 7–10), Tan and Wang (2004, 11–12), Li (2004, 35–37) and Chen et al. (2009, 323–343) suggest that with parents migrating abroad in large numbers and the phenomenon of children left behind or posted now becoming a common occurrence, the school performance of the migrants' children tends to decline. Correspondingly, Phillips and Gleeson (2007) show that parental absence contributes to the problems of adjustment of children. As a result, maladjustment due to parental absence plays a role in the poor educational performance of school children.

The European Commission Report (2008) observed that the degree of parental participation is a significant indicator of the quality of schooling and tuition to which children may have access to. Harris, Furstenberg and Marmer (1998, 201–216) found that children who live with both parents who are fully involved in their upbringing have high educational attainment, social competence, self-esteem and life satisfaction. Conversely, children who are brought up in families without their biological parents face various degrees of challenges, some of which include malfunctioning and maladjustment (Dankyi 2011, 133–162). Owing to the effects of maladjustment and malfunctioning, children left behind tend to experience poor educational performance as a result of the international migration of their parents.

The kind of family a child lives in also has a role to play in the educational performance of the child. On the average, in the United States, children from single families perform poorly on standardized tests and are not likely to complete high school. As a result, such children may not attain any further formal education as compared to their counterparts who live with both parents (Astone and McLanahan 1991, 309–320, Downey 1994). In the same vein, poorer educational outcomes are experienced by children growing up in families where fathers are absent. The absence of fathers is typically associated with lower levels of socioeconomic status as well as inconsistent levels of discipline and supervision (McLanahan and Booth 1989, McLanahan and Sandefur 1994). According to Downey (1994, 129–147), single-father families may have more economic resources than single-mother families; however, there is no difference in the academic performance of children from these families. In addition, these two categories of children are outperformed by children from two-parent families. In an attempt to explain the reason behind this occurrence, Downey further argues that the educational difficulties of children from single-mother and single-father families can best be explained by some intervening processes. The lack of economic resources aids in understanding the educational performance of children from single-mother families while interpersonal deprivation, or the lack of interpersonal parental resource explains the poor performance of children from single-father families (Downey 1994, 129–147). Demuth and Brown (2004, 58–81) also argue further that economic factors are better predictors of school performance among children in single-father families, whereas interpersonal resources (e.g., parental involvement and supervision) play a larger role among children from single-mother families.

In the same vein, most studies have mixed outcomes as to whether the participation of parents in the education of children yields desirable or undesirable results. Desforges and Abouchaar (2003, 14) uncovered that the direct involvement of parents in the educational processes of children can enhance or diminish pupils' achievement under some circumstances. Parental participation may take various forms which include good parenting in the home, preschool nurturance (which provides a good foundation of skills, values, attitudes and self-concept); helping with homework; visits to school and talking to teachers to gather relevant information and establish good parent-teacher relationships; holding discussions with teachers to keep abreast with the child's progress or to discuss emergent problems (Ibid). This shows that parental participation is not limited to the school environment; some aspects of parental involvement take place at home, while the rest are executed in the school in response to some prevailing circumstances in the school.

3.0 EFFECTS OF PARENTAL MIGRATION ON EDUCATIONAL OUTCOMES

Migration was previously often associated with fathers moving out; hence there has been a long-standing concern about the absence of fathers in children's lives (Mintz 1998), but the attention is now moving to the mother's absence due to the fact that migration is becoming more feminized. The literature now brings to bear the fact that mothers and fathers are conspicuously absent and may be unaware of the educational life of their own children or may not care about it. The impact of parental participation on the education of children cannot be taken for granted considering the enormous consequences it has for the educational outcome of children.

The potential challenge in the education of children arising from the absence of one or both parents due to migration have been postulated by a range of scholars including Battistella and Conaco (1998). Children of migrant parents more often than not tend to be affected by the parental separation which causes detrimental effects on their school performance. According to Battistella and Conaco (1998, 220–241), Filipino children of migrants fared worse academically in relation to nonmigrants' children. The class ranks of children with one or both parents absent were below that of their counterparts with both parents present (Battistella and Conaco 1998, 220–241). A UNICEF report on Ecuador by Cortes (2008, 21) also confirmed the adverse effect of parental migration on the education of children left behind. According to Cortes, female children of migrant children are more affected compared to boys due to the added time dedicated to the performance of household chores in the absence of mothers which dimishes their school performance (Cortes 2008, 17). These studies in the Philippines and Mexico are further corroborated by a study of left-behind children by Yeoh and Lam (2007, 120). Their interaction with the headmistress of one school, revealed that ten out of seventy-three children in a class who were left behind did not do well in school and thus dropped out of school at the end or turned to crime in their parent's absence. These findings are supported by Cortes (2008) who says that pupils with migrant parents perform worse than children who live with their parents.

Studies have also revealed that the situation of children left behind is not unique to only left-behind children in Mexico and the Philipines. Giannelli and Mangiavacchi (2010) in their study of left-behind children in preschool and primary and secondary schools in Albania stated that migration impacts on the school attendance of children left behind and they are even at risk of dropping out of school. School attendance, retention and completion are also major factors which surfaced in the literature on left-behind children. There were much higher cases of truancy and dropout among the children of migrant households than children from nonmigrant households because left-behind children lacked the necessary supervision of their academic activities (Batistella and Conaco 1998, Cortes 2008,Yeoh and Lam 2008, 220–241).

In Moldova, some children considered the lack of parental supervision and monitoring as the reason behind the declining performance in their education. They also complained that they could not always rely on caregivers, who were not always available to follow their performance. Among other reasons, they mentioned that in some cases after the departure of their parents, they had to take care of daily household duties and had little time left for their studies (Lozinksi 2006, Cortes 2008).

There are other factors that may influence the educational performance of children left behind, for instance, in a study in Mexico on "an appraisal of the effect of parental migration on family left behind," Cortes (2008) pointed out that children left behind, who are mostly in their adolescence, often harbor the desire of migrating to join their parents and as a result begin to perform poorly in school and also have a higher probability of dropping out of school. Bakker, Elings-Pels and Reis (2011, 11) also add that, the "waiting to migrate or waiting for papers syndrome" in order to reunite with their parents harms the academic performance of children; when the waiting period is too long, "attendance, concentration or overall motivation at school" reduces (Bakker, Elings-Pels, and Reis 2011, 11). Other studies also portray international migration as a dent on the image of children left behind which results in them being discriminated against in their own societies. Cortes (2007) revealed that in some expensive schools in small cities in Ecuador, having migrant parents attracts a negative connotation which affected children's academic performance. They are seen as children of cowards who run out of the country when conditions were not favorable.

Notwithstanding these issues, the migration of parents can have positive effects on the left-behind children. Kuhn (2006, 183–209) highlights this in his study in Bangladesh which showed that the emigration of fathers and male siblings often resulted in improvements in the education of children left behind in rural areas in Bangladesh. Moreover, public school children in migrant households in Ecuador are well recognized and often become leaders in their class because they have access to more money than children with nonmigrant parents and are able to purchase household gadgets for themselves (Cortes 2008, 18). Studies conducted in Mexico further suggest that the receipt of remittances generally facilitates children's access to schooling which would not have been possible if the parents had stayed behind (Borraz 2005, 13, López 2005 as cited in Cortes 2008, 16). The receipt of remittance ensures that children of migrant parents have access to the best schools in their community but the ability to remit and the amount to remit are all dependant on the migration staus of the parents, their economic engagement since irregular status tends to influence their ability to send home remmitance.

Correspondingly, a study conducted in the Philippines in 2003 revealed that most migrants' children were enrolled in private schools and they performed well and were generally happy at school in their elementary school years compared to some children of nonmigrant parents. Increased school enrolment, retention and performance are positively connected to the migration of parents (Cortes 2008). Surveys in Pakistan also attribute higher school enrolment among children of migrants to remittances from migration; it found that children in migrant households had higher levels of enrolment and lower dropout rates, attended school more frequently and progressed in school better than children in nonmigrant households. Mansuri (2006) added that in Pakistan, the dropout rates of girls in migrant households were lower than that in the control group. The education of children left behind by the migration of either one or both parents is obviously an issue of concern in most of the migration literature but as to whether the impact is negative or positive is difficult to tell.

A clear debate ensues at this point as to whether parental migration enhances or worsens the education of children left behind. There is no consensus as to whether children of migrants do better than children of nonmigrants in school, because studies in countries such as Mexico, Philippines, Ecuador and Moldova focused on absenteeism and lack of supervision as a consequence of parental absence which cause children to perform poorly in school, while other studies in countries such as Bangladesh, Pakistan and the Philippines focused on how remittances enabled children to attend better quality schools and remain in school. This study seeks to offer clarity on the matter in the Ghanaian context by focusing on academic achievement of children from migrant and nonmigrant households.

4.0 ACADEMIC PERFORMANCE OF CHILDREN OF MIGRANT AND NONMIGRANT PARENTS

4.1 Sociodemographic Characteristics

Out of the total sample for this study, 116 were children of migrants while 97 were children of nonmigrants. The numbers of male and female respondents were also fairly similar, 107 were male and 106 female. Among the 116 children of migrant parents, 60 of them were females and 65 were males and out of the 97 children of nonmigrants 50 of them were males and 46 were females. The ages of the children in all ranged between 10 and 16 years. Majority of them (71.4%) were between 13 and 15 years old. Most of the children (42%) were in Junior High School Form 2. One-fifth of the children (19%) came from public schools while the rest came from private schools. With respect to the living arrangements of children left behind, the majority of them were living with mothers only because they had migrant fathers. Those with both parents abroad lived with kin relations and a few with non-kin relations. All the children of nonmigrant parents lived with both parents in Ghana.

4.2 Academic Performance of All Children

As shown earlier in this chapter, studies have postulated that the educational performance of children left behind tends to be adversely affected by the migration of one or both parents compared to the academic performance of children who live with both parents under the same roof. It is based on this assertion that this chapter intends to ascertain the existence of any difference in the educational outcome of children left behind by migrant parents and children who live with both parents in Ghana. This is to find out whether there is any association between children's living arrangement, migration status of children's parents and children's educational outcome. The findings of the interviews conducted with children, teachers and caregivers were used in the analysis to support the survey findings gathered from the children involved in the study.

4.3 Results

An independent samples *t*-test aimed at ascertaining any statistically significant difference between the academic performances of children left behind by migrant parents and children of nonmigrants was not significant at 0.05. However, further comparative analysis, using logistic regression shows that children of migrant parents are 0.2 times more likely to perform better in school than children of nonmigrant parents. Refer to Table 5.1.

Table 5.2 further highlights the average academic performance of children from both migrant households and nonmigrant households in english, mathematics, integrated science and social studies. The table does not show any significant variation in terms of the average academic performance in the four selected subjects among the two groups of children. The average academic performance of children from both migrant households and nonmigrant households in english, mathematics, integrated science and social studies indicates that, statistically, there is no difference in the performance of both groups of children. Therefore, the educational outcomes of children of migrant and nonmigrant parents are statistically not significant. The results of the *t*-test shows that there is no significant difference in the academic performance between these two groups of children [$t\ (211) = 1.547$, $p = 0.123$, $\alpha = .05$]. The lack of a significant relationship between the average academic

Table 5.1 Logistic Regression Result and Odd Ratios

	β	*S.E*	*Df*	*Wald*	*(p-value)*	*Odd Ratio*
Migration status of parent	0.189	0.457	1	0.171	0.679	
Nonmigrant (RC)						1.000
Migrant						1.208
Constant	2.079	0.294	1	49.967	0.000	8.000

Source: Author's fieldwork, November 2011; Significance Level: 0.679

Table 5.2 Migration Status of Children's Parents and the Average Academic Performance of Children

Academic Performance (Average Performance)	*Migration Status of Children's Households*				
	Migrant Households		*Nonmigrant Households*		
	Frequency	*Percent*	*Frequency*	*Percent*	*Total*
80–100	25	22	30	31	55
70–79	48	41	45	46	93
60–69	29	25	13	14	42
50–59	13	11	6	6	19
>49	1	1	3	3	4
Total	116	100	97	100	213

Source: Author's fieldwork, November 2011

performance of children and the migration status of children's parents as portrayed by the quantitative data advances the argument that there is no significant difference in the educational outcome of children left behind and children of nonmigrant parents. This finding is supported by the qualitative data collected from selected left-behind children, caregivers and teachers.

The qualitative findings indicate that the migration status of children's parents has no influence on the educational performance of children. Afi, a JHS 3 girl in one of the in-depth interviews stated that, "My father left when I was in class four and my mother joined him a year-and-half later, but I will say my performance in school has not changed so much, I am still in the first ten in my class" (Afia, Sunyani, November 2011). Afi's assertion does not mean that the academic performance of migrants' children is always high. Some of the teachers interviewed in-depth stated that the performance of children of migrant parents is not always the best or up to standard, but it is not necessarily as a result of the absence of the parents. The following are sentiments of Mr. Armah, one of the teachers:

> The migration status of parents is not the issue because, nowadays most parents hardly spend much time with their children, even parents in Ghana do not see their children within the week, and it is the maids who care for the children. (Mr. Armah, Accra, Novemebr 2011)

Neither did the children trace poor school performance to the migration of the parents. Some of them admitted that they were not pleased with their current school performance but they did not attribute their nonperformance to parental absence. In the opinion of these children, the parental absence has even enhanced their educational outcome. When asked if his poor performance was not as a result of the absence of his parents, Mumuni a JHS 2 pupil, laughed and said:

> oh no, now, I am doing well when I compare my performance to when I was with my parents. Now, my grandmother will tell me to go and learn and stop watching TV but I was free to do whatever I wanted when I was with my parents. I think because of that I was not serious with my studies; my freedom caused my poor performance at that time. (Mumini, Accra, November 2011)

Yaa, whose mother has been out of the country for seven years and is currently living with her father and her siblings also said,

> My grades are good, even though my mum is not in the country. My Daddy transferred me to this school and said it is a good school after my mum travelled. When I was in my former school my Mum wasn't around but my grades were good, so it is not that but if she were to be around I think she will help me to do better. (Yaa, Accra, November 2011)

In essence, there may be other factors (personal and environmental) which influence the performance of children of migrants in school. As the children indicated, their performance cannot be attributed solely to their status as coming from migrant households. This was emphasized by one of the teachers who noted: "there are children who live with their parents yet they perform poorly, could this be attributed to parental absence? Obviously, this is not the case."

The study also attempted to find some of the possible factors that may influence the academic performance of children from migrant households other than the direct effect of parental absence. In this regard, some teachers were interviewed to find out if the assertion by Cortes (2008) that, in Ecuador, being a child of a migrant parent attracted negative remarks from teachers and pupils in private schools which negatively influenced their school performance and even led to school dropouts holds in their schools because they are considered as children of unpatriotic cowards who ran out of the country when conditions were tough. All the teachers interviewed disagreed with the notion that children could be stigmatized because of their parents' migrant status. A teacher from one of the selected private schools added that "being a migrant's child is rather a privilege and a prestige in Ghana but we do not treat children based on this criterion, they are all equal." Another teacher, Mr. Duah noted:

> in this school, we have rules that every child should abide by. We don't consider whether your parent is in America or Ghana, you must obey the rules in the school, so we treat them all equally and the children also behave as such towards each other, so we don't hail anybody here neither do we condemn anybody. (Mr. Duah, Sunyani, November 2011)

This response led to a further probe to find out from the teachers if the children of migrant parents whose performance is not up to standard received any preferential treatment, favor or assistance at some point in time because their parents are migrants. Most of the teachers in Accra answered in the affirmative but were quick to add that, it is an informal arrangement between the teachers and the migrant parents or the caregivers but this opportunity is open to all children and not children of the migrant parents alone. Mr. Armah, a teacher said:

> at times it happens and when that happens, normally the only assistance given is that, the parents or the care givers see the teacher after school for some private assistance but we don't give them any special assistance because if they sit in the class with their colleagues and they do not utilize the opportunity very well why should we favour them? (Mr. Armah, Accra, November 2011)

Mr. Kabu, another teacher interviewed on his part explained it further thus:

> what normally happens is that since their parents are abroad and they can afford extra tuition for their children so they even communicate with teachers, I want you to give my child extra tuition especially when they send the reports to them. They will call and say oh my child is not good in this area, can you help? Then it means that the teacher has to give extra attention to the child. (Mr. Kabu, Accra, November 2011)

One of the teachers also added that migrant parents normally entrust some care and supervisory responsibilities to teachers. They make telephone calls or come to teachers for updates and advice whenever they visit the country. They are, most of the time, asked to supervise the children's work in the school, make sure their notes and homeworks are up to date, and ensure that they have all the required textbooks. In some cases, the teachers are asked to visit the children at home from time to time to see the conditions in which they live. In the words of the said teacher,

> yes, some will engage you in extra duties, sometimes they will tell you, check on my ward on weekends to see that the homework is done, make sure that his notes are up to date and other duties, so it is your duty to at least visit the child on Saturday after five or Sunday after church. (Mrs. Addo, Accra, November 2011)

Thus, children of migrant parents may be given some form of assistance, but this is not because they have their parents abroad. The assistance may be given based upon the request of either their biological parents or their caregivers and this is not limited to the children who have their parents abroad but other children may also be offered such assistance should their parents appeal to the teachers for assistance. Since there was no statistical relationship between the average academic performance of children from migrant and nonmigrant households, an attempt was made to find out if there are any differences in the school attendance of children from migrant households and children from nonmigrant households.

4.4 School Attendance of Children of Migrant and Nonmigrant Households

There has been divergent opinions in the migration literature on the effects of the migration status of children on their school attendance. Some studies have shown that parental migration tends to have untoward impact on the rate at which children left behind attend school after the migration of their parents (see Hanson and Woodruff 2003). Other researchers argue that parental migration rather has an innocuous impact on school attendance due to the receipt of remittance and the role that it plays in the provision of home and educational supplies (Meyerhoefer 2011, 379–396,Borraz 2005, 13, Lopez-Cordova 2006).

This study revealed that the majority of the children (46%) were not absent from school in the last term (seeTable 5.3). Out of this number, about half of the children (55%) with migrant parents and 45 percent of the children with nonmigrant parents attended school for all the days of the term. However, children of migrant parents formed 56 percent and 51 percent of the children who were not in school for one to two times and three to four times, respectively, in a term. In terms of absolute numbers, the findings show that both children have equal chances of not attending school for a week or more and different reasons could be attributed to this phenomenon rather than parental migration.

The chi-square technique was used to test the significance of the association between the migration status of the parents of the children and their school attendance. The result shows that there is no statistically significant association between these two variables too. The *P*-value is 0.969 ($x^2 = 0.249$; df = 3; $p > 0.05$).

The findings from this study indicated that there is no difference in the school attendance of children whether they have migrant or nonmigrant parents. The qualitative study disclosed that children of migrant parents have similar favorable living arrangements and care as the children of nonmigrant parents; they receive all the support that their biological parents would have given them, so the effects of the parental absence are nonexistent. This revelation is contrary to the findings in some of the migration literature which indicates that children of migrant parents lack parental supervision; perform household chores which keep them out of school, as compared to children who have nonmigrant parents (Cortes 2008, McKenzie and Rapoport 2007, 18–20, Mansuri 2006).

Table 5.3 Children's School Attendance and Migration Status of Children's Parents

Number of Times Absent from School	*Migration Status of Children's Parents*				*Total*
	Nonmigrant Parent(s)	*Percent*	*Migrant Parent(s)*	*Percent*	
None	44	45	54	47	98
1–2	32	33	40	34	72
3–4	15	15	16	14	31
>5	6	7	6	5	12
Total	97	100	116	100	213

Source: Author's fieldwork, November 2011

The majority of the children left behind (about three-quarters) indicated that migration of their parents did not affect their school performance though they feel they could perform better if their parents were present. All the four teachers interviewed in Accra reacted in unison saying that parental migration does not necessarily affect children's performance adversely if certain conditions prevail. They suggested that what matters is proper care by the caregiver which include frequent supervision of homework; ensuring that children revise their notes before coming to school and a comfortable home for the children. One teacher who indicated that he has taken particular interest in children left behind and "posted children" said children left behind and "posted children" do perform well when caregivers show interest in the work of the children and adequately supervise them at home. He was quick to add that good care and supervision is essential not only to children of migrant parents but to children of nonmigrant parents as well.

> supervision at home is key in the education of the children and this is what I usually tell parents. A few of the children who have their parents abroad, who do not do well in class because they lack this supervision, they usually do not do homework and when they do, it is poorly done. It is when you invite their caregivers that you get to know that their parents are not around, it is difficult to take good care of someone's child and this is also the same with parents who are all working and do not have time for their own children, their children are cared for by their maids, how can they do well? (Mr. Armah, Accra, November 2011)

Another teacher also observed that:

> The care is very important and this depends on the guardian who is taking care of the child, maybe the guardian will say because he is not my child I will not concentrate on whether he is doing well or not, we have a problem with that so when you realize it, you call them so that you will talk one-on-one. There are some children in our school whose performance is not good but they live with their own biological parents and they bring them to school every day. What can we say about that? So it depends on the child, the guardian and some other reasons which I cannot tell. (Auntie Esi, Sunyani, November 2011)

The teachers also noted that, they need the support of caregivers and even parents in their quest to discharge their duties effectively. According to one of them, Mr. Armah,

> yes, there are so many things that hinder children's performance in school. If you don't get support and cooperation from the parents, when you give them homework and when they take them home and parents don't ask if they were given homework, children can be lazy, they can leave the homework and go and play, so teachers and the parents have to collaborate. Even when you give

> homework, there is a column that the parent has to sign to make sure that the child has done the homework so they will not come to school early in the morning and come and do it. So, in order for them to perform there has to be this collaboration. (Mr. Armah, Accra, November, 2011)

5.0 CONCLUSION AND POLICY RECOMMENDATIONS

Children living without one or both parents in the home country have generally been portrayed to have the worse educational performance compared to other children living with both parents in the home country (Battistella and Conaco 1998, 220–241, Cortes 2008,Giannelli and Mangiavacchi 2010). On the contrary, it is also clear that parental migration has also enhanced school enrolment, retention and improved educational outcomes (Kuhn 2006, 183–209, Mansuri 2006, Cortes 2008, 16). This study found that the outcome of parental migration is locus specific and reliant on the sociocultural and economic practices prevailing in the areas where these studies were carried out. In the cases studied in Ghana, parental migration did not adversely impact on the academic performance of children from migrant households because of the high level of support that extended kin in the Ghanaian context provided to such children (Dankyi 2011, 133–162). This is unlike studies in Ecuador where left-behind children were considered as children of unpatriotic citizens and treated with disdain (Cortes 2008). A second explanation for this discrepancy lies in the fact that countries which recorded negative impact of parental migration on the educational outcomes of left-behind children attributed it to the dominance of female migration (Cortes 2015, 62–78, Jampaklay 2006, 93-102).

However, in this study, most of the migrant parents were the fathers while the mothers were the caregivers. Since mothers are the primary caregivers in the Ghanaian context, left-behind children were not necessarily deprived of parental care and attention. Those who had both parents being migrants also lived with kin relations who cared for them as if they were their own children in accordance with the typical Ghanaian extended family system. Migrant parents ensured that they entrusted the care of their children to people who could bring them up well. It was therefore not surprising that some of the children attested to the improvement of their educational outcomes after the migration of their parents. The communal care for children in most Ghanaian communities, especially where this study was conducted, ensured that children received adequate care just as their biological parents would have cared for them.

In actual sense, holding all factors constant it is not expected that there would be any variance in the educational outcome of children of migrant and children of nonmigrant parents. This shows that role of the extended family in the nurturance of children support the growth and welfare of children. The extended family can be entrusted with the responsibility of cogent education of children left behind to attain their complete developmental potentials while the migrant parent being aware of this will get the peace of mind, work hard and possibly remit more to finance the educational and subsequent professional development of the children.

In view of the crucial role played by the Ghanaian extended family system in the nurturance of children even in the absence of their biological parents, it is recommended that policies regarding the welfare of children in Ghana should be formulated toward the upholding and sustenance of the Ghanaian family values which encourage equal care for all children by family members and not only the biological parents.

REFERENCES

Astone, Nan M, and Sara S. McLanahan. 1991. "Family Structure, Parental Practices and High School Completion." *American Sociological Review* 56(3).

Asima, Prosper P D., 2010. "*Continuities and Discontinuities in Gender Ideologies and Relations: Ghanaian Migrants in London.*" PhD diss., Unpublished DPhil Dissertation, University of Sussex, UK.

Bakker, Caroline, Martina Elings-Pels, and Michele Reis. 2011. *The Impact of Migration on Children in the Caribbean.* UNICEF.

Battistella, Graziano, and Ma Cecilia G. Conaco. 1998. "The Impact of Labour Migration on the Children Left Behind: A study of elementary school children in the Philippines." *SOJOURN: Journal of Social Issues in Southeast Asia*: 13(2), 220–241.

Bledsoe, Caroline. 1990. "The politics of children: fosterage and the social management of fertility among the Mende of Sierra Leone," *in Births and power: Social change and the politics of reproduction*, edited by W. P. Handwerker, 81–100. Boulder, CO: Westview Press.

Borraz, Fernando. 2005. "Assessing the Impact of Remittances on Schooling: The Mexican Experience." *Global Economy Journal* 5(1).

Chen, Xinxin, Qiuqiong Huang, Scott Rozelle, Yaojiang Shi, and Linxiu Zhang. 2009. "Effect of Migration on Children's Educational Performance in Rural China." *Comparative Economic Studies* 51(3).

Córdova, Ernesto. 2006. *Globalization, Migration and Development: The Role of Mexican Migrant Remittances (Working Paper ITD= Documento de Trabajo ITD; n. 20)*. 20. BID-INTAL.

Cortenraad, J. 2009. Transnational Families in Ghana: NWO Grant for Research into the Effects of Migration.

Cortes, Patricia. 2015. "The Feminization of International Migration and its Effects on the Children Left Behind: Evidence from the Philippines." *World Development* 65.

Cortes, Rosalia. 2008. "Children and Women Left Behind in labour sending countries: an appraisal of social risks." *New York: United Nations Children's Fund (UNICEF), Policy, Advocacy and Knowledge Management Section, Division of Policy and Practice.*

Cortes, Rosalia. 2007 *Remittances and Children's Rights: An Overview of Academic and Policy Literature.* Division of Policy and Planning. Working Paper. UNICEF.

Dankyi, Ernestina. 2011. "Growing Up in a Transnational Household: A Study of Children of International Migrants in Accra". *Ghana Studies* 14.

Demuth, Stephen, and Susan L. Brown. 2004. "Family Structure, Family Processes, and Adolescent Delinquency: The Significance of Parental Absence Versus Parental Gender." *Journal of Research in Crime and Delinquency* 41(1).

Desforges, Charles, and Alberto Abouchaar. 2003. *The Impact of Parental Involvement, Parental Support and Family Education on Pupil Achievement and Adjustment: A literature review.* Vol. 433. Nottingham: DfES Publications.

Downey, Douglas B, James W. Ainsworth-Darnell, and Mikaela J. Dufur. 1998. "Sex of Parent and Children's Well-Being in Single-Parent Households." *Journal of Marriage and the Family.*

Downey, Douglas B. 1994. "The School Performance of Children from Single-Mother and Single-Father Families: Economic or Interpersonal Deprivation?" *Journal of Family Issues* 15(1).

Ghana Living Standard Survey. 2010. Ghana Statistical Service Report, Accra.

Ghana Transnet. Accessed June 20, 2007. http://www2.fmg.uva.nl/ghanatransnet/program.

Gianneli G. C, and L. Mangiavacchiy. 2010. *Children's Schooling and Parental Migration: Empirical Evidence on the "Left Behind" Generation in Albania.* IZA Discussion Paper No. 4888.

Global Commission on International Migration. 2005. *Migration in an interconnected world: new directions for action.* The Commission, 2005.

Hakim, Catherine. 2003. *Models of the family in modern societies: Ideals and realities.* Aldershot: Ashgate.

Hanson, Gordon H, and Christopher Woodruff. 2003. *Emigration and educational attainment in Mexico.* Mimeo., University of California at San Diego, CA, USA.

Harris, Kathleen Mullan, Frank F. Furstenberg, and Jeremy K. Marmer. 1998. "Paternal Involvement with Adolescents in Intact Families: The Influence of Fathers Over the Life Course." *Demography* 35(2).

Jampaklay, Aree. 2006. "Parental Absence and Children's School Enrolment: Evidence From a Longitudinal Study in Kanchanaburi, Thailand." *Asian Population Studies* 2(1).

Klugman, Jeni. 2009. Human development report 2009. Overcoming barriers: Human mobility and development.Kuhn, Randall. 2006. "The effect of fathers' and siblings' migration on children's pace of schooling in Bangladesh," *Asian Population Studies*, 2(1): 69–92.

Kuhn, Randall S, Bethany Everett and Rachel Silvey. 2011. "The effects of children's migration on elderly kin's health: A counterfactual approach," *Demography*, 48(1): 183–209.

Li, X. 2004. "The Investigation on the Rural Migrant Children (in Chinese)." *Journal of Women Study in China* 10.

Lopez-Cordova Ernesto, 2006. "*Globalization, Migration and Development: The Role of Mexican Migrant Remittances.*" Working Paper 20. Institute for the Integration of Latin America and the Caribbean—INTAL ITD. Inter-American Development Bank.

Lozinksi, Vladimir. 2006. "Lack of jobs in Moldova leaves children without parental care." Moldova: UNICEF.

Manuh Takyiwah. 2006. *Ghana Migration Profile.* Consultancy Report Prepared for The Ministry of Finance and Economic Planning.

Mansuri, Ghazala. 2006. "Migration, School Attainment, and Child Labor: Evidence from Rural Pakistan." *World Bank Policy Research Working Paper* 3945.

McKenzie, David, and Hillel Rapoport. 2007. "Network Effects and the Dynamics of Migration and Inequality: Theory and Evidence from Mexico" *Journal of development Economics* 84(1).

McLanahan, Sara, and Gary Sandefur. 1994. *Growing Up with a Single Parent. What Hurts, What Helps.* Cambridge: Harvard University Press.

Meyerhoefer, Chad D, and Chen. C, J. 2011. "The effect of parental labor migration on children's educational progress in rural China," *Review of Economics of the Household,* 9(3): 379–396.

Mintz, Steven. 1998. "From Patriarchy to Androgyny and Other Myths: Placing Men's Family Roles in Historical Perspective", in Men and families: When do they get involved? What difference does it make?, edited by Alan Booth and Ann Crouter, 3–30. New Jersey: Lawrence Erlbaum Associates.

Nukunya, Godwin K. *Tradition and Change in Ghana: An Introduction to Sociology.* Accra: Ghana Universities Press.

Phillips, Susan D, and James P. Gleeson. 2007. *What We Know Now That We Didn't Know Then about the Criminal Justice System's Involvement in Families with Whom Child Welfare Agencies have Contact.* Center for Social Policy and Research.

Shinn, David H. 2008. *African Migration and the Brain Drain.* Accessed June 20, 2010. http://sites.google.com/site/davidhshinn/Home/african-migration and-the-brain-drain.

Tan, S, and X Wang. 2004. "The Study on the Migrant Children (in Chinese)." *Journal of Education in Hubei* 20.

UN-DESA, O. E. C. D. 2013. "World migration in figures." *A Joint Contribution by UN-DESA and the OECD to the United Nations High-Level Dialogue on Migration and Development.*

United Nations, Department of Economic and Social Affairs, Population Division. 2013.*Trends in International Migrant Stock: The 2013 Revision - Migrants by Age and Sex.*(United Nations database, POP/DB/MIG/Stock/Rev.2013/Age)

Yeoh, Brenda SA, and Theodora Lam. 2007. "The costs of (im) mobility: Children left behind and children who migrate with a parent." *Perspectives on gender and migration* (2007): 120–149.

Wang, Y, and X Wu. 2003. "A Case Study of the Migrant Children (in Chinese)." *Investigation of the Youth* 4.

Chapter 6

Brain Drain or Brain Gain?

The Contribution of Skilled Migrants to Development in Kenya

Jane Mwangi

1.0 INTRODUCTION: THE BRAIN DRAIN VS. BRAIN GAIN DEBATE

The emigration of highly skilled professionals is one of the highly debated issues in the migration literature, as scholars try to understand whether it constitutes benefits or losses to the countries of origin. Both theoretical and empirical evidence shows that the migration of skilled professionals presents both challenges and opportunities for the countries of origin (Adepoju 2010, Ghai 2004).

Various scholarly works have highlighted how the emigration of highly skilled professionals leads to brain drain in the countries of origin, and/or brain waste in destination countries (Kirigia et al. 2006, Oyelere 2011). According to Global Knowledge Partnership on Migration and Development (KNOMAD), tertiary-educated emigrants from sub-Saharan Africa (SSA) were 33.4 percent of total emigrants in OECD countries in 2011. The health profession is one of the most affected professions by massive emigration (Newland 2007). The emigration rate of physicians trained in SSA rose from 18.4 percent in 2000 to 28.0 percent in 2010 (World Bank [WB] 2011). Farrant et al. (2006) have documented that three quarters of doctors in Zimbabwe migrate within the first few years of completing medical school. Similarly, Global Commission on International Migration (GCIM) (2005) also shows that there are more Malawian doctors practicing in Manchester than in Malawi.

The effects of brain drain are more severe in developing countries where education is usually heavily subsidized and therefore the migration of highly skilled professionals represents a loss of returns from public investment in human capital (Farrant, MacDonald and Sriskandarajah 2006, Newland 2007, Taylor 2006). When highly skilled persons migrate, their home country loses thousands of dollars spent on their education (Taylor 2006). Emigration of highly skilled professionals also represents loss of talented people who could have contributed to the growth and productivity of the economy, thus hampering the ability of the country to develop (Farrant, MacDonald and Sriskandarajah 2006, Ghai 2004, Sriskandarajah 2005). Countries of origin are also robbed of potential tax revenue that the migrants would have paid if they were working in the country (Farrant, MacDonald and Sriskandarajah 2006, Newland 2007).

The brain drain arguments have been refuted by some scholars. Hugo (2003), for instance, contends that even though these negative impacts cannot be denied, there is limited information on the impact of migration on countries of origin and is therefore difficult to ascertain the overall effect of the emigration of skilled labor. Similarly, Bauer et al. (2005) maintain that it is unclear whether the countries of origin experience brain drain or not. Their argument is that although emigration of highly skilled professionals may have negative effects on countries of origin in the short term, migration increases the demand for education thus leading to accumulation of human capital in the long run. De Haas (2009) also questions the brain drain hypothesis. According to him, there are only a few countries that experience true massive brain drain and this is only in specific sectors like healthcare. He also argues that people who migrate may have been underutilized or even unemployed if they stayed. He gives the example of the Maghreb countries, which have high unemployment rates of university graduates. He explains that in such cases, emigration of highly educated people is "a useful economic safety valve" to reduce unemployment pressure (De Haas 2009).

In recent times, the brain drain debate has been challenged by assertions about "brain gain" and "brain circulation" (Wouterse 2011). Parthasarathi (2006) explains that although the flow of highly skilled professionals from less industrialized to more industrialized countries in the 1960s and 1970s was seen as negative to the countries of origin, these same countries later benefited from reverse flows of remittances and knowledge and skills, as well as networks. Other scholars also support the view that migrants are of benefit to their home countries through remittances, skills and technology transfer, trade and investment, among others things (Ratha et al. 2011). Parthasarathi (2006) advocates for the promotion of brain circulation as a way of tackling the brain drain problem. He argues that the reason why many highly skilled professionals are hesitant to return to their country of origin is because of fear of being unable to carry on their professional practice at home due to lack of adequate facilities, administrative hassles and restrictions on return visa. He thus proposes the provision of flexible visas to highly skilled professionals to allow circulation of scientific talent between developing and developed countries.

The assertions about brain gain and brain circulation have been strengthened by transnational perspectives on migration, which have modified how the migration process is viewed (Portes 2006). Migration is no longer viewed as a one-way process where migrants settle permanently in their host society, but migrants can now maintain ties with their home countries and engage in social, economic and political life across borders (Dade 2004, Glick-Schiller 2003, Levitt 2004, Portes 2001, Portes 2006). These new possibilities in migration have been opened up by advancement in transport and communication technologies that greatly facilitate contacts across borders (Portes 2006). In terms of development in countries of origin, this means that migrants no longer have to wait until they return home permanently in order to transfer human, financial and social capital to their home countries (Adepoju 2010, Castles and Delgado Wise 2008, Chappell and Glennie 2010, Saxenian 2002, Saxenian 2005). Saxenian (2005) attributes the emergence of India as a leading exporter of software programming and development to Indian professionals who, after migrating to Silicon Valley in the United States, have become transnational entrepreneurs linking US firms with India thus promoting "brain circulation" between the two countries.

Those who are cautious about the brain gain and brain circulation views warn that although highly skilled migrants may send back home remittances, investment and skills and technology, these resources may not offset the losses caused by their emigration, if their home countries do not have adequate economic and financial infrastructure that enable them to harness the development potential of these resources (Adepoju 2010, Oyelere 2011, Rothgang and Schmidt 2003, Simmons 2005).

Most recent studies on brain gain focus on how expected return to human capital fosters education investment in countries of origin (brain gain) (Beine, Docquier and Rapoport 2009, Beine, Docquier and Rapoport 2008). Some studies have also used return migration of highly skilled migrants to measure brain gain (Mayr and Peri 2008). Nonetheless, the existing theoretical literature suggests that a country of origin can experience brain gain when its migrants contribute to national development by engaging in transnational activities that result in skills and knowledge transfer, increased trade and investment as well as financial flows (Plaza 2013, Saxenian 2002, Saxenian 2005).

The purpose of this chapter is to show that highly skilled migrants contribute to development in their countries of origin through development-oriented transnational activities like remittance transfers, investment and return visits. This work is based on a study I carried out in 2012 and 2013, where I looked at the transnational engagement of Kenyans living in Ghana, United States, United Kingdom and Canada. The latter three were selected for the study because they are the leading sources of diaspora remittance flows to Kenya

(Central Bank of Kenya (CBK) 2010, WB 2011), while Ghana was selected because it is a leading destination of Kenyans in Africa, beyond Kenya's traditional trade partners and neighbors in Common Market for Eastern and Southern Africa (COMESA), East African Community (EAC) and Intergovernmental Authority on Development (IGAD) (Kinuthia 2013). The study focused on three main development-oriented transnational activities: remittance transfers, investment and return visits. This work looks at the relationship between migrants' level of education (independent variable) and their involvement in remittance transfers, investment and return visits (dependent variables). In order to get a comprehensive analysis of the migrants' transnational activities, I used concurrent mixed methods, where I converged both qualitative and quantitative methods. I used web survey to collect quantitative data, while I collected qualitative data using in-depth interviews, focus group discussions (FGDs) and observation.

The rest of the chapter is organized as follows: section 2 gives a brief overview of Kenyan migration dynamics. Section 3 gives a descriptive analysis of the level of education, employment status, area of expertise, annual income and reasons for migration of the Kenyan diaspora in the four selected countries. This is followed by bivariate and multivariate analyses of migrants' level of education versus remittances, investments and return visits. The final section provides the concluding remarks and policy implications.

2.0 KENYAN MIGRATION DYNAMICS

In the 1950s, 1960s and 1970s, only a few Kenyans migrated for education and training and returned back home after acquiring their education, to participate in national development (Black, Hilker and Pooley 2004, Musonda 2006, Okoth 2003). Nevertheless, between the 1980s and early 2000s, the country experienced a severe economic downturn and political repression that led to the exodus of both highly skilled and semi-skilled Kenyans to various countries in the world (Ghai 2004, International Organization for Migration (IOM) 2010, Musonda 2006, Okoth 2003). As the country started experiencing steady economic recovery and political reforms from the mid-2000s, Kenya began to witness an increase in return migration (Oucho, Oucho and Ong'ayo 2013). This notwithstanding, Kenya has a net emigration rate of -0.22 per 1,000 persons (IOM 2015). Although the exact size of Kenyan emigrants varies according to the source and definition used (Regional Mixed Migration Secretariat (RMMS) 2013), it is estimated that there are about 3 million Kenyans living outside the country (IOM 2015, Republic of Kenya 2014). This includes persons of Kenyan origin as well as non-resident Kenyans (Republic of Kenya 2014).

Kenya is an important source of highly skilled migrants; professionals, technicians and business people (IOM 2010, 2015, Oucho, Oucho and Ong'ayo 2013, RMMS 2013, WB 2011). According to WB estimates, Kenya was among countries with the highest emigration rate of tertiary-educated population in SSA in 2000, 38.4 percent (2011). The skilled emigration rate is estimated at 35 percent (IOM 2015). The health profession is among the most affected by this high emigration rate with about 51 percent of physicians leaving the country (WB 2011). The high emigration rate of skilled professionals raises valid brain drain concerns (IOM 2015).

The key reasons for emigration are better employment opportunities and further studies (Ghai 2004, IOM 2010, 2015, Nguvulu 2010, Okoth 2003). It is important to note that Kenya has high rates of unemployment, especially youth unemployment (IOM 2015). Europe, North America, Australia, New Zealand and East and Southern Africa are the preferred destinations of many skilled professionals, including medical professionals, lecturers, accountants, engineers, managers and business entrepreneurs (Adepoju 2008, Ghai 2004, IOM 2010, Oucho, Oucho and Ong'ayo 2013, WB2011). In South Africa, Kenyans are among the leading highly skilled professionals (Adepoju 2008). Apart from Kenyans who migrate independently, the government has also been involved in bilateral labor arrangements with other countries to help Kenyans get employment opportunities abroad (Black et al. 2004, Musonda 2006, Okoth 2003, Zoomers and van Naerssen, 2007). Youth Employment Scheme Abroad (YESA) is one of the government initiatives, which help to match the skills of Kenyans with employment opportunities abroad (IOM 2015). Between 2008 and 2013, the YESA helped over 15,000 young people to find employment (IOM 2015). Countries with labor export arrangements with Kenya include South Africa, Seychelles, Congo, Rwanda, Burundi, the United States, Canada, EU countries, and the Gulf States (Black et al. 2004, Musonda 2006, Okoth 2003, Zoomers and van Naerssen 2007). Most of the emigrants involved in bilateral labor arrangements are employed as high school and elementary school teachers as well as in other middle-level jobs (Musonda 2006, Okoth 2003, Adepoju, Zoomers and Naerssen 2008).

There is also a growing number of semi-skilled and low-skilled professionals like drivers, domestic servants and security guards migrating for jobs in Middle East countries like Saudi Arabia, Bahrain and Qatar (Black, Hilker and Pooley 2004, Ghai 2004, IOM 2010, Musonda 2006, Okoth 2003, RMMS 2013). There has been reported cases of labor exploitation, trafficking and smuggling among Kenyans working in the Middle East (RMMS 2013). There are also a few semi-skilled and low-skilled migrants who migrate irregularly to developed countries (IOM 2010).

Kenyans who travel for further studies go to various universities abroad (Ghai 2004, IOM 2010,Nguvulu 2010, Okoth 2003). In 2007, Kenyan students abroad were estimated to be more than 13,000 (Nguvulu 2009). The leading destinations for Kenyans who travel for further studies are the United States and the United Kingdom. However, the UK's attractiveness to students has been decreasing steadily due to employment restrictions for students (Okoth 2003). Some of these migrants settle down in their host countries after completing their studies (Ghai 2004, IOM 2010, Nguvulu 2010, Okoth 2003).

3.0 DESCRIPTIVE RESULTS

In this section, I briefly describe migrants' level of education, employment status, area of expertise and annual income. I have also presented migrants' reasons for leaving their country of origin.

3.1 Migrants' Level of Education, Employment Status, Area of Expertise and Annual Income

Most of the migrants were highly skilled professionals with a minimum of a bachelor's degree (see Table 6.1). The number of migrants with at least a first degree was especially high among migrants living in the United Kingdom, United States and Canada (86%). Migrants with postgraduate degrees were also quite many (39%). Similarly, most of these people were employed (83%) and were earning a high income. Thirty seven percent of the migrants were earning USD 90,000 and above per year.

In terms of type of employment and income, there was a clear distinction between migrants in Ghana and those in the three developed countries. Most high-income earners in Ghana were mostly in executive and other top management positions in multinational companies and other organizations. However, their counterparts in the three developed countries had difficulties finding jobs that matched their training and were therefore doing jobs that were beneath their qualifications. Therefore they had to do more than one job to earn high income. Jonathan, an economics graduate narrated how he had to sell pizza in the United States after leaving an executive job as a banker in Kenya. Later on, he had to do nursing certificate courses to be able to earn a decent living. His wife also narrated how she had to do odd jobs to make a living before she decided to venture into a totally different occupation from her university training.

3.2 Migrants' Reasons for Migrating

The leading cause of emigration was education, followed by employment and better opportunities (see Table 6.2). The term "better opportunities" meant

Table 6.1 Migrants' Level of Education, Employment Status, Area of Expertise and Annual Income

	Country				
	UK	*US*	*Canada*	*Ghana*	*All Countries*
Variables	*n (%)*	*n (%)*	*n (%)*	*n (%)*	*n (%)*
Level of Education					
Primary/High/Tech School	1(3)	14(16)	3(23)	31(41)	49(24)
Bachelors	10(35)	34(40)	4(31)	27(36)	75(37)
Master/PhD	18(62)	38(44)	6(46)	17(23)	79(39)
Total	29(100)	86(100)	13(100)	75(100)	203(100)
Employment Status					
Employed	24(83)	72(92)	11(100)	50(69)	157(83)
Student	5(7)	6(8)	0(0)	22(31)	33(16)
Total	29(100)	78(100)	11(100)	72(100)	190(100)
Area of Expertise					
Business Administration	12(34)	24(10)	3(18)	32(33)	71(21)
Education & IT	7(14)	21(17)	2(18)	10(18)	40(13)
Health & Community Services	10(34)	37(43)	5(45)	16(27)	68(38)
Total	29(100)	84(100)	11(100)	58(100)	182(100)
Income per Annum (USD)					
Less than 50,000	7(35)	14(22)	2(20)	16(41)	39(30)
50,000–89,000	9(45)	24(39)	5(50)	5(13)	43(33)
90,000 & above	4(20)	24(39)	3(30)	18(46)	49(37)
Total	20(100)	62(100)	10(100)	39(100)	131(100)

Source: Fieldwork, 2012–13

Table 6.2 Reasons for Migrating

	Country				
	UK	*US*	*Canada*	*Ghana*	*All Countries*
Variables	*n (%)*	*n (%)*	*n (%)*	*n (%)*	*n (%)*
Employment & Better opportunities	18(42)	48(38)	7(39)	42(51)	115(42)
Studies (self/children/spouse)	19(44)	67(52)	7(39)	29(35)	122(45)
Other	6(14)	13(10)	4(22)	11(14)	34(13)
Total	43(100)	128(100)	18(100)	82(100)	271(100)

Source: Fieldwork, 2012–13

different things to migrants in different destinations. For the migrants in the United Kingdom, United States, and Canada, "better opportunities" meant better system of government, a higher sense of security, better social facilities, better infrastructure and other amenities. However, for the migrants in Ghana, "better opportunities" meant investment opportunities and expatriate job positions and not necessarily better amenities.

Most of the migrants in Ghana were lured to migrate with expatriate salaries which were higher than what they were earning in Kenya as local employees. They had already secured jobs in Ghana before leaving Kenya. Some of them went there on secondment, while others were posted to Ghana as expatriates. The few who went in search for jobs in Ghana were mostly spouses and other dependents of the working migrants. Although the percentage of those who migrated to Ghana for studies looks impressively high, most of them were taken to Ghana by one church organization to study theology and only a few were studying in other institutions.

Nine out of the eleven respondents interviewed in the United States said that they migrated in pursuit of education and job opportunities. Genevieve, for instance, explained her reasons for migrating as follows: "I came here because of both job and education opportunities,"

When the respondents were asked whether they had achieved their objectives of migration, most of them (82%) answered in the affirmative. Canada had the highest percentage of those who had not yet achieved their objectives of migration (31%), followed by Ghana (22%) and the UK (15%). Most of the people who indicated that they had not achieved their objectives went further to explain that the pursuit of their objectives was in progress. Those who migrated for studies, for instance, explained that they were still pursuing their education.

One of the reasons given for the delay in achieving migration objectives was that pre-migration expectations did not match the reality the migrants found at the destination. Some of the people who migrated for studies for example, realized they had to work as well. This stretched the study period longer than anticipated. This is what Danielle, a Kenyan living in the United States, said in response to the question on whether she had achieved her migration objectives:

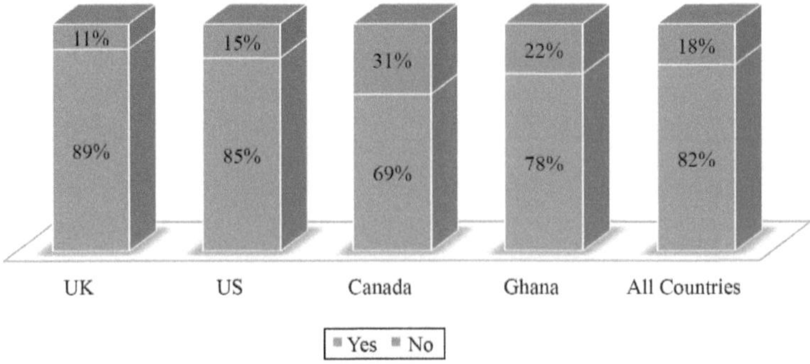

Figure 6.1 Have you achieved your objective of migration? *Source*: Fieldwork Data, 2012–13.

I have not yet achieved my objective for migrating; I haven't finished my Masters yet and this was my objective of coming here. I have got two kids; this place is not like Kenya where you have opportunities to get somebody watch over your children. Here they have children control up to the age of 18 (Danielle, July 2012, USA).

4.0 BIVARIATE RESULTS

4.1 Test of Association Between Level of Education and the Dependent Variables

Table 6.3 presents the cross tabulations and chi-square analyses that were done to ascertain the significant associations between the dependent variables (remittance transfer, investment and frequency of return visits) and the independent variable (level of education).

There was a significant association between migrants' level of education and remittance transfers (χ^2 = 27.976, p = 0.000) and investments (χ^2 = 14.291, p = 0.001). Cross tabulations showed that more migrants with a bachelor's degree (91%) were involved in sending remittances compared to migrants who had only primary, high school or technical school education (53%). Similarly, higher proportions of migrants who had postgraduate (70%) and bachelor's degree (62%) had invested in Kenya compared to those who only had primary, high school and technical qualifications (33%). However, the association between migrants' level of education and frequency of return visits was not significant (χ^2 = 2.464, p = 0.292).

Further analyses were done using logistic regressions to assess whether a migrant's involvement in remittance transfers, investment and return visits (dependent variables) was affected by their level of education (independent variable) (Table 6.4).

Table 6.3 Test of Association Between Level of Education and the Dependent Variables

	Remittance Transfers		*Investment*		*Frequency of visits*	
	Yes	*No*	*Yes*	*No*	*Once every ≥2 years*	*≤1year*
Primary/High Sch./Tech.	52.5	47.5	33.3	66.7	65	35
Bachelors	91.0	9.0	62.5	37.5	45.3	54.7
Masters/PhD	88.2	11.8	70.3	29.7	46.8	53.2
N	142	33	98	69	66	69
	$\chi2$ = 27.976 *p* = 0.000* df = 2		$\chi2$ = 14.291, *p* = 0.001* df = 2		$\chi2$ = 2.464 *p* = 0.292 df = 2	

Source: Computed from Fieldwork data, 2013
* Significant association $p < 0.05$

Table 6.4 Estimated OR of Migrants' Level of Education Versus Remittances, Investment and Return Visits

	Remittance Transfers	*Investment*	*Return Visits*
	OR (95% CI[2])	OR (95% CI)	OR (95% CI)
High/Tech/ Pry Sch (BC[1])	1	1	1
Bachelor	9.198*** (3.241–26.108)	3.333*** (1.444–7.692)	2.244 (0.773–6.517)
Masters &PhD	6.786*** (2.588–17.793)	4.737*** (2.015–11.137)	2.113 (0.743–6.012)
Constant	1.105	0.500	0.538

Source: Computed from Fieldwork data, 2013
*** $p < 0.01$; ** $p < 0.05$; *$p < 0.1$
[1]Base Category
[2]CI—Confidence Interval

Migrants' level of education had a significant association with remittance transfers. Migrants who had a bachelor's degree (*OR* = 9.198; *CI* =3.241–26.108; p = 0.000) were 9.2 times as likely to send remittances as those who had only high school or technical or primary education. Similarly, those with postgraduate degrees (*OR* = 6.786; *CI* =2.588–17.793; p = 0.000) were 6.8 times more likely to send remittances than those who had no degree. The level of education also had an influence on migrants' investment. Migrants who had a postgraduate degree (*OR* = 4.737; *CI* =2.015–11.137; p = 0.000) were 4.7 more likely to invest in Kenya than those with primary, high school and technical education, while migrants with a bachelor's degree (*OR* = 3.333; *CI* =1.444–7.692; p = 0.005) were 3.3 times as likely to invest in Kenya as those who had no degree. The level of education also affected migrants' frequency of return visits. Migrants who had a bachelor's degree were 2.2 times more likely to visit Kenya frequently than those who had attained only high school or technical or primary education. Also, those with a master's degree or PhD were 2.1 times as likely to pay frequent visits to Kenya as those who did not have a degree.

5.0 MULTIVARIATE RESULTS

5.1 Multivariate Analyses of Level of Education (Independent) Versus Dependent Variables

Multivariate logistic regression analyses were conducted to find out the effect of migrants' level of education on remittance transfers, investments and return visits, while controlling for sex, marital status, employment status and annual income.

Table 6.5 presents estimated odds ratios (ORs) of level of education (predictor variable) versus remittances (dependent variable) and the control variables. Controlling for sex, marital status, employment status and annual income has changed the associations between level of education and remittance transfers. The association between remittance transfer and level of education remained highly significant, however, in the bivariate analyses the ORs reduced from 9.2 to 2.7 for migrants with postgraduate degrees and from 6.7 to 1.5for migrants with postgraduate degrees. Among the control variables, men were 1.6 times as likely to send remittances as women. Employment status showed no significant association between those who were employed and those who were not, but migrants who were students were about 3 times more likely to send remittances than those who were not employed.

Table 6.6 shows estimated ORs of level of education versus investment, while controlling for sex, marital status, employment status and annual income. There was still a strong association between investment and level of education. However, the introduction of control variables reduced the ORs from 3.3 to 2.2 for migrants with a bachelor's degree and from 4.7 to 3.0 for migrants who had a master's or PhD degree. Among the control variables, men were 3.9 times as likely to invest in Kenya as women. Employment status showed no association between having a job and investing in Kenya, even though students were 1.1 times as likely to invest as migrants who were not employed.

The estimated ORs of level of education (predictor variable) versus return visits (dependent variable), while controlling for sex, marital status,

Table 6.5 Estimated ORs of Independent Variables Versus Remittances

Variables	*Remittances*
	OR (95% CI[2])
Sex (Female[1])	1
Male	1.643 (.358–7.532)
Marital Status (Unmarried[1])	1
Married	0.57*** (0.007–0.477)
Employment Status (Not employed[1])	1
Employed	0.989 (0.024–40.205)
Student	2.991 (0.281–31.838)
Level of Education (High/Tech/ Pry Sch[1])	1
Bachelor	2.686 (0.322–22.388)
Masters & PhD	1.467 (0.158–13.589)
Annual Income (Less than $15,000[1])	1
$15,000–29,000	0.940 (0.062–14.371)
$30,000 and above	0.667 (0.072–6.169)
Constant	13.203

Source: Computed from Fieldwork data, 2013
***$p < 0.01$; **$p < 0.05$; *$p < 0.1$
[1]Base Category
[2]CI—Confidence Interval

Table 6.6 Estimated ORs of Independent Variables Versus Investment

Variables	*Investment*
	OR (95% CI[2])
Sex (Female[1])	1
Male	3.876*** (1.519–9.894)
Marital Status (Unmarried[1])	1
Married	0.252*** (0.100–0.635)
Employment Status (Not employed[1])	1
Employed	0.831 (0.051–13.515)
Student	1.148 (0.169–7.782)
Level of Education (High/Tech/ Pry Sch[1])	1
Bachelor	2.212 (0.594–8.239)
Masters & PhD	3.015 (0.784–11.591)
Annual Income (Less than $15,000[1])	1
$15,000–29,000	1.089 (0.150–7.883)
$30,000 and above	2.384 (0.423–13.438)
Constant	0.889

Source: Computed from Fieldwork data, 2013
***$p < 0.01$; **$p < 0.05$; *$p < 0.1$
[1]Base Category[2]CI—Confidence Interval

Table 6.7 Estimated ORs of Independent Variables Versus Return Visits

Variables	*Return visits*
	OR (95% CI[2])
Sex (Female[1])	1
Male	0.701 (0.300–1.636)
Marital Status (Unmarried[1])	1
Married	0.980 (0.412–2.332)
Employment Status (Not employed[1])	1
Employed	0.613 (0.021–17.819)
Student	0.309 (0.030–3.152)
Level of Education (High/Tech/ Pry Sch[1])	1
Bachelor	1.946 (0.495 7.654)
Masters & PhD	1.898 (0.493–7.309)
Annual Income (Less than $15,000[1])	1
$15,000–29,000	0.867 (0.112–6.716)
$30,000 and above	5.350 (0.558–51.258)
Constant	1.913

Source: Computed from Fieldwork data, 2013
***$p < 0.01$; **$p < 0.05$; *$p < 0.1$
[1]Base Category
[2]CI—Confidence Interval

employment status and annual income are shown in Table 6.7. The predictor variable showed a significant association with migrants' return visits. Nonetheless, controlling for sex, marital status, employment status and annual income decreased the ORs from 2.2 to 1.9 for migrants with a bachelor's degree and from 2.1 to 1.8 for those with a postgraduate degree. It is only annual income among the control variables that showed a significant association with migrants' return visits. Migrants whose annual income was USD 30,000 and above were 5.3 times more likely to visit Kenya than those who earned less than USD 15,000.

6.0 CONCLUSION AND POLICY IMPLICATIONS

Findings from this study showed that most of the study respondents were highly skilled emigrants who had a minimum of a bachelor's degree. This validates the findings that the leading cause of the emigration of Kenyans was quest for education and the majority of the respondents had achieved this objective. These findings corroborate Ghai's work, which describes Kenyan migrants as highly qualified professionals (2004). The fact that many of the respondents migrated to acquire education means that some of the skills they possess were actually acquired abroad and they did not necessarily deplete existing skills at home. Eventually, this leads to brain gain and brain circulation when the migrants return home temporarily, permanently or even virtually, bringing with them new ideas, attitudes, skills and technology.

The study results revealed that highly skilled professionals were more likely to participate in development-oriented transnational activities like remittance transfers, investment and return visits, than migrants with low levels of education. This cumulatively contributes to the development of their communities of origin as well as the macro economy. The migration literature seems to suggest that the participation of skilled migrants in development-oriented transnational activities can only be sustained if there are available investment and other opportunities in the home countries. Ghosh (2006) explains that when there are investment opportunities at home, highly educated migrants tend to send more money to their home countries than people with low levels of education. Nonetheless, when there are few opportunities available at home, the migrants tend to save and invest in their destination countries. This awareness is important in designing effective diaspora engagement strategies. Such strategies should include the creation of diaspora-targeted opportunities that are attractive to the highly skilled migrants. This is especially important for a country like Kenya with a sizable number of highly skilled emigrants.

Most of the respondents were employed at the time of the study, but many of them were not working in jobs that matched their training, and some were doing jobs that were beneath their qualifications. These findings raise valid "brain waste" concerns. However, it is important to note that these migrants left Kenya because they needed better jobs than what was available at home. This means that when they were in Kenya, they were either unemployed or dissatisfied with the jobs they were doing. Migration therefore gave them an opportunity to explore job opportunities outside Kenya. Therefore, the presence of highly skilled professionals in other countries may not automatically lead to brain drain and/or brain waste in the country of origin. It may actually mean "brain utilization"—when people who were unemployed or underemployed in their countries of origin find jobs elsewhere.

In the current age of globalization, it is untenable to prevent skilled migrants from migrating, but it is paramount to find ways of enhancing their contribution to development at home. Availability of investment opportunities, for instance, is crucial in attracting the human, financial and social capital of skilled migrants to their home country. Countries of origin should therefore create diaspora-targeted investment and other opportunities to tap into the resources of their diaspora. It is also important to adequately disseminate information about these opportunities.

REFERENCES

Adepoju, Aderanti. 2008. 'Migration in Sub-Saharan Africa'. The Nordic African Institute. Accessed October 14, 2015. http://www.diva-portal.org/smash/record.jsf?pid=diva2:241148.

Adepoju, Aderanti. 2010. *International Migration Within, to and from Africa in a Globalised World.* Ghana: Sub-Saharan Publishers.

Adepoju, Aderanti, Annelies Zoomers, and Ton van Naerssen, eds. 2008. *International Migration and National Development in Sub-Saharan Africa. Viewpoints and Policy Initiatives in the Countries of Origin.* Leiden: Brill. http://pub.uni-bielefeld.de/download/2318318/2319935.

Bauer, Thomas K, John P. Haisken-DeNew, and Christoph M. Schmidt. 2005. 'International Labour Migration, Economic Growth and Labour Markets: The Current State of Affairs'. In *The New Demographic Regime: Population Challenges and Policy Responses*, 111–135. Geneva: United Nations.

Beine, Michel, Frederic Docquier, and Hillel Rapoport. 2008. 'Brain Drain and Human Capital Formation in Developing Countries: Winners and Losers'. *The Economic Journal* 118 (528): 631–652.

———. 2009. 'On the Robustness of Brain Gain Estimates'. Centre for Research and Analysis of Migration (CReAM). Accessed March10, 2017. http://www.cream-migration.org/publ_uploads/CDP_17_09.pdf.

Black, Richard, Lyndsay Hilker, and Claire Pooley. 2004. *Migration and pro-Poor Policy in East Africa*. Development Research Centre on Migration, Globalisation and Poverty, University of Sussex. Accessed January 12, 2016. http://www.migrationdrc.org/publications/working_papers/WP-C7.pdf.

Castles, Stephen, and Raúl Delgado Wise, eds. 2008. *Migration and Development. Perspectives from the South.* Geneva: International Organization for Migration.

Central Bank of Kenya (CBK). 2010. 'Diaspora Remittances'. Accessed January 10, 2011. https://www.centralbank.go.ke/index.php/diaspora-remittances?yr=2010.

Chappell, Laura, and Alex Glennie. 2010. "Show Me the Money (and Opportunity): Why Skilled People Leave Home—and Why They Sometimes Return." *Migration Information Source*. Accessed January 10, 2016. http://www.migrationpolicy.org/article/show-me-money-and-opportunity-why-skilled-people-leave-home-%e2%80%94-and-why-they-sometimes-return/.

Dade, Carlo. 2004. 'Transnationalism, Foreign Assistance, Domestic Communities: New Opportunities and New Challenges for Canada and the United States'. *FOCAL Point*, Special Edition on Migration. Accessed January 18, 2016. http://focal.ca/pdf/focalpoint_se_march2004.pdf.

De Haas, Hein. 2009. *Mobility and Human Development*. UNDP, Human Development Reports, Research Paper 2009/01. Accessed September 9, 2016. https://mpra.ub.uni-muenchen.de/19176/.

Farrant, Macha, Anna MacDonald, and Dhananjayan Sriskandarajah. 2006. *Migration and Development: Opportunities and Challenges for Policymakers*. Edited by Ise Pinto-Dobernig. 22. Geneva: United Nations Publications.

Ghai, Dharam. 2004. 'Diasporas and Development: The Case of Kenya'. *Global Migration Perspectives* 10. Global Commission of International Migration. Accessed October 14, 2015. http://www.migrationdevelopment.org/fileadmin/data/resources/general/research_papers/GMP_No10_01.pdf.

Ghosh, Bimal. 2006. *Migrants' Remittances and Development: Myths, Rhetoric and Realities*. Geneva: International Organization for Migration (IOM).

Glick-Schiller, Nina. 2003. 'The Centrality of Ethnography in the Study of Transnational Migration: Seeing the Wetland instead of the Swamp America Arrivals'. In *American Arrivals: Anthropology Engages the New Immigration*, 99–128. Santa Fe: School of American Research Press.

Global Commission on International Migration (GCIM). 2005. *Migration in an Interconnected World: New Directions for Action*. Global Commission on International Migration. Accessed January 6, 2016. http://www.queensu.ca/samp/migrationresources/reports/gcim-complete-report-2005.pdf.

International Organization for Migration (IOM). 2010. *Harnessing the Development Potential of Kenyans Living in the United Kingdom*. International Organization for Migration (IOM). Accessed October 14, 2015. http://unitedkingdom.iom.int/sites/default/files/doc/publications/Kenya%20Diaspora%20Report%20(Web%20Version).pdf.

International Organization for Migration (IOM). 2015. *Migration in Kenya: A Country Profile 2015*. International Organization for Migration (IOM). Accessed January 12, 2016. https://publications.iom.int/system/files/pdf/migration_profile_kenya.pdf.

Kinuthia, Bethuel K. 2013. *Spotlight on the Young and Skilled: Kenyan Diaspora Members in the South*. International Organization for Migration (IOM) and ACP Observatory on Migration, Observatory on Migration No. ACPOBS/2013/PUB07. Accessed March 17, 2016. https://publications.iom.int/system/files/pdf/spotlight.pdf.

Kirigia, Joses M., Akpa R. Gbary, Lenity K. Muthuri, Jennifer Nyoni, and Anthony Seddoh. 2006. 'The Cost of Health Professionals' Brain Drain in Kenya'. *BMC Health Services Research* 6 (1): 89.

Levitt, Peggy. 2004. *Transnational Migrants: When "home" means More than One Country*. Migration Information Source. Accessed January 18, 2016. http://www.migrationpolicy.org/article/transnational-migrants-when-home-means-more-one-country/.

Mayr, Karin, and Giovanni Peri. 2008. *Return Migration as a Channel of Brain Gain*. National Bureau of Economic Research. Accessed March 9, 2017. http://www.nber.org/papers/w14039.pdf.

Musonda, Flora. 2006. *Migration Registration in East Africa*. International Labour office (ILO). Accessed October 14, 2015. http://www.ilo.org/wcmsp5/groups/public/---ed_protect/---protrav/---migrant/documents/publication/wcms_201465.pdf.

Newland, Kathleen. 2007. *A New Surge of Interest in Migration and Development*. Migration Information Source. Accessed January 11, 2016. http://www.migrationpolicy.org/article/new-surge-interest-migration-and-development.

Nguvulu, K. 2010. *Overview on South-South Migration and Development Trends and Research Needs in Kenya*. ACP Observatory and International Organization for Migration (IOM). Accessed October 14, 2015. https://environmentalmigration.iom.int/overview-south-south-migration-and-development-kenya-trends-and-research-needs.

Okoth, Kenneth. 2003. *Kenya: What Role for Diaspora in Development*? Migration Information Source. Accessed October 14, 2015. http://www.migrationpolicy.org/article/kenya-what-role-diaspora-development.

Oucho, J, Oucho , L, and Ong'ayo, A. 2013. *The Biggest Fish in the Sea? Dynamic Kenyan Labour Migration in the East African Community*. ACP Observatory on Migration and International Organization for Migration. Accessed October 14, 2015. https://publications.iom.int/system/files/pdf/dynamic_kenyan.pdf.

Oyelere, Ruth U. 2011. 'Brain Drain, Waste or Gain? What We Know About the Kenyan Case'. *Journal of Global Initiatives: Policy, Pedagogy, Perspective* 2 (2): 113–129.

Parthasarathi, A. 2006. *Turning Brain Drain into Brain Circulation. Immigration Policies Can Be a Ticket for Scientific Talent to Recirculate among Countries*. Accessed January 12, 2016. https://inis.iaea.org/search/search.aspx?orig_q=RN:38058809.

Plaza, Sonia. 2013. 'Diaspora Resources and Policies'. In *International Handbook on the Economics of Migration*, edited by Amelie F. Constant and Klaus F. Zimmermann, 505–529. Cheltenham, UK: Edward Elgar Publishing. http://www.iza.org/MigrationHandbook/27_Plaza_Diaspora%20Resources%20and%20Policies.pdf.

Portes, Alejandro. 2001. 'Introduction: The Debates and Significance of Immigrant Transnationalism'. *Global Networks* 1 (3): 181–194.

Portes, Alejandro. 2006. *Migration and Development: A Conceptual Review of the Evidence*. The Center for Migration and Development/Princeton University, Working Paper. Accessed January 18, 2016. http://meme.phpwebhosting.com/~migracion/rimd/bellagio/2.pdf.

Ratha, Dilip, Sanket Mohapatra, Çaglar Özden, Sonia Plaza, and William Shaw. 2011. *Leveraging Migration for Africa: Remittances, Skills, and Investments*. Washington DC: World Bank Publications.

Regional Mixed Migration Secretariat (RMMS). 2013. *Mixed Migration in Kenya: The Scale of Movement and Associated Protection Risks*. Regional Mixed Migration Secretariat (RMMS), Migration Research Series. Accessed June 20, 2016. http://www.regionalmms.org/fileadmin/content/rmms_publications/series_booklettwo.pdf.

Republic of Kenya. 2014. *Kenya Diaspora Policy*. Ministry of Foreign Affairs and International Trade. Accessed October 14, 2015. http://www.mfa.go.ke/policy-matters/Kenya%20Diaspora%20Policy.pdf.

Rothgang, Michael, and Christoph M. Schmidt. 2003. 'The New Economy, the Impact of Immigration, and the Brain Drain'. In *New Economy Handbook*, 583–625. Amsterdam: Elsevier Academic Press. https://www.econbiz.de/Record/the-new-economy-the-impact-of-immigration-and-the-brain-drain-rothgang-michael/10001832259.

Saxenian, AnnaLee. 2002. 'Brain Circulation. How High-Skill Immigration Makes Everyone Better off'. *Brookings Review* 20 (1): 28–31.

Saxenian, AnnaLee. 2005. 'From Brain Drain to Brain Circulation: Transnational Communities and Regional Upgrading in India and China'. *Studies in Comparative International Development* 40 (2): 35–61.

Simmons, Alan B. 2005. *Globalization and Migration*. International Migration and the Millennium Development Goals. Accessed January 11, 2016. http://www.unfpa.org/sites/default/files/resource-pdf/migration_report_2005.pdf#page=177.

Sriskandarajah, Dhananjayan. 2005. *Migration and Development*. Global Commission of International Migration (GCIM). Accessed January 11, 2016. http://iom.ch/jahia/webdav/site/myjahiasite/shared/shared/mainsite/policy_and_research/gcim/tp/TP4.pdf.

Taylor, J. Edward. 2006. *International Migration and Economic Development*. Citeseer. Accessed October 21, 2015. http://citeseerx.ist.psu.edu/viewdoc/download?doi=10.1.1.452.9164&rep=rep1&type=pdf

World Bank. 2011. *Migration and Remittances Factbook 2011*. 2nd Edition. Washington DC: World Bank.

Wouterse, Fleur. 2011. *Continental Vs. Intercontinental Migration: An Empirical Analysis of the Impacts of Immigration Reforms on Burkina Faso*. OECD. Accessed January 11, 2016. http://search.oecd.org/dev/poverty/47908790.pdf.

Chapter 7

The Repatriation of Destitute Nigerians in Colonial Ghana

Omon Merry Osiki

1.0 THE EMERGENCE OF "UNDESIRABLE IMMIGRANTS" DURING THE COLONIAL PERIOD

Since the precolonial era, many West African communities have played host to a large number of foreigners who have settled down to live, spread religion and education as well as carry out economic and commercial activities. While some of these immigrants came periodically to work in their host communities, others stayed on for several years (Peil 1971, 1974). In essence, long-distance migration has been a feature of the West African subregion for centuries (Azarya 1980). Hence, there were permanent stranger communities in many West African societies during the precolonial period (Skinner1963). In that connection, we can easily recall that the Wangara, who spread Islam from Mali and the Saharan region to Asante, were well established as itinerant traders before the arrival of Europeans in West Africa. Similarly, the Yoruba and the Hausa have also traded over a wide area for well over a century, just like the Fanti fishermen came from Ghana and plied their trade from the Cameroons to Sierra Leone. In the same way, their Igbo counterparts worked on Cameroonian and Equatorial Guinea (Fernando Po) plantations, among others (Wilks 1965, Lovejoy 1978, Akinwumi and Raji 1990, Adekunle 1994, Law 1995, Massing 2000).

Fundamentally, the basic reasons for the huge twentieth-century West African migrations may be found in the overall redirection, in colonial times, of economic activity away from the precolonial production and trade centers to production, administrative and commercial centers established or promoted by the colonial regimes. As observed elsewhere, the imposition of taxes, the introduction of various goods and services that had to be purchased with European currencies and other related reasons "literally forced people to move away from those areas which could not provide them with adequate cash income" (Sudarkasa 1977).

Interestingly, this pattern of migration became more formalized during the colonial period. Some studies have attributed the reason for its formalization to "the political stability of the colonial period (which) made possible a great increase in migration (as) 'strangers'- foreigners to the local political unit-were no longer liable to be enslaved . . ." (Peil 1971, Stapleton 1959). In addition to the regular migrants, swarms of other people, responding to the advantages of colonialism, moved continuously on the travel routes in West Africa. As time went on, immigrant settlements gained momentum throughout the subregion.

Whatever the case, the point to stress is that trans-border migration received a boost during the colonial period and climaxed in a booming intra-West African migration and settlement. It is in this context that we can understand and analyze the emergence of a category of people known as "undesirable immigrants" whose plight had been worsened by destitution caused by the complex nature of the colonial socioeconomic and related migration issues. This work analyzes these important migration issues to capture the relationship between destitution and repatriation in the context of colonial West Africa. The work conceptualizes destitution as a state of extreme poverty or abandonment that threatens the life of an immigrant unless relieved, while repatriation is perceived as the process of returning "undesirable immigrants" to their countries of origin or citizenship. In addition, the related matter of the attraction offered by the Gold Coast to immigrants from Nigeria, and vice versa is relevant to our understanding of destitution in the West African subregion.

The study is also interested in determining the extent to which the policy of repatriation addressed the issue of destitution in the Gold Coast. For instance, how did the stakeholders-government, parents and immigrants-work out workable repatriation strategies and how effective were they in addressing destitution in the Gold Coast? This study adopts the historical style of presentation to discuss these interesting issues because as noted by I. L. Claude, "the historical approach is important, first of all for the obvious reason that the present cannot be adequately understood, nor future prospects reasonably assessed, without a grasp of the tendencies and continuities which emerge from the past" (Claude Jr 1971, 5).

2.0 THE ATTRACTION TO THE GOLD COAST

Ghana is a tropical country and one of the former British colonies in West Africa. Formerly known as the Gold Coast due to the vast presence of gold deposits in the area, Ghana was gradually conquered and became a British colony in 1874. The British also extended their rule inland from the coast to cover the Asante Empire and the various communities in the north. Thereafter, the entire area became known as the Gold Coast Colony and Protectorate. At independence in March 1957, the name Ghana was adopted to reflect the glory of the medieval Ghana Empire of West Africa (Mauny 1954, Ajayi and Crowder 1971, Levtzion 1973, Lange 2004).

The migration of Nigerians to the Gold Coast (later Ghana) started long before the country gained its independence in 1957. Colonial legacies and natural resources were the major factors that attracted West African immigrants to Ghana. In one important respect, Ghana was among other things the world's largest producer of cocoa beans, in addition to its impressive reserve and exploitation of mineral resources, such as bauxite, gold, diamonds and manganese. Additionally, Ghana's physical infrastructure such as network of rail lines and motor roads that connected its major cities with one another are believed to be the best developed in West Africa in the late 1950s. This was in addition to its impressive labor force, especially its Western-educated professionals. Therefore, given the scenario above, Ghana provided a ready magnet for Africans of all descriptions. Hence, in the 1940s, several Nigerians traveled to the Gold Coast to eke out a living (Osiki 2015).

Although most West African countries have received migrants since the precolonial times, Ghana appears to have been one of the preferred destinations during the colonial period. This was because of its relative wealth compared to those of many other West African countries. For instance, its mines and cocoa farms depended on labor supply from West African countries such as Upper Volta and workers from neighboring countries, especially Togolese farmers and craftsmen who flocked to Ghana in the 1920s, 1930s and 1940s. Peil's study has indicated that one in eight of the adults in Ghana by 1960 was a descendant of an immigrant, and an additional 2 percent were African foreigners born in Ghana. In addition, 22 percent of the adult population of Accra were foreigners. Besides, there were over 100,000 each of Togolese, Voltaics, and Nigerians out of the recorded total of 827,000 immigrants in Ghana during the late 1960s (Peil 1971, 207–209).

Moreover, during the colonial period, the expansion of cash crops and mining helped to intensify labor flows to major colonial centers. For instance, the Gold Coast's mining sector was probably the biggest under British colonial rule in West Africa. It offered a range of opportunities for employment for which Ghanaians minimally took part (Yaro 2008, Akurang-Parry 2001, 365–84). In addition, the colonial era also witnessed dramatic changes occasioned by industrialization and commercialization in Europe, which provided socioeconomic momentum in different ways in the colonies, affecting levels of wealth, urbanization, industrial growth and other related spheres. In that connection, Ghana and Nigeria served as attractive centers to African migrants.

However, beginning in the 1930s, the global economic crisis caused more people to migrate across West African cities in search of job opportunities. For instance, in October 1943, 176 Nigerians applied for new travel permits and 30 others already in possession applied for exit permits to travel to the Gold Coast. In November, the figures were 115 and 30 respectively, and in each of these months, 95 percent of these persons were going to Ghana (CSG 36005/206, 10 August 1943). Furthermore, according to census statistics in Ghana for the years 1921, 1931 and 1960, Nigerians constituted 44 percent, 23 percent and 24 percent respectively, of African immigrants resident in Ghana, while about 40 percent of female traders in the Kumasi market were of Yoruba ethnic extraction from Nigeria. Besides, based on the 1921 and 1931 census figures, Nigerians constituted the single largest group of African immigrants in the Gold Coast and by the second quarter of the twentieth century, as much as 96 percent of immigrants from other British West African colonies resident in the Gold Coast were Nigerians (Bosiakoh 2012, 15–18). Both A. Adepoju (2005) and T. Bosiakoh (2012) agree that the colony's relative affluence in the subregion during the period made her the "Gold Coast" for thousands of migrants from countries within the subregion, particularly Nigeria, Togo and Burkina Faso.

Moreover, a colonial report indicates that the Nigerian immigrant community had a lengthy history of activities in the Gold Coast (CSG 21/14/36, 1936). This agrees with the findings by Yaro (2008) that the relatively prosperous economies of the Ghana-Côte d'Ivoire migration axis attracted large numbers of internal migrants as well as international migrants from countries such as Togo, Nigeria, Guinea, Burkina Faso, Niger and Mali since the inception of the colonial economy. Essentially, the common push and pull factors, which took cognizance of socioeconomic and political factors, were basic to this pattern of migration. However, the fact that the global economic crisis had ripple effects across the world made life unbearable for the unemployed immigrants in West Africa. Indeed, countries were hard hit by the fall in demand occasioned by the declining purchasing power of the wealthier industrial nations. In addition, prices of raw materials and agricultural produce fell more alarmingly than the prices of manufactured commodities (Mathias 1983). While it may be argued that there were cases of destitution in colonial West Africa before the 1930s, there is no gainsaying the fact that the phenomenon reached a high proportion during the period of the Great Depression because the depression produced some immediate results that affected immigrants in West Africa.

In addition, the colonial authorities also recorded that there were more Nigerians traveling illegally whose movements were ostensibly facilitated by agents in Nigeria who passed the people, especially young girls, on to their network of migration and human trafficking which they established in the Gold Coast (CSG 36005/205, 1943). Thus, undocumented migration was well established between the Gold Coast and Nigeria during the period.

3.0 METHODOLOGY

In reconstructing the history of destitute Nigerians and their repatriation from the Gold Coast, it is important to place emphasis on some sources that are useful and helpful in the analysis of the events that shaped the processes of destitution and repatriation of Nigerians in that part of West Africa. Therefore, the qualitative method and from within it the historical method is adopted in this study. Indeed, as noted by I.L. Claude (1971), the historical approach is important because of the obvious fact that the present cannot be adequately understood, nor future prospects reasonably assessed without a grasp of the past.

The historical methodology of data collection and analysis covers the use of both primary and secondary sources. This may include oral information, focused-group discussions, archival documents and newspaper reports. For the purpose of the current study, emphasis is placed on archival documents and newspaper reports that are considered reliable and invaluable in the understanding of the history of destitution in colonial Ghana. In addition, secondary sources such as scholarly journal articles, books, conference and seminar papers, dissertations and other works on migration and deportation have also been very useful. They have been critically assessed and analyzed for a historical reconstruction of the history of migration, destitution and repatriation of Nigerians from the Gold Coast. In addition, information from these sources has complemented the primary materials used in the study. Moreover, the mode of presentation consciously combines the narrative, descriptive and analytical styles of writing. The structure of the work is thematic.

4.0 THEORETICAL FRAMEWORK

Both the causes and occurrence of destitution can be defined by social processes and structures. Although different people may share a similar exposure to social problems, the problems could have varying consequences for them. This is largely because they have different capacities and abilities to cope with the problems. The social vulnerability theory can adequately address the problem of destitution and repatriation, which are partly the products of social inequalities.

The concept of social vulnerability is often understood as the opposite of resilience. Historically, the concept of social vulnerability emerged within the discourse on natural hazards and disasters. These include earthquake, plague, flood and provoked mass movements, among others. A variant of the social vulnerability theory is the theory of marginalization. The theory examines the process by which individuals, social groups and ideas are made peripheral to the mainstream by relegating or confining them to the outer edges or periphery of society.

Interestingly, the theory of marginalization is also called social exclusion theory. Social exclusion is the process in which individuals or entire communities of people are systematically blocked from (or denied full access to) various rights, opportunities and resources that are normally available to members of a different group (Silver 1994). Obviously, the theory implies social disadvantage and relegation of a group or individuals to the fringe of society. In addition, alienation or disenfranchisement that may result from social exclusion is often connected to a person's social class, including educational status, citizenship and related issues. As a multidimensional process, social exclusion detaches groups and individuals from social relations and institutions. Similarly, it could prevent them (the lumpen proletariat-a conglomeration of beggars, discharged soldiers, prostitutes, vagabonds, etc.) from full participation in the prescribed activities of the society in which they live (Silver 1994).

The problem of social exclusion can intensify social problems such as destitution, poverty and unequal access to basic social amenities. With respect to the immigrant community, social exclusion may lead to or aggravate insufficient access to social rights, limited social participation, material deprivation and a lack of normative integration, among others. These factors act to undermine the capacity of the immigrant community for self-protection, block or diminish access to social protection, and so on. In all, when people are socioeconomically and politically disadvantaged, their vulnerability is exacerbated further.

5.0 DESTITUTE NIGERIANS IN THE GOLD COAST

The migration and settlement of Nigerians in the Gold Coast had its own obvious challenges and contradictions. First, because they left their families at home, immigrants needed basic social facilities such as shelter and clothing to meet up with the conditions in their new settlement. After all, it was the rush to fill a vacuum and enjoy greener pastures that propelled more and more Nigerians to migrate to the Gold Coast. Second, a substantial number of Nigerian women and young men migrated to the Gold Coast for one form of socioeconomic activity or another. Many of them went there on their own accord, while the movement of others was facilitated by their relatives and friends who had already established strongholds in the area.

Third, some other Nigerians went to the Gold Coast in the company of foster fathers and mothers. A few of them were recruited from their poor parents and transported to the Gold Coast for use as domestic servants. For instance, in 1927, one Mr. George Ato Aba, a native of Ikpetim in the Calabar Province of Nigeria encouraged Mr. Henry Okai Tetteh, a Ghanaian (or Gold Coaster) then residing in Nigeria, to take his ten-year-old son, Joe George to the Gold Coast. According to Mr. Tetteh,

> I was in Nigeria during 1924. In the year 1927, I returned to the Gold Coast. I know one Mr. George Eto Aba of Ikpetim in Calabar. He was friend (*sic*). When I was returning to the Gold Coast Mr. Aba gave me his son to bring to the Gold Coast . . . The boy, Joe George who had now adopted the name of "Jonas George Tetteh" stay (*sic*) with me in Ghana. (CSG 21/14/36, 1936)

Interestingly, George's father allowed his son to travel with Mr. Tetteh hoping that he would be enrolled in a school in the Gold Coast. Rather than enroll George in school, Mr. Tetteh preferred to employ the young George as an apprentice in his workshop. He also encouraged George to do his domestic activities. The situation of George's servitude in the Gold Coast was leaked to his father in Nigeria by a kindhearted fellow. Accordingly, in 1936 George's father protested to the colonial authorities in Lagos, calling for the repatriation of his son to Nigeria (CSG 21/14/36, 1936). George confirmed in his statement to the police on 10 February 1936 that he was used as a domestic servant and an apprentice by Mr. Tetteh. Consequently, he consented to his father's application for voluntary repatriation on his behalf.

From the details of the statement given by George to the police, it appears that the young man was coerced to declare that he was in good health in the Gold Coast to frustrate his father's application for his repatriation. In other words, he was guided in his statement by Mr. Tetteh to paint a picture of a cordial relationship between him and Mr. Tetteh (CSG 21/14/36, 1936). The truth is that George was a semi-illiterate who dropped out of school in standard III to learn carpentry. His father, who relied on information from his relatives in the Gold Coast, refused to believe that George was not subjected to slavery and exploitation by Mr. Tetteh and therefore insisted on his being repatriated to end his period of destitution in the Gold Coast.

Therefore, in his protest letter, which he sent to the office of the Chief Secretary to the Colonial Government in Lagos, Mr. Ato Aba complained that he kept up a correspondence with Tetteh and that in 1929 he asked Joe to be sent back. However, Tetteh refused to comply with his request unless money for the passage was remitted (CSO 21/14/36, 1936).

Moreover, in order to end the quagmire occasioned by the case, Ato Aba declared his readiness to bear the cost of his son's repatriation provided the colonial authorities were willingly to facilitate the repatriation process (CSO 21/14, 1936). Based on Mr. Aba's willingness to bear the cost of the repatriation, the police in Accra finally ensured that George was repatriated to Nigeria via the S.S. Edward Blyden, through Port Harcourt on 3 September 1936 (CSO21/14, 1936). The responsiveness of the relevant colonial authorities in the repatriation of George Aba proved effective in similar cases that involved destitute Nigerians in the Gold Coast.

In a related sense, the story of George Aba typified the worrisome occurrence of destitute immigrants in the Ghanaian society during the colonial period. For instance, because some Ghanaian cities started to experience the signs of burgeoning metropolitan settlements, immigrants had to encounter different socioeconomic problems and were affected by unhealthy conditions. Further, while many were perennially unemployed, others were underemployed and found it difficult to make headway in their socioeconomic struggles. For instance, the story of one James Ajayi Jumbo, who was taken to the Gold Coast by Mr. Joseph Henry Smith for engagement as a domestic help, is a clear example of trafficking in minors from Nigeria to Ghana during the colonial period (CSO 21/14/106, 1937). According to the information supplied by Jumbo in his letter of application for voluntary repatriation, he was brought to the Gold Coast from Lagos based on an arrangement between his poor mother, Mary Williams of 12 Thomas Street, Lagos and his master, Mr. Smith in March 1936. He was initially engaged as a domestic servant by Mr. Smith (CSO 21/14/106, 1937). Shortly after they arrived in the Gold Coast, Mr. Smith died leaving young Jumbo at the mercy of his wife.

From the investigations carried out by the relevant security operatives in the Gold Coast, it was revealed that as a pensioner, Mr. Smith took Jumbo to the Gold Coast so that he would help him and his wife in household chores and related services as a domestic servant. Unfortunately, Mr. Smith died on their arrival in the Cape Coast. When it was obvious that Mrs. Smith could not take care of Jumbo, the boy had to apply for voluntary repatriation. Interestingly, Mrs. Smith refused to contribute to the cost of repatriating Jumbo on the excuse that the sum of £14.11.8d in respect of unpaid pension to Mr. Smith was on deposit in the District Treasury at the Cape Coast and that the debts left behind by her husband exceeded the amount she was to inherit (CSO 21/14/106, 1937). Consequently, Jumbo was left on his own to face the difficult situation.

The character of Mrs. Smith provides an interesting insight into the plight of abandoned or destitute Nigerian youths in the Gold Coast. It beats imagination why Mrs. Smith, a wife of a retired senior registrar of the Supreme Court of Nigeria, was callous toward Jumbo. In addition, it is not stated whether the debts she alluded to were incurred in Nigeria or in Ghana. Moreover, there is no information regarding the nationality of Mr. Smith, except that he was described as a "Nigerian pensioner . . . and appeared to have been employed by the Nigerian and not Gold Coast Government" (CSO 21/14/101B, 1936).

Furthermore, it is not clear why Mrs. Smith, also known as Abbah Georgi, a Ghanaian (or Gold Coaster), decided to discontinue with the services of young Jumbo after the death of her husband bearing in mind that there is no indication that Jumbo was on their payroll financially (CSO21/14/101,1937). However, it can be speculated that Jumbo requested voluntary repatriation to Nigeria because he was no longer comfortable with Mrs. Smith. The information contained in the colonial record indicates that the "boy now appears to be stranded in the Cape Coast" (CSO21/14/101, 1937).

In Jumbo's own letter to the District Commissioner in Accra, he complained that he was a British subject by birth, having been born in Lagos, Nigeria, and a 14-year-old boy. He also said:

> He was brought to this town by late Mr. J. H. Smith . . . from Lagos . . .on the 28th March, 1936 and landed at Accra on 29 March 1936. On the same day, we arrived Cape Coast by car. Mr. Smith took me as his boy without wages. . . . (CSO 21/14/43, 1943)

Due to the content of his petition, the Colonial Secretary in Accra suggested that enquiry be made from the Colonial Secretary in Lagos whether in view of the circumstances to which James Ajayi Jumbo had found himself, if he should be repatriated to Lagos at the expense of the Government of Nigeria or that of the Gold Coast as the case might be (CSO 892/31, 1937). Following the inquiry, the authorities of the Cape Coast secured the willingness of their Nigerian counterpart to pay for the cost of repatriating Jumbo to Nigeria, though the money was less than what was required to cover his travel expenses. The payment was made through the official channels in which the government declared it was "willing to bear the cost of repatriating James Ajayi Jumbo from Accra to Lagos . . .the cost of repatriating the boy (being fixed) at £17.0d (which was) to be deposited to this administration in the usual manner" (CSO 21/14/4, 1937).

In the end, Jumbo was handed over to Messrs West African Lighterage and Transport Company Limited for 17/3 pounds, being the cost of the repatriation (CSO 21/14/264, 1937). As noted above, the amount offered by the Nigerian government was less than the amount it earlier promised the government of the Gold Coast. As a result of this, the authorities of the Gold Coast resolved the problem by obtaining a passage to Lagos at half the normal rate as the boy was under eighteen years of age (CSO 21/14/264, 1937).

Interestingly, Jumbo's case raises the question of the responsibility of the colonial authorities to social welfare, education or at least of general social attitude of Africans. In addition, it clearly shows a lack of grant of public fund to support the education of the youths, whether citizens or immigrants. Certainly, this proved one of the problems of adolescent destitution in colonial West Africa (Achola, 2006, Fourchard, 2006). The next problem was the absence of a working social welfare system, which invoked the whole structure of the colonial economy. It should be stressed that the extraordinary quest for profit made interest in social welfare system a secondary consideration, where and when it existed.

An even more pressing illustration of absence of a social welfare system can be gleaned from the case of involuntary migration that involved one Nuada Minadrichiawan who was nicknamed Ambah. Mrs. Minadrichiawan was a native of Opobo in southeast Nigeria. She already had a son and a daughter by her European husband, Mr. Palmer before she traveled to the Gold Coast. The names of her children were Albert and Allanamba, respectively (CSO 892/31/s.4, 1933). Nuada Minadrichiawan was deceived to abandon her family and travel to the Gold Coast around 1930 possibly to practice commercial sex work, though available records are silent on her mission in the Gold Coast. However, shortly after her arrival in Accra, Mr. Okine, who facilitated her movement, duped her and abandoned her to her fate.

In her account to the police, Mrs. Minadrichiawan made the following revelations:

> I have one son and a daughter at Opobo. I was brought in to Accra by one man called Okine for a very long time. On our landing Okine stole my box containing my property and ran away with it. I lodged with late Ga Manche called Yaboi. He and his people looked after me, as I had nothing. (CSO 892/31/s.4, 1933)

Moreover, from the information supplied by Mrs. Minadrichiawan, there is no indication that Okine was her lover. Consequently, we can speculate that Okine might have operated an outfit that specialized in organizing trips for young women between Nigeria and the Gold Coast in order to swindle them (CSO 892/31/s.4, 1933). From the report made available to the police, it is obvious that he was good at deceit and manipulation. However, this was an oversimplification of the modus operandi of Mr. Okine and his likes. In fact, the colonial authorities were dazzled by the ease with which he carried out his nefarious activities. However, their inability to track him down shows a number of shortcomings, notably ineptitude, bureaucratic inefficiency and carelessness. More importantly, the fundamental factors for the failure of the authorities to arrest Mr. Okine might have also been due to their seemingly indifference in the affairs of the "natives" provided their basic socioeconomic and political interests were not affected. Despite their seemingly lip service to the plight of Africans, the colonial authorities were ever ready to embrace the policy of self-repatriation, which they found irresistible for obvious reasons.

The case of Miss Christiana MorinolaAjayi was similar to that of Nuada Minadrichiawan in the sense that both of them were deceived to migrate to the Gold Coast in the hope of acquiring a better standard of living in that colony. Precisely in October 1936, Miss Ajayi sailed with a woman friend by name Maria Asukor from Lagos to Accra on board S. S. Abosso without the knowledge of her parents. Although Miss Ajayi did not state in her statement her intended mission in Accra, it can be inferred from her account that she was deceived into traveling to the Gold Coast and might not have known what awaited her in that place (CSO: 892/31/5A, 1937).

Nevertheless, the little she disclosed to the police revealed that, "about two weeks after our arrival at Accra, I had palava (*sic*) with my lady friend and she quitted me off from her house. I became lonely in the Gold Coast and hired a house of myself" (*sic*) (CSO: 892/31/5A, 1937). Thereafter, Miss Ajayi was repatriated to Nigeria with the assistance of her father, Mr. A. Oke Ajayi, a worker in the British Cotton Growing Association, Challowa via Kano in Northern Nigeria. To facilitate the repatriation process, Mr. Ajayi drew a bank draft no. 64/6828 of 10/3/37 for the sum of five pounds (£5) in the name of the Government of the Gold Coast, Accra for the repatriation of her daughter to Nigeria (CSO: 21/14/105/SF22, 1937). Following the payment of the passage fare, Miss Ajayi sailed from Accra on 1 April 1937 for Lagos by the M.V. Adda. The cost of her passage was deducted from the amount remitted by her father and the balance was paid to her for miscellaneous purposes (CSO: 21/14/105/892/31,1937).

In a similar case, one Mr. Jos B. Ogbebor Obasuyi was in financial distress and needed to be repatriated to Nigeria. He was a staff of the United African Company (UAC) Lighterage Department in Winneba in the 1930s. He applied for self-repatriation in June 1938. Surprisingly, however, as an interesting sidelight to the whole issue, Mr. Obasuyi disclosed that his movement would be based on the willingness of his father to assist him offset his debts as well as his preparedness to meet the voyage expenses (CSO: 892/31/SF.24/12,1938). Furthermore, Mr. Obasuyi disclosed that once the funds for the settlement were sent by his father, one Mr. Matthew Bannerman, a typist with the UAC, would be responsible for the distribution of the debt repayment while he would be on his way to Nigeria. Consequently, in his letter to the monarch (Oba) of Benin, Mr. Obasuyi enumerated his debts and challenges in the Gold Coast and why he found it difficult to be repatriated without offsetting his debts. The quantitative analysis of his debts is as follows: Loan from Papafio (£54.0); Messrs Arnold Riley & Co. Bradford V/s Sekyi and Bank (£4.18.9); Messrs Askham London V/s Brew and Bank (£5.6.0); Gold Smith balance (£6.9.0); Mr. Doberty's cash for re-stamped agreement (£5.0.0); Messrs Sawyer & Swatson (£2.0.0); Mr. Annerman, Takoradi (£2.0.0); London Book Club due to Rit (£1.17.0) and Miscellaneous Account (£5.9.9). This totaled £87.0.6 (CSO: 892/31/SF.24, 1938).

A cursory look would indicate that Obasuyi's debts were not due to his inability to meet basic necessities such as shelter, food and clothing, but rather to what may be considered his "exotic" life style. Indeed, a critical look at the items contained in the debt profile reflects leisure and pleasure, and the material culture associated with them. His expectation was that his father would eagerly offset his debts on the flawed assumption that he was desperate about the repatriation of his son to Nigeria. In addition, important in Obasuyi's calculation was that his father would lack the knowledge to decipher the true situation of things in the Gold Coast. However, contrary to Obasuyi's expectation, his father, Chief Aiehioba of Benin declined to pay his debts until he had seen him. Obasuyi's request for debt settlement may have added credence to his father's suspicion that his son wanted to defraud him.

Nevertheless, Obasuyi's father proposed that, "his son should pay him a short visit without bringing his wife or belongings so that matters may be discussed" amicably (CSO: 892/31, 1938). In addition, in order to match words with actions, Obasuyi's father, Chief Aiehioba agreed to defray Obasuyi's traveling expenses both ways in connection with the proposed visit. Accordingly, he deposited the necessary travel expenses with the Benin Native Treasury, because he was unwilling to send money direct to his son (CSO: 892/31, 1938). The underlying message here is that vigilant parents were rarely swindled in the name of repatriation. On the other hand, there was a mutuality of interaction between parent and son on the desirability of the latter's quest for repatriation.

In a cursory look, Obasuyi's father's attitude may appear unreasonable. However, one of the key deficiencies of this conclusion is that it fails to take cognizance of the situation of things with respect to trust between "unwanted immigrants" and their relatives in their home countries. Sincere and sensible scholars will agree that conscious parents had the right to defend themselves against their children who exploited their ignorance to defraud them in the name of self-repatriation. However, even more distressing is the fact that Mr. Obasuyi appears to be interested in benefiting from his own misfortune, which in fact he seems to have done. It may be confidently asserted that he assumed that his father was bound by tradition to take care of him. Indeed, the issue of self-indulgence or acquisitiveness cannot be completely ruled out of his intention. As is already evident, it is fair to say that Obasuyi's father's action might have been guided by realistic altruism coupled with the need to be circumspect, family emotion notwithstanding. This appears to have been a straightforward response to Obasuyi's behavior. Yet, this does not undercut the fact that Obasuyi was insolvent and needed to be repatriated like other destitute Nigerians in the Gold Coast during the period.

There were other interesting cases of destitution and application for self-repatriation by Nigerians. For instance, like the case of Mr. Obasuyi, Mrs.

UsekpimiOgunje was eager to shoulder the cost of repatriating her destitute pregnant daughter, Rebecca Odarley Johnson, from Accra to Nigeria. Hence, she applied through the Colonial Secretary in Accra for Rebecca to be sent to her in Warri by the boat that was due to leave Accra on or about 16 April 1936. Her intention was for her to connect with the M.V. "Calabar" passing through Warri. To show her readiness, Mrs. Ogunje forwarded the sum of £3 (three pounds) in British postal order for her daughter's passage and the likely incidental expenses (CSO: 892/S.F.16/31, 1936).

However, contrary to Mrs. Ogunje's expectation, Rebecca declined her mother's request on the ground that her mother needed to settle the issue with her father, Mr. J.B. Johnson before she could proceed to Nigeria (CSO: 892/S.F.16, 1936). Following this clarification, the colonial authorities refunded her £3, less 1 shilling for the commission on the postal orders. Thereafter, she was advised to ensure that future communication was done directly with her daughter (CSO: 21/14/100, 1936). The amazing thing is that the colonial authorities did not want to be caught up in the growing complexity of requests for repatriation from parents. It cannot be emphasized too strongly that some requests were sometimes made in bad faith. It was after the issue had been settled between her parents that the question of repatriating her was put to rest.

Her case contrasted sharply with that of Giboh Hausa, an abandoned ex-soldier from Sokoto in Nigeria who resided in the Takoradi area of the Gold Coast. Delighted to see that Mr. Hausa left Takoradi, the District Commissioner of Ahanta-Nzima in Sekondi expressed the willingness to take care of the expenses for his repatriation as follows: (a) passage expenses from Takoradi to Lagos (b) money order for £1.7.3 for his estimated expenses for movement between Lagos and Sokoto, including train fare from Lagos to Guzan-16/6 shillings; lorry fare for Guzan to Sokoto-5/6 shillings; and (c) feeding/chop money for seven days at 9d per day-5/3 shillings (CSO: 2106/5A/1923, 1941).

His case was that of poverty, which deprived him of good health, adequate feeding and certainly influence over his environment. This made the difference between whether he was truly living in good condition or merely surviving. Obviously, he was highly vulnerable and found it difficult to cope with economic downturns that faced the Gold Coast during the period. In addition, the loss of livelihood had dreadful impact on him (Watts and Hans 1993, 43-67, Sen 1981). Eventually, he was repatriated to Nigeria.

Mr. Hausa's case resembled the picture presented previously, but with some exceptions. Like that of Mrs. Ambah, they were both incapacitated by health challenges. On the one hand, Mrs. Ambah was reported to be suffering from an incurable affection of the legs and was unable to walk. In addition, following the death of her husband, she was forced to beg because she had no relations in the Gold Coast. Based on her statement that her father was the "Chief Judge" of Opobo, the colonial authorities in Accra requested to know if any of her relatives in Nigeria would be willing to defray the cost of her repatriation to Nigeria or whether the government of Nigeria would be ready to meet such expenses (CSO: 92/31/S.4/4, 1937). When help was not forthcoming, the potential for confusion over Mrs. Ambah's pedigree became particularly enormous. In the end, both colonial authorities agreed to share the responsibility of repatriating her to Nigeria.

The same fate of ill health confronted one Moses N. Ochukpa. He was reported to be "mentally deranged" and was under an illusion that "the Ibos and the Efiks in the Gold Coast instructed everyone to refuse employing him" (CSO: 892/31/21/14/100A, 1936). He was a native of Abariba in the Owerri Province of Nigeria. The colonial authorities agreed that Ochukpa's statements were incorrect, but they were impressed by his intelligence as he answered most of the questions put to him (CSO: 892/31/21/14/100A, 1936). However, it was clear that Ochukpa was living "upon the charity of Nigerians living in Accra" (CSO: 892/31/s.17/4, 1936). In essence, he was a victim of an economy that was struggling to absorb its labor force. Consequently, he was compelled to tackle the twin problems of joblessness and poverty and was almost swept away in a terrible storm of hopelessness without any governmental authorities ready to turn the page for him.

However, the main issue with respect to Ochukpa's case was not whether he was intelligent or a victim of economic crisis, but that he was a destitute or an "undesirable immigrant" that should be repatriated. With respect to Ochukpa's case, the need to understand destitution as a socioeconomic problem makes sense, yet the option of repatriation was attractive in the face of lack of an alternative strategy. However, Ochukpa was eventually repatriated to Nigeria at the cost of £1.6 via Messrs Holland West Africa Lijn N.V. at the expense of the Nigerian government (CSO: 865/42/14/1936, 1937, CSO: 892/31/s.17/8, 1937).

6.0 RECIPROCAL REPATRIATION OF DESTITUTE GHANAIANS IN NIGERIA

Just as there were destitute Nigerians in the Gold Coast, there were also some Ghanaians who were stranded in Nigeria due to financial, employment and other related problems. The case of Anyetei, an only son of his parents stood out. He was reported to the relevant colonial authorities for immediate repatriation to the Gold Coast when it was obvious he was dependent on others. He was reported to be 27 years of age at the time his father wanted him to be repatriated to the Gold Coast. He was initially employed by "a certain

European then resident in Nigeria as his washerman" (CSO: 1493/29, 1938). Matters became worse for Anyetei when he was out of job probably because his employer relocated from Nigeria. Consequently, he was reported to be living in Lagos "under financial stress and extreme abject circumstances; and . . . decided not to return home in his disgraceful and impecunious state" (CSO: 1493/29, 1938). Anyetei's father, Labadi Ambessey, was prepared to deposit Anyetei's "passage home" together with such sum of money as would cover other financial expenses, which might facilitate his early return home.

Moreover, Mr. H.R.E. Browne, the Acting Commissioner of the Colony at the time who responded to the request, arranged to repatriate Anyetei via a deck passage onboard M.V. "Adda," which was billed to leave Lagos on 4 February 1939 (CSO: 1493/vol.III/387, 1939, CSO: 06312/s.55/5, 1939). Based on the arrangement put in place, Anyetei left for Accra by M.V. "Adda" which sailed on Saturday, 4 February, 1939 (CSO: 1493/vol. III/392, 1939).

The case of Kwesi Appiatsi was slightly different from that of Anyetei. He came to Lagos in 1917 with the purpose of securing employment and was engaged by a number of firms such as the Elder Dempster and co., Ltd., Lagos, as clerk. In 1923, he resigned his appointment and secured a job with the African and Eastern Trade Corporation based in Warri. He was retrenched in 1929 because of constant illness and other undisclosed reasons. He returned to Lagos in 1930 and was out of job. He started to live "a hand to mouth existence" (CSO: 1493/40/1137/270, 1940). Consequently, he was largely dependent on the generosity of his friends and countrymen. Besides, he was seldom able to pay his house rent and had to move from one location to another, leaving unpaid debts behind him. Expectedly, he was reported to be "a frequenter of palm wine bars where he sponges on others for his drinks" (CSO: 1493/40/1137/270, 1940). His lifestyle compelled him to be dependent perpetually on others.

Nevertheless, the colonial authorities acknowledged that there were no crimes or convictions recorded against him. Yet, he was regarded as "an undesirable person who should be deported from Nigeria" (CSO: 1493/40/1137/270, 1940). Several questions face this attitude of the colonial authorities. First, it exposes government's inability to provide employment to the numerous unemployed in society. Second, it gives the impression that government had limited strategies to cope with the problems of unemployment and destitution generally. Interestingly, the government was willing to repatriate him if it could be "arranged without a cost to this government" (CSO: 1493/11/40, 1940). This suggests that the thing to be explained with respect to the plight of the poor was the economic hardship that faced West African cities during the period and not necessarily the problem of destitution.

Understandably, Kwesi Appiatsi was very willing to be repatriated in the event that the government was unable to get him a job of any kind in Nigeria

(CSO: 1493/11/40, 1940). However, the most limiting factor for most destitute immigrants interested in self-repatriation was transport cost and related expenses. Surprisingly, in 1940, Kwesi Appiatsi disappeared from the radar of the police because he "appears to have left Lagos" (CSO: 1493/40, 1940). This may be a convenient way of saying that the police lost interest in the case. Again, we are driven back to the whole question of whether the police had sufficient logistic to track him down or not. Curiously, there was no specific indication or reference to how the police intended to locate Kwesi Appiatsi for repatriation from Nigeria. Perhaps, it would have been inspiring if the police had successfully handled the repatriation of Kwesi Appiatsi to give a coherent indication that they were up to the task of successful repatriation exercises. This is a valid and useful suggestion, although it must be admitted that the police authorities had their own challenges as well.

7.0 CONCLUSION

The Gold Coast's thriving socioeconomic sectors were the major motivation for the attraction of Nigerians and other West Africans to the area during the colonial period. While it offered the proverbial greener pastures to the immigrants, it had its own difficulties that made life unbearable for the destitute ones among them. To these people, they had obviously reached the line where dreams clashed with reality. Indeed, their world was characterized by imbalances in access to wealth and resources, in safety and in opportunities for betterment. This observation gives insight into the understanding of the connection between destitution and repatriation. This can be seen in the cases examined in this work.

On the part of the destitute Nigerians, some reasons for despondency existed. Lack of employment and rising cost of living combined as a fatal mix for the immigrants and exacerbated the disequilibria, which they faced. While they struggled to cope with the impact of urbanization in the Gold Coast, the period examined in this work was conterminous with the Great Depression of the interwar years as well as the period of the Second World War (1939–1945) with their attendant socioeconomic crises across the world. Therefore, the flurry of destitution and repatriation that became the order of the day was not unexpected. More generally, certain socioeconomic trends of the period were simply unfavorable to underprivileged members of the immigrant community in West Africa who were deprived of the minimum approximation of social welfare. Their disadvantages were aggravated by the fact that they were far away from home. This conclusion is reinforced by the understanding of the problem of social exclusion faced by the immigrant community. Indeed, social exclusion theory examined in this work agrees that the conditions of the immigrant community may be further worsened or intensified by social problems such as destitution, poverty and unequal access to basic social amenities, which privileged citizens may be spared of.

Finally, how effective the repatriation exercises were in addressing the menace of destitution in colonial West Africa is another matter entirely. Largely, they were important as symptoms of a socioeconomic sector in distress. In that regard, the switch to repatriation mostly served as a means to an end, the end being to cut down on the number of "undesirable immigrants" in West African cities. Nevertheless, a critical look at the reactions of the colonial authorities reveals a trend that was diverse, tentative and sometimes complex in accordance with colonial urban influences and complexities. In that case, the immigrants appeared to have been treated as mere scapegoats.

The above conclusion calls for some policy recommendations to address the difficulties posed by destitution and repatriation. First, immigrants should be encouraged to return to their countries of origin once it is obvious they are unable to secure a meaningful livelihood. Second, the practice of allowing foster parents to travel with minors to another country should be discouraged as much as possible. The cases examined in this study indicate that such minors usually bear the brunt of whatever socioeconomic crises that may affect their foster parents. Lastly, while the practice of self-repatriation is encouraged, national governments must be ready to alleviate the financial burdens associated with repatriation of stranded immigrants.

REFERENCES

Achola, Milckl A. 2006. "Youth, Poverty and Destitution in Colonial Nairobi." Paper presented at a Conference on Youth, Nyeri, Kenya, June.

Adekunle, Julius O. 1994. "Borgu and Economic Transformation 1700–1900: The Wangara Factor." *African Economic History* 22: 1–18.

Adepoju, Aderanti. 2005. "Patterns of Migration in West Africa." In *At Home in the World? International Migration and Development in Contemporary Ghana and West Africa*. Edited by Takyiwaa. Manuh. Accra: Sub-Saharan Publishers.

Ajayi, Jacob F. A. and Michael Crowder. 1971. *History of West Africa*. London: Longman.

Akinwumi, Olayemi, and Adesina Y. Raji.1990. "The Wangarawa Factor in the History of Nigerian Islam: The Example of Kano and Borgu." *Islamic Studies* 29/4: 375–385.

Akurang-Parry, Kwabena O. 2001. "'We Cast about for a Remedy': Chinese Labor and African Opposition in the Gold Coast, 1874–1914." *International Journal of African Historical Studies* 34/2: 365–384.

Azarya, Victor. 1980. "Traders and the Center in Massina, Kong, and Samori's State." *The International Journal of African Historical Studies* 13/3: 420–456.

Bosiakoh, Thomas A. 2012. "'In Unity Lies Our Strength': Exploring the Benefits and Entitlements in Nigerian Migrant Associations in Accra, Ghana." *Global Journal of Human Social Science: Sociology, Economics and Political Science* 12/9: 15–18.

Claude, Inis L. (Jr.). 1971. *Swords into Plowshares: The Problems and Progress of International Organizations* (4th Edition). New York: Random House.

Fourchard, Laurent. 2006. "Lagos and the Invention of Juvenile Delinquency in Nigeria." *The Journal of African History* 47/1: 115–137.

Lange, Dierk. 2004. *Ancient Kingdoms of West Africa*. Dettelbach, Germany: J.H. Roll.

Law, Robin. 1995. "'Central and Eastern Wangara': An Indigenous West African Perception of the Political and Economic Geography of the Slave Coast as Recorded by Joseph Dupuis in Kumasi, 1820." *History in Africa* 22: 281–305.

Levtzion, Nehemiah. 1973. *Ancient Ghana and Mali*. London: Methuen.

Lovejoy, Paul E. 1978. "The Role of the Wangara in the Economic Transformation of the Central Sudan in the Fifteenth and Sixteenth Centuries." *The Journal of African History* 19/2: 173–193.

Mathias, Peter. 1983. *The First Industrial Nation: The Economic History of Britain* (2nd Edition). London: Routledge.

Massing, Andreas W. 2000. "The Wangara, an Old Soninke Diaspora in West Africa? (Les Wangara, unevieille diaspora soninked'Afrique de l'Ouest?)." *Cahiers d'Études Africaines* 40/158: 281–308.

Mauny, Raymond A. 1954. "The Question of Ghana." *Journal of the International African Institute* 24/3: 200–213.

Osiki, Omon M. 2015. "Xenophobia and Press Reportage of the 1969 Immigrant Expulsion from Ghana: The Nigerian Experience." *Journal of Applied Thought* 4/1: 177–178.

Peil, Margaret. 1974. "Ghana's Aliens." *International Migration Review* 8/3: 367–381.

Peil, Margaret. 1971. "The Expulsion of West African Aliens" *The Journal of Modern African Studies* 9/2: 205–229.

Sen, Amartya. 1981. *Poverty and Famines: An Essay on Entitlement and Deprivation*. London: Oxford University Press.

Silver, Hilary. 1994. "Social Exclusion and Social Solidarity." *International Labour Review* 133/5–6: 531–578.

Skinner, Elliott P. 1963. "Strangers in West African Societies." *Africa: Journal of the International African Institute* 33/4: 307–320.

Stapleton, Brian G. 1959. "Nigerians in Ghana." *West Africa* 2184.

Sudarkasa, Niara. 1977. "Women and Migration in Contemporary West Africa." *Signs* 3/1: 178–189.

Watts, Michael J, and Hans G. Bohle.1993. "The Space of Vulnerability: The Causal Structure of Hunger and Famine." *Progress in Human Geography* 17/1: 43–67.

Wilks, Ivor. 1965. "A Note on the Early Spread of Islam in Dagomba." *Transactions of the Historical Society of Ghana* 8: 87–98.

Yaro, Awetori J. 2008. *Migration in West Africa: Patterns, Issues and Challenges*. University of Ghana, Legon: Centre for Migration Studies.

9.0 ARCHIVAL SOURCES

CSG 36005/206. 1943. "From the Colonial Secretary's Office (CSO) to the Governor of Nigeria, Lagos." National Archive, Ibadan (NAI).

CSG 21/14/36. 1936. "Gold Coast Police, Headquarters, C.I.D. Accra Station, Eastern Province, 'Statement', by Mr. Henry Okai Tetteh, Boundary Road, Accra, 10th day of February, 1936." Public Records and Archives Administration Department (PRAAD), Accra.

CSG 36005/205. 1943. "From the Colonial Secretary's Office to the Governor of Nigeria, Lagos." NAI.

CSG 21/14/36. 1936. "Gold Coast Police, Headquarters, C.I.D. Accra Station, Eastern Province." PRAAD.

CSO 21/14. 1936. "From the Chief Secretary's Office, Lagos, Nigeria, to the Honourable, the Colonial Secretary, Gold Coast." PRAAD.

CSO21/14. 1936. "From the Inspector-General of Police, Headquarters, Accra, to the Honourable, the Colonial Secretary, Victoriaborg, 'Joe George-Repatriation of to Nigeria'." PRAAD.

CSO 21/14/101B. 1936. "From the District Commissioner's Office, Cape Coast, to the Honourable, the Treasurer, Victoriaborg, Accra, 'Estate of Mr. J.H. Smith, Pensioner-Deceased'." PRAAD.

CSO 21/14/106. 1937. "From the Colonial Secretary, Accra, to the Honourable, the Chief Secretary to the Government of Nigeria, Lagos, 'Repatriation of Destitute Africans from the Gold Coast, James Ajayi Jumbo, repatriation of, to Nigeria'." PRAAD.

CSO 21/14/4. 1937. "From Chief Secretary's Office, Nigeria, Lagos, to the Honourable, the Colonial Secretary, Gold Coast, Accra." PRAAD.

CSO 892/31/s.4. 1933. "Gold Coast Police, Accra, 'Statement of Mrs. Nuada Minadrichiawan.'" PRAAD.

CSO 892/31/5A. 1937. "From Gold Coast Police, Accra Station, Eastern Province, Christiana Morinola Ajayi, 'Miss Christiana Morinola Ajayi-repatriation of, to Nigeria'." PRAAD.

CSO 21/14/105/SF22. 1937. "From A. Oke Ajayi, c/o the British Cotton Growing Association, Challowa via Kano, Northern Nigeria, to His Merjesty (*sic*), the Gold Coast Government, Accra, Gold Coast." PRAAD.

CSO 21/14/105/892/31/S.22/9. 1937. "From the Colonial Secretary, to Mr. A. Oke Ajayi, c/o the British Cotton Growing Association, Challowa via Kano, Northern Nigeria." PRAAD.

CSO 892/31/SF.24/12. 1938. "From the Commissioner's Office, Accra, to the Honourable Colonial Secretary, Victoriaborg/Accra, "Obasuyi Ogbebor." PRAAD.

CSO 21/14/264/C.P.353/23. 1937. "From Provincial Commissioner's Office, Cape Coast, to the Honourable, the Colonial Secretary, Victoriaborg, Accra, 'James Ajayi Jumbo-Repatriation of'." PRAAD.

CSO: 892/31/SF.24. 1938. "From Jos B. O. Ogbebor, to the Oba of Benin, Benin City." (NAI).

CSO 892/31/SF.24/03028/S.877/11. 1938. "From the Acting Chief Secretary to the Government of Nigeria, to the Honourable Colonial Secretary, Gold Coast." NAI.

CSO 892/31/pf.24/03028/S.877/4. 1938. "From the Acting Chief Secretary to the Government, to the Honourable Colonial Secretary, Gold Coast." NAI.
CSO 892/S.F.16/31. 1936. "From Usekpimi Ogunje, Seton House, Warri, Nigeria, to the Honourable Colonial Secretary, Gold Coast, Accra." NAI.
CSO 892/S.F.16.1936. "From Rebecca Odarley Johnson, to the Gold Coast Police, Accra." NAI.
CSO 892/31/21/14/100A. 1936. "Repatriation of Moses N. Ochukpa." NAI.
CSO 892/31/s.17/4. 1936. "From the Acting Colonial Secretary, Accra, to the Chief Secretary to the Government of Nigeria, Lagos." NAI.
CSO 1493/29. 1938. "Anyetei-Application for Repatriation of to the Gold Coast." NAI.
CSO 1493/vol.III/387. 1939. "From the Honourable, the Chief Secretary to the Government, Lagos, to the Acting Commissioner of the Colony, 'Anyetei-Repatriation of to the Gold Coast'." NAI.
CSO 1493/40/1137/270. 1940. "From the Superintendent of Police of the Colony, Lagos, to Commissioner of the Colony, Lagos, 'Kwesi Appiatsi: Repatriation of'." NAI.
CSO 1493/11/40. 1940. "From the Honourable Chief Secretary to the Government, Lagos, to the Commissioner of the Colony, Lagos, 'Application for Repatriation by Kwesi Appiatsi to Gold Coast.'" NAI.
CSO 06312/s.55/5. 1939. "From the Chief Secretary to the Government, Lagos, to the Colonial Secretary, Gold Coast, Accra, 'Anyetei-Application for Repatriation of to the Gold Coast.'" NAI.
CSO 21/14/100. 1936. "From the Colonial Secretary, Accra, to Madam Usekpimi Ogunje, Seton House, Warri, Nigeria." NAI.
CSG 36005/206. 1943. "From the Colonial Secretary's Office (CSO) to the Governor of Nigeria, Lagos." NAI.
CSG 21/14/36. 1936. "Gold Coast Police, Headquarters, C.I.D. Accra Station,
Eastern Province, 'Statement, by Mr. Henry Okai Tetteh,' Boundary Road, Accra, 10th day of February, 1936." PRAAD.
CSG 36005/205 and CSG 36005/203/ C. 0836/77. 1943. "From the Colonial Secretary's Office (CSO) to the Governor of Nigeria, Lagos." NAI.
CSG 21/14/36. 1936. "Gold Coast Police, Headquarters, C.I.D. Accra Station, Eastern Province." PRAAD.
CSO: 21/14, File No. 03028/s.864/3. 1936. "From the Chief Secretary's Office, Lagos, Nigeria, to the Honourable, the Colonial Secretary, Gold Coast." PRAAD.
CSO 21/14, 696/42/3/1936. 1936. "From the Inspector-General of Police, Headquarters, Accra, to the Honourable, the Colonial Secretary, Victoriaborg, 'Joe George-Repatriation of to Nigeria.'" PRAAD.
CSO 21/14/106. 1937. "From the Colonial Secretary, Accra, to the Honourable, the Chief Secretary to the Government of Nigeria, Lagos, 'Repatriation of Destitute Africans from the Gold Coast, James Ajayi Jumbo, repatriation of, to Nigeria.'" PRAAD.
CSO 21/14/101B, 1931/224/1921. 1936. "From the District Commissioner's Office, Cape Coast, to the Honourable, the Treasurer, Victoriaborg, Accra, 'Estate of Mr. J.H. Smith, Pensioner-Deceased.'" PRAAD.

CSO 21/14/101. 1937. "From the Provincial Commissioner's Office, Cape Coast, to the Honourable, the Colonial Secretary, Victoriaborg, Accra, 'James Ajayi Jumbo-Application of, for Repatriation to Nigeria.'" PRAAD.

CSO 21/14/43,892/31/SF.21. 1943. PRAAD.

CSO 21/14/4, File No. 892/31/of 21. 1937. "From Chief Secretary's Office, Nigeria, Lagos, to the Honourable, the Colonial Secretary, Gold Coast, Accra." PRAAD.

CSO 21/14/264, C.P.353/23. 1937. "From Provincial Commissioner's Office, Cape Coast, to the Honourable, the Colonial Secretary, Victoriaborg, Accra, 'James Ajayi Jumbo-Repatriation of.'" PRAAD.

CSO 892/31/s.4. 1933. "Gold Coast Police, Accra, 'Statement of Mrs. Nuada Minad-richiawan.'" PRAAD.

CSO 892/31/5A. 1937. "From Gold Coast Police, Accra Station, Eastern Province, Christiana Morinola Ajayi, 'Miss Christiana Morinola Ajayi-repatriation of, to Nigeria.'" PRAAD.

CSO 21/14/105/SF22. 1937. "From A. Oke Ajayi, c/o the British Cotton Growing Association, Challowa via Kano, Northern Nigeria, to His Majesty (*sic*), the Gold Coast Government, Accra, Gold Coast." PRAAD.

CSO 21/14/105/892/31/S.22/9. 1937. "From the Colonial Secretary, to Mr. A. Oke Ajayi, c/o the British Cotton Growing Association, Challowa via Kano, Northern Nigeria." PRAAD.

CSO 892/31/SF.24/12. 1938. "From the Commissioner's Office, Accra, to the Honourable Colonial Secretary, Victoriaborg/Accra, 'Obasuyi Ogbebor.'" NAI.

CSO 892/31/SF.24. 1938. "From Jos B. O. Ogbebor, to the Oba of Benin, Benin City." NAI.

CSO 892/31/SF.24/03028/S.877/11. 1938. "From the Acting Chief Secretary to the Government of Nigeria, to the Honourable Colonial Secretary, Gold Coast." NAI.

CSO 892/31/pf.24/03028/S.877/4. 1938. "From the Acting Chief Secretary to the Government, to the Honourable Colonial Secretary, Gold Coast." NAI.

CSO 892/S.F.16/31. 1936. "From Usekpimi Ogunje, Seton House, Warri, Nigeria, to the Honourable Colonial Secretary, Gold Coast, Accra." NAI.

CSO 892/S.F.16. 1936. "From Rebecca Odarley Johnson, to the Gold Coast Police, Accra." NAI.

CSO 21/14/100. 1936. "From the Colonial Secretary, Accra, to Madam Usekpimi Ogunje, Seton House, Warri, Nigeria." NAI.

CSO 2106/5A/1923. 1941. "From District Commissioner's Office, to the District officer, Lagos." NAI.

CSO 92/31/S.4/4. 1937. "From the Colonial Secretary, Accra, to the Honourable Chief Secretary, Lagos." NAI.

CSO 892/31/s.17/4. 1936. "From the Acting Colonial Secretary, Accra, to the Chief Secretary to the Government of Nigeria, Lagos." NAI.

CSO 1493/29. 1938. "Anyetei-Application for Repatriation of . . . to the Gold Coast." NAI.

CSO 1493/vol.III/387. 1939. "From the Honourable, the Chief Secretary to the Government, Lagos, to the Acting Commissioner of the Colony, 'Anyetei-Repatriation of to the Gold Coast.'" NAI.

CSO 06312/s.55/5. 1939. "From the Chief Secretary to the Government, Lagos, to the Colonial Secretary, Gold Coast, Accra, 'Anyetei-Application for Repatriation of to the Gold Coast.'" NAI.

CSO 1493/vol. III/392. 1939. "From the Acting Commissioner of the Colony, Lagos, to the Honourable Chief Secretary to the Government, Lagos, 'Anyetei-Application for Repatriation of to the Gold Coast.'" NAI.

CSO 1493/40/1137/270. 1940. "From the Superintendent of Police of the Colony, Lagos, to Commissioner of the Colony, Lagos, 'Kwesi Appiatsi: Repatriation of.'" NAI.

CSO 1493/40/1137/270. 1940. "From the Superintendent of Police of the Colony, Lagos, to Commissioner of the Colony, Lagos." NAI.

CSO 1493/11/40. 1940. "From the Honourable Chief Secretary to Government, Lagos, to the Commissioner of the Colony, Lagos, 'Application for Repatriation by Kwesi Appiatsi to Gold Coast.'" NAI.

CSO 1493/11/40. 1940. "From the Honourable Chief Secretary to the Government, Lagos, to the Commissioner of the Colony, Lagos." NAI.

CSO 1493/40. 1940. "From the Superintendent of Police of the Colony, Lagos, to the Commissioner of the Colony, Lagos, 'Kwesi Appiatsi- Repatriation of.'" NAI.

Chapter 8

From Seasonal Migrants to Settlers

Climate Change and Permanent Migration to the Transitional Zone of Ghana

Peter Bilson Obour, Kwadwo Owusu and Joseph K. Teye

1.0 INTRODUCTION: SEASONAL AND PERMANENT MIGRATION

Seasonal migration is an important livelihood strategy practiced by labor migrants across the world (Pham and Hill 2008, 62-70, Jülich 2011, 195–196, Martin et al. 2014, 100–101). Over the years, environmentally induced seasonal migration has been of great interest to researchers (van der Geest 2011, 81–84). The drivers of this type of population movement have been categorized into "slow-" and "sudden-onset" depending on how they propel migration (Dun and Gemenne 2008, 5–10). The sudden environmental drivers, such as floods and storms, are usually swift and cause involuntary migration. The slow-onset environmental drivers, such as drought and land degradation, are gradual and tend to induce voluntary migration as a long-term coping strategy (van der Geest 2011, 81–88, Fritz 2010, 2–10).

As many parts of the world are experiencing both "rapid-onset" and "slow" climatic events, migration flows to destinations where conditions are favorable are expected to increase (Fritz 2010, 2–10). In Africa, climate-related environmental changes, characterized by warmer and drier conditions, have resulted in changes in cropping seasons among rural farmers in the Sahelian region. These changes are projected to reduce rain-fed agricultural yields by 50 percent in some countries (IPCC 2007). This is expected to force farmers to migrate in search of job opportunities in other rural and urban communities to enable them remit portions of their incomes to sustain their families back home (Hunter 2007). Although the nexus between climate change and migration is highly contested, there is a consensus that climate-driven migration, combined with socioeconomic and political drivers, induce seasonal and permanent migration, particularly among rural populations (Martin et al.

2014, 101–105). For instance, in Ethiopia, migration serves as an important long-term coping strategy to environmental changes (Meze-Hausken 2000, 397–401). Similarly, most rural farmers in dry regions of Burkina Faso are likely to move to wetter regions in order to continue with their farming activities (Henry, Schoumaker and Beauchemin 2004, 446–447).

In Ghana, labor mobility from the north to the south is an important livelihood strategy (Anarfi et al. 2003, 8–14, Black, Kniveton, and Schmidt-Verkerk 2013, 37–43). In spite of the dynamics with the north-south migration, it has been argued that both voluntary and involuntary migration (such as forced migration through labor recruitment during the colonial times) enabled laborers from the north to take up agricultural and non-agricultural jobs in the south (Cleveland 1991, 222–225, Rademacher-Schulz, Schraven, and Mahama 2014, 47–51). Seasonal migration of labor from the north also has a long history which reflects the differences in the timing and onset of the rainy season between the north and the south. The long dry season (October–March) in the north is characterized by dry soils, dry vegetation and unavailability of water, which temporally shuts agricultural activities, because most people in the north practice rain-fed agriculture (van der Geest 2004, 4–8). In response to this, farm labor moves to the middle and southern part of Ghana, where climatic conditions are suitable, to search for on-farm and off-farm jobs, and return to their farm-based regions during the onset of the rainy season (van der Geest 2011, 81–88). This trend of migration enabled the migrants to sustain their livelihoods and that of their households. Over the past decades, there have been shifts in the seasonal migration patterns of farm labor from northern Ghana (van der Geest 2011, 84–85). It has been observed that most farm laborers from northern Ghana now tend to settle permanently in the middle belt (Sow, Adaawen and Sheffran 2014, 388–390).

Previous studies have shown that the combined effects of climate change/variability and politicoeconomic factors explain the emerging trend of farm labor migration from the north to the south in Ghana (van der Geest 2011, 82–87, Abu, Codjoe and Sward 2014, 342–347, Sow, Adaawen and Sheffran 2014, 388–387). The effects of this new form of permanent migration on livelihoods and the challenges faced by this group of permanent migrants are quite poorly understood. This chapter therefore examines the changing trends in the migration of farmers from the Upper West Region to three districts—Ejura-Sekyedumase, Nkoranza South and Techiman—in the transitional zone of Ghana within the last ten years. Farm labor migrants from the Upper West Region provide an appropriate case study for exploring the shift in migration trends because they have a long history of north-south seasonal migration (van der Geest 2011, 81–86). Apart from analyzing the causes of these migration trends, we also examined the effects of these emerging migration patterns on livelihoods in the study communities.

2.0 THE NEXUS BETWEEN CLIMATE CHANGE AND MIGRATION

Different models have been designed to explain the relationship between climate change and migration. The behavioral model explains the linkage between the two concepts using cognition and new economics of labor migration theories (Martin et al. 2014, 90–91). The agent-based model (Kniveton 2011, 36–39) and the agent migration adaptation to rainfall change model (Kniveton 2012, 444–446) adopt psychosocial theories, namely theory of reasoned action (Ajzen and Fishbein 1980, 240–248) and theory of planned behavior (Ajzen 1991, 181–185), to explain human migratory trends under climate change and variability. Most of the existing models suggest that climate change combines with other non-climate-related drivers to induce migration (Martin et al. 2014, 89–92). In this case, migration can be considered as an adaptive livelihood strategy (Rademacher-Schulz, Schraven, and Mahama 2014, 50–51).

Against this background, we propose a conceptual framework for climate-induced permanent farm labor migration (see Figure 8.1).

In this framework, we postulate that farm labor faced with climate change effects, acting as a single driver or combined with other non-climatic socio-economic, political and cultural stressors would opt to remain in situ or migrate to a more suitable destination. The decision to move is, however, influenced by the individual's socioeconomic characteristics, experiences and by making a rational thought (Kniveton 2011, 35–36). There are also external influences from household/family, peers and migrants' social network. The migrants' ability to make a rational decision is also influenced by how much information is available about the driving factor, in this case climate change effect. For instance, information about prolonged droughts and its severity in the long term in the home region compared to destination areas may influence migrants to embark on permanent migration as a long-term adaptation strategy. The movement could involve either the individual migrant or the entire family. The choice of destination is determined by the migrants' experiences from past visits, social network, employers (Jülich 2011, 194–195) and self-exploration at the intended destinations. We argue that permanent migration offers migrants an opportunity to sustain their livelihoods and those of their households and families. There is also a trickle-down effect on the economy and development in the destination region as well as the home region, for instance through remittances.

The study was conducted in three districts in Ghana: Ejura-Sekyedumase District of the Ashanti Region, Nkoranza South District and Techiman Municipal in the Brong Ahafo Region located in the forest-savannah transition zone. It coincides with Zone C in the agro-ecological classification of the

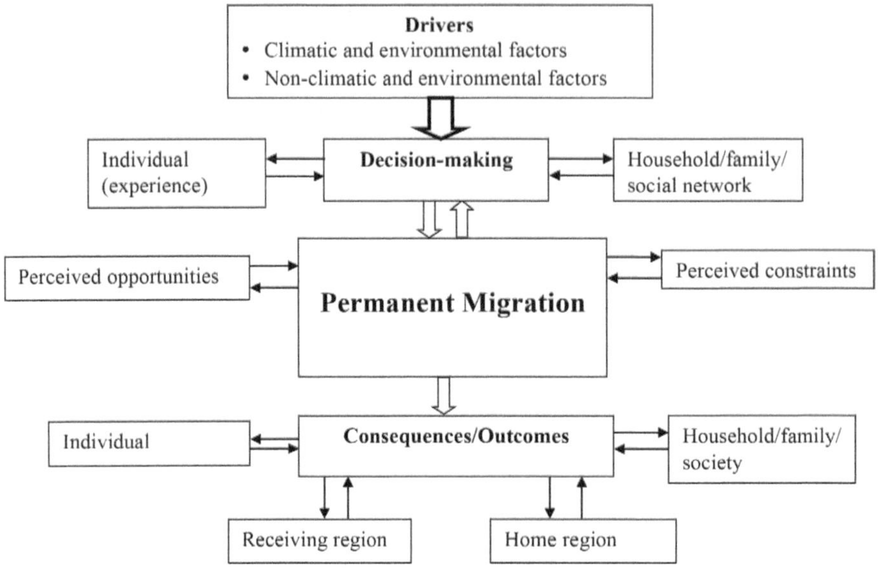

Figure 8.1 Conceptual framework for climate-induced permanent farm labor migration. Created by author.

Ghana Meteorological Agency (GMet) (Klutse et al. 2013, 395–396, Owusu and Waylen 2012, 202–203) (shown in Figure 8.2). The zone has a bi-modal rainfall pattern with a mean annual rainfall total between 1,200 and 1,500 mm (Klutse et al. 2013, 395–396). The major rainy season starts from late March/early April to June. This is interspersed by a short dry spell from July/August. The minor rainy season sets in between September and October (Isaac 2014, 57–58), allowing two cropping seasons a year without irrigation.

The population of Ejura-Sekyedumase District is about 85,446 while Nkoranza South District and Techiman Municipal have populations of about 100,929 and 206,856, respectively (Ghana Statistical Service 2012, 101–102). For each of the three selected districts, five communities were purposively selected for the study: Ejura, Sekodumasi, Sekyekumase, Dwenewoho and Kyenkyenkura for Ejura-Sekyedumase District; Nkoranza, Nkwabeng, Ahyiaem, Donkro-Nkwanta and Yefri for Nkoranza South District; and Techiman, Nsuta, Fiaso, Mangoase and Nkwaeso for Techiman Municipal. Primary data were obtained from migrant farmers using a combination of quantitative and qualitative research techniques. Semi-structured questionnaires were used to interview 190 people (150 males and 40 females) randomly selected from the three districts. In addition, focus group discussions (FGDs) and key informant interviews were used to collect qualitative data. Quantitative data were analyzed using SPSS version 16.0 and qualitative data by using content analysis approach (Mayring 2014, 39–53).

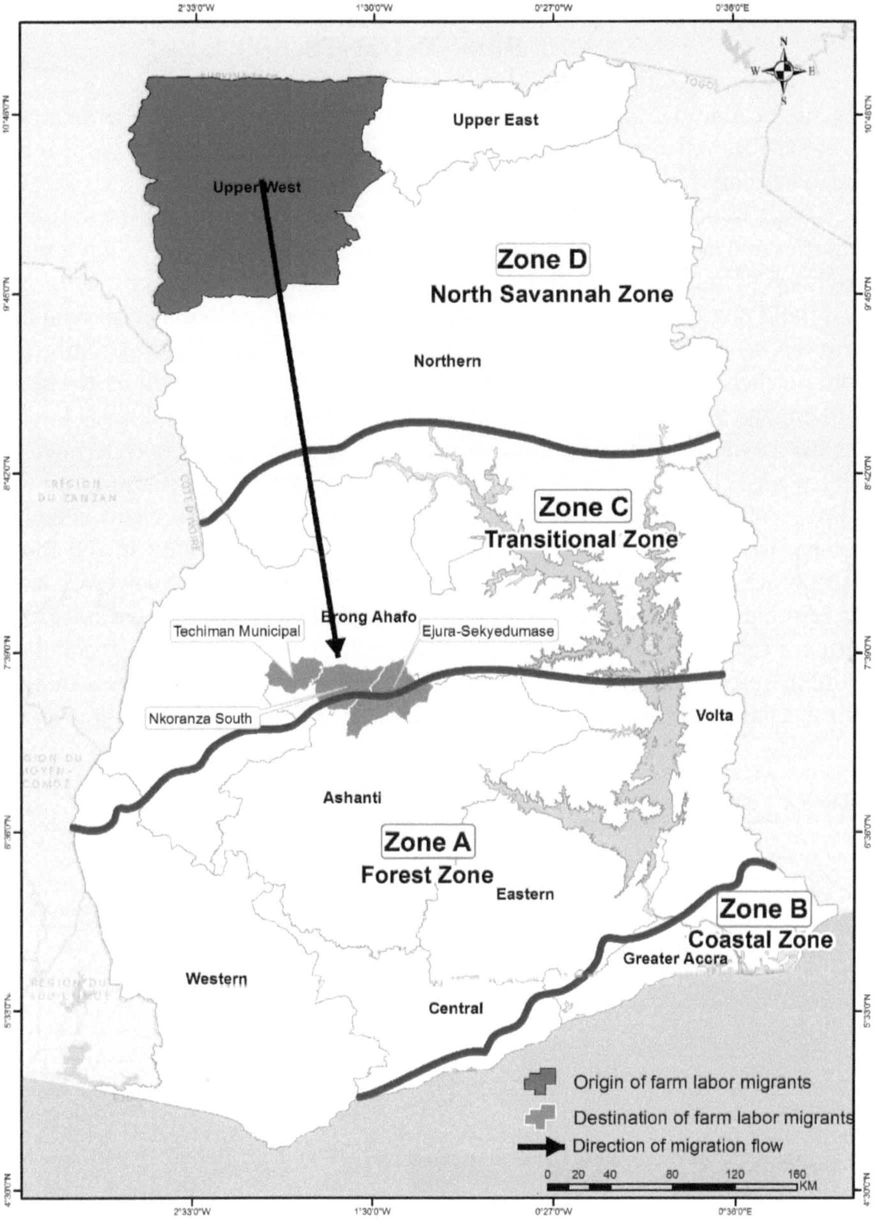

Figure 8.2 Origin and Destinations of Farm Labor Migrants. Created by author.

3.0 SOCIODEMOGRAPHIC CHARACTERISTICS OF RESPONDENTS

The socioeconomic characteristics of the 190 survey respondents are shown in Table 8.1. All the 40 females and 115 out of the 150 males were married. The interviews indicated that majority of the respondents were married because it is quite difficult for a single person to carry out all the farming activities and domestic work. According to the male respondents, "being married helps to make farm work pretty easy, because the women take care of the household chores, including preparing food while the men concentrate on the farm work." Unlike the situation whereby young unmarried women migrate from northern Ghana to work as head porters (popularly known as *kayayei*) or to engage in domestic work in urban Ghana (Kwankye et al. 2009, 11–12), females have difficulty migrating alone to engage in seasonal and permanent farm work. This could be because of the type of activities involved and the many arrangements migrants have to make before they can settle permanently in the destination region. For instance, poor migrants arriving in the three districts are required to work for other farmers or raise money to acquire land for farming. Other important barriers to independent female migration from northern Ghana to the transition zone were child care and lack of capital. It could therefore be argued that unlike other forms of north-south labor migration in Ghana (Adaawen and Owusu 2013, 41–42), permanent migration of

Table 8.1 Background Characteristics of Respondents

	District/Municipality (n = 190)			
Background characteristics	*Ejura-Sekyedumase*	*Nkoranza South*	*Techiman*	*Percentage*
Average age (years)	38	42	46	–
Married				
Males	38	45	32	77
Females	15	12	13	100
Not married				
Males	13	0	22	23
Females				
Household size	7	5	6	–
Occupation				
Food crop farming	55	56	59	89
Food crop farming and animal keeping	5	10	5	11
Pito brewing*	8	12	15	88
Average number of years at destination	8	7	10	–

*Only women were engaged in production
Source: Authors' own data from fieldwork

farm labor from the north to southern Ghana is predominantly a male-driven activity.

On the average, the household size is between 5 and 7 people. The migrants have settled in the respective communities for at least eight years. There is little intra-district movement among the respondents, an indication that once the migrants settled in a specific community, they barely relocate to another community or district. The main reasons they stated for this was the cost of movement and the fact that such frequent movements would interrupt their children's education. There was no major difference between the male and female migrants in terms of the number of years of settling in the destination. This substantiates the earlier assertion that once migrants decide to move permanently, the entire household moves together at a go.

In cases where an adult male moves ahead of the remaining household members, they will usually follow shortly after the male member has finally settled in the destination region. Food crop farming, involving the production of cereals, root and tuber crops and vegetables, was the major economic activity of all respondents. Production was mainly subsistence and involved the use of family and hired labor. Yam and maize were the predominant cash crops produced by the settler farmers. Some of the respondents also keep poultry for household consumption and sale. For the females, in addition to assisting their husbands with farm work, they are also engaged in *pito*[1] brewing as an alternative source of income for their households.

4.0 RESULTS AND DISCUSSIONS

4.1 Historical Analysis of Seasonal Migration to the Transitional Zone

As has already been mentioned in several studies, seasonal migration among farm laborers from the north to middle and southern Ghana is not a new phenomenon. Many researchers have documented how seasonal migration has been used as a livelihood strategy by residents of northern Ghana (Radermacher-Schulz 2014, 50–51). Historically, seasonal movement usually occurred during the long dry period in the north (October–March). This movement has several benefits, including the provision of income and food. Some of the money earned by the migrants was sent back home to cater for their nuclear and extended family members. The migrants also save some part of the money earned and use it to make new farms after they have returned to the north during the rainy season.

Traditionally, young men dominated seasonal migration streams. For families, it was the men who moved while the women took care of the rest of the family in the origin region. Key informant interviews suggest that the decision to migrate was and is still informed by a multiplicity of factors. Personal factors, for example, include the need to earn money for one's education. Among unmarried men, the decision is highly influenced by their parents, while for married men it was usually a collective decision by the man and his wife or wives. It was reported that leaving the rest of the family behind helped to relieve the men of economic burden during the early days in the destination region. It also kept families stable without disrupting the work of the wife or wives and the education of their children and wards. Seasonal migration was also influenced by the social unit to which the migrant belonged as well as social network and peer pressure as has been reported elsewhere by Kwankye et al. (2009, 20–28). While seasonal migration, historically, involved the movement of individual household members rather than families (Dungumaro 2013, 46–49), this is changing in nature in response to environmental changes. In the sections that follow, we discuss some of the important changes to seasonal migration and the major characteristics of permanent migration. We then proceed to discuss the drivers and challenges of permanent farm labor migration.

4.2 From Seasonal Migrants to Settler Migrants

As shown in Table 8.2, majority of the male respondents reported that prior to migrating permanently to their current location, they had engaged in seasonal out-migration to southern Ghana in the last twenty years. One of the respondents summarized these migration shifts in the following words:

> The first time I moved from the north (Nandom) to mid-Ghana was way back in 1997 and this was when it was dry season in the north. I came with three of my friends to work as farm laborer in several farms in Ejura and its surroundings. We moved back (to the north) to continue work on our own farms. This cycle of movement more or less became annual event. When I found that conditions in the north were not improving, I asked myself, "why don't I move with my

Table 8.2 Migration Characteristics of Respondents

	District/Municipality (n=190)			
Migration characteristics	*Ejura-Sekyedumase*	*Nkoranza South*	*Techiman*	*Percentage*
Respondents engaged in seasonal migration prior to permanent migration				
Males	50	50	50	100
Females	–	–	–	–
Respondents living with household in present location	52	50	53	82

Source: Authors' own data from fieldwork

family to settle here (Ejura) where we can do proper farming on our own instead of being a laborer? . . . (FGD at Kyenkyenkura, December 20, 2014)

On the other hand, none of the females interviewed in all the communities had ever engaged in seasonal migration from the origin region. This may be explained by the fact that women tend to move as accompanying wives.

The current trend of permanent migration from northern Ghana to the forest-transitional zone involves both men and their wives. Most of the respondents explained that they migrated with their families because they had no intention of returning to their home regions, given that the climate there is worsening. Some of the respondents also reported that they migrated with their families because such a practice provides them with the opportunity to start a new life in the new location. On the other hand, the females reported that they joined their husbands in the new location because it was a family decision to relocate permanently. As shown in Table 8.3, the main drivers of permanent migration from the Upper West Region to the transitional zone reported by the respondents included unreliable rainfall and high temperatures; landlessness and land degradation; high cost of living; lack of economic opportunities, and rising cost of living at the region of origin. Most migrants also wanted to use migration to move out of poverty.

Decline in Rainfall and Frequent Dry Spells

The decline in rainfall and long dry spells were the major reasons given by the respondents (88%) for the new migration trends. The respondents complained that rainfall in northern Ghana is very low and unreliable for farming activities. They indicated that the single rainfall maxima over the Upper

Table 8.3 Drivers of Permanent Migration of Labor (multiple responses)

	District/Municipality (n = 190)			
Reasons for relocating permanently	*Ejura-Sekyedumase*	*Nkoranza South*	*Techiman*	*Percentage*
Environmental				
Decline rainfall and long dry spell	55	55	57	88
Socioeconomic				
Landlessness	30	27	29	45
Cost of living in origin region	56	54	53	86
Less economic opportunities	34	32	33	52
Psychological				
High aspirations	22	24	21	35

Source: Authors' own data from fieldwork

West and northern Ghana in general, which occurs from April–September has become too short, erratic and sometimes occurs in torrents. These, they claimed, have adverse implications on agronomic activities in the area. Moreover, the frequency of dry spells and their duration have also increased. In order to corroborate the accounts of the settler farmers, rainfall data for Wa from 1960–2011 (representing the source region) were analyzed as shown in Figure 8.3. There is clear indication that rainfall in the region is associated with high inter-annual variability. The highest rainfall was recorded in 1962 and 1968 (1404 mm and 1534 mm, respectively), while the years 1983 and 1986 recorded the lowest amount of rainfall (670 mm and 523 mm, respectively). The dry conditions in the Upper West Region and in many parts of the world were linked with the El-Niño-Southern Oscillation (ENSO) event (Owusu, Waylen and Oiu 2008, 202–204).

The respondents emphasized that because they lacked irrigation facilities to enable them cope with rainfall variability and long periods of drought, out-migration from the unsuitable agro-climatic conditions becomes an attractive option to maintain their farming activities. It came out during the FGDs that in the past, seasonal migration was attractive, but the migrants returned home to produce crops during the rainy season. Today, however, rainfall is unreliable even during the rainy season and as such many migrants have decided to settle at the destination area permanently.

Landlessness

Some of the respondents (45%) reported that lack of access to land in the origin areas influenced their decision to migrate. Landlessness was attributed to the competition for land for agricultural and non-agricultural purposes. The respondents complained that scarcity of land has worsened due to population

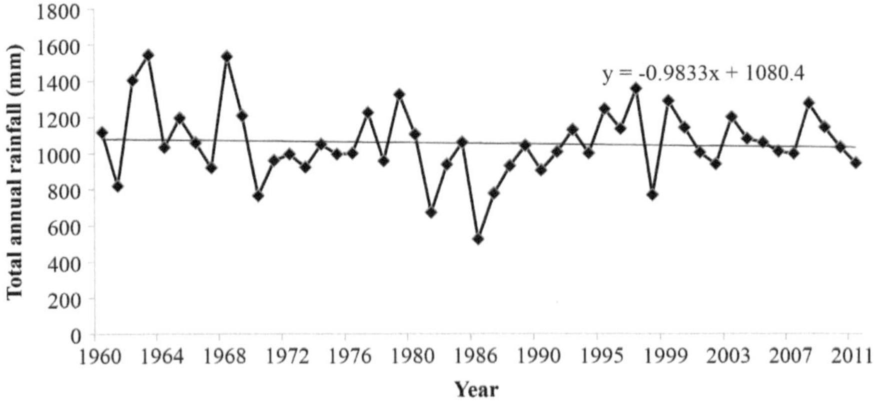

Figure 8.3 Total Annual Rainfall of Wa (1960–2011). Created by author.

pressure and land fragmentation which make long periods of fallow practically impossible. Another cause of landlessness in the origin region is land degradation due to soil erosion and rampant bush burning. As a result, most farmlands are no longer able to support agricultural activities. Participants in the FGDs in some of the communities explained that because most farmers at the origin are poor and cannot afford fertilizers, agricultural production has declined in recent years and these make farmers in northern Ghana very poor. According to the respondents, although the problem of land degradation appears to be a nationwide problem, farmlands in middle and southern parts of Ghana are still more suitable for agricultural activities compared to those in northern Ghana. One of the respondents reported this in the following words:

> I think the problem of land degradation is increasingly becoming a major obstacle to farming activities—it occurs everywhere in the country (Ghana) due to human and natural factors. But I can say that the effects of land degradation are more severe in the north than in middle and southern part of Ghana. (FGD in Mangoase, December 10, 2014)

High/Rising Cost of Living in Origin Region

Generally, the cost of living in farming communities in Ghana is quite low because most farming households depend on food and meat from their farms for household consumption. The respondents, however, complained that as a result of climate variability, food production has declined in the origin areas. Consequently, the cost of living has been rising, and it is therefore not surprising that 52 percent of the respondents mentioned high and rising cost of living as the main reason for permanent migration. Further interviews suggested that the high cost of living in the Upper West Region has also been heightened by increasing pressure from family members due to the high level of poverty among the populace. As a result, the level of dependency on the few *"well to do persons"* in the family or society is often high. This corroborates a study by the Ghana Statistical Service (2012, 8–10), which found high poverty and dependency levels in the Upper West Region compared to the other two northern regions of the country. During the interviews, one of the respondents emphatically stated that he decided to move permanently with his family to the destination region to escape family pressures for money. Although almost all the respondents take care of their families and friends who remain in the origin areas, a cross-section of them reported that family demands for money is lesser when they live outside the region than when they lived in their home towns and villages.

Lack of Economic Opportunities at the Origin Areas

The absence of many on-farm and off-farm economic opportunities in the origin region was also a key factor mentioned as being responsible for permanent migration to the destination areas. Half of the participants reported that seasonal agriculture in the origin region is restricted to the production of similar crops, namely sorghum, millet, and groundnut, which often fetched lower market prices due to overproduction. However, in the destination region, environmental conditions support the cultivation of a variety of crops (for example, yam, maize, cassava) with high yields. Additionally, the major and minor rainy seasons support the growing of crops twice in a year. It was also mentioned that off-farm economic activities are more viable at the destination than at the origin areas. For instance, female migrants who were involved in *pito* brewing mentioned that it provides an important source of income generation for their household, because there are fewer producers (*pito* brewers) in the destination region compared to the origin region. Trading activities were also reported to be more profitable in the transitional zone as a result of a larger market.

High Aspirations

A few of the migrants (35%) also reported that their decision to migrate permanently was to a lesser extent informed by psychological reasons. The most important factor was to meet their aspirations and goals. For instance, one respondent in Dwenewoho in the Ejura-Sekyedumase District summarized this point in the following words:

> Personally, I set several goals and objectives in life. . . . For instance, I wanted to build a house where my family can live comfortably. Another goal was to be able to cater for my children in school. . . . But I realized none of these goals would be met if my family and I continued to live in Nandom (origin). Because environmental conditions were increasingly becoming unfavorable for agricultural activities each season. . . . Finally, we moved here (Dwenewoho). . . . I think situations are better here; at least my children are in school and I hope very soon I will be able to start building a house. . . . (Expert interview at Dwenewoho, December, 15, 2014)

The above statement implies that some of the respondents migrated because they wanted to achieve short and long-term goals in their lives. Similar findings have been reported elsewhere among agricultural labor migrants in Punjab in India (Kaur et al. 2011, 461–465). A recent study shows that many people who migrate from northern Ghana to slums in Accra believed that migration gives them a hope of moving out of poverty (Awumbila, Owusu and Teye 2014, 26–31).

Effects of Environmentally induced Permanent Migration on Migrants' Livelihoods

The benefits of environmentally induced permanent migration on migrants' livelihoods were examined in this study. There was a general consensus among all the respondents that shifting from seasonal to permanent migration has significantly increased their incomes and well-being. This was substantiated by comparing the average annual incomes of the respondents over three years, before and after migrating permanently from the destination region. Results from the statistical analysis showed that average household incomes have slightly increased (P=0.049) after permanent migration. The average income rose from 1,110 Cedis[2] before migration to 1,650 Cedis after permanent out-migration. On the other hand, household average annual expenditure has significantly reduced (P=0.019) after permanent migration (1,050 Cedis) compared to before (1,320 Cedis). These results also support the respondents' observation that there are many economic opportunities in the destination region. Some of the participants also stated that the set of environmental and economic conditions that favor agricultural production have improved their household nutritional needs and earnings from agriculture. A few of the respondents (12%) periodically send foodstuffs to extended family members and friends in the origin region. A majority of the respondents (92%) feel that their livelihoods have improved after migrating to the transitional zone. During the FGDs and in-depth interviews, most of the migrants asserted that they have been able to finance their children's education, engaged in secured jobs and were able to assist their extended families and friends back home (origin region), which show that their lives have improved in the destination region. These findings are consistent with those reported by Awumbila, Owusu and Teye (2014, 26–31), who demonstrated that over 80 percent of people who migrated from northern Ghana to slums in Accra felt that their livelihoods have improved after migration. Similar findings have also been reported among labor migrants from northern Ghana to the south (Tanle 2014, 583–586). In addition, some of the migrants reportedly contribute to socioeconomic development in the origin and destination regions. In almost all the study communities, the migrants have formed associations that support households and communities back at home. They meet periodically to deliberate on development issues in the origin region. They also contribute in cash and in kind to support development projects such as community infrastructure in both the origin and destination regions.

5.0 CHALLENGES FACED BY MIGRANTS—THE ROLE OF POLICY

From the foregoing discussion, it could be argued that shifting from seasonal to permanent migration serves as a strategy which enables migrants to adapt to environmental and socioeconomic changes. It also enables migrants to contribute to economic and food security in the origin and destination regions. Notwithstanding these, some challenges were reported by the migrants interviewed (Table 8.4). There was no major difference among the challenges outlined by the respondents across the district.

Lack of accessibility to land and land tenure complications in the destination region was the major challenge stated by all the participants interviewed. They attributed it to the high influx of people from areas in the north and elsewhere in the country to engage in agricultural activities such as livestock keeping, cashew plantation and other agro-business enterprises in the destination region. According to the respondents, most land owners in their respective communities prefer to lease their farmlands to people who require land for large-scale production, instead of subsistence farming which is predominantly practiced by the migrants. Lands leased to migrants are also often planted with cash crops, like mango and cashew, which render the land unusable for food crop production after a few years. There are complications associated with access to family lands in which different members of the family claim the rightful ownership to the same land after it has been leased out. A cross-section of the respondents (25%) who have experienced such land tenure problems reported that they have had to abandon their farms even after spending so much money to develop them.

Another challenge faced by the migrants is accommodation, particularly during the early months of their arrival in the destination region. As stated earlier, because permanent migration, unlike seasonal migration, usually involves the whole nuclear family, lack of accommodation creates discomfort for the immigrant's household. A few of the respondents (28%), however, stated that they made contacts with people at the destination prior to their arrival to make sure accommodation issues were resolved. In some cases, a member from the household, usually the man or son would travel to the proposed destination to make housing arrangements or acquire land to build simple structures before the entire family moved in. Over 25 percent of the respondents said they lived with friends upon arrival before searching for their own accommodation.

Table 8.4 Constraints of Permanent Migration of Labor

Challenges faced by migrants	*District/Municipality (n = 190)*			
	Ejura-Sekyedumase	*Nkoranza South*	*Techiman*	*Percentage*
Lack of access to land	50	50	50	100
Accommodation	47	42	48	72
High cost of living	46	43	40	68
Shortage of labor	37	33	35	55
Low accessibility to credit facilities	28	30	29	46

Source: Authors' own data from fieldwork

The high cost of living and shortage of labor in the destination region were also mentioned as major problems that affect the livelihoods of the migrants. Even though the cost of living is reportedly lower in the destination areas because the farmers produce more food, it is rising in recent years as a result of inflation and the depreciation of the Ghanaian cedi. The majority (68%) of the respondents acknowledged the high cost of living as a national problem that the government needs to resolve as quickly as possible. However, the high cost of labor was attributed to the high out-migration of local people to urban areas in search of greener pastures. The study showed differences in perspectives between the immigrants from the Upper West Region and the indigenous population. Whereas the immigrants see their new destinations as places to improve their livelihoods, the indigenous people have the perception that their livelihoods can only be improved by migrating to urban areas. Another reason for the shortage of labor was the fact that most migrants now prefer to make their own farms instead of working as farm laborers. In view of this challenge, most of the respondents have formed "*nnoboa*" (communal) groups to assist members with farm work. The wives of the migrants also provide additional hands, especially during sowing and harvesting periods.

Another challenge, which was actually mentioned by 46 percent of the respondents, was their inability to access credit facilities. This challenge emanated from the fact that most of the communities where the migrants live are either remote or lack financial institutions where the farmers can seek financial assistance. Financial institutions, such as credit unions and rural banks located in the bigger settlements usually have strict and cumbersome requirements for giving out loans to their clients. It was reported that some of the institutions require collateral security such as houses, plantations and other high-value assets to guarantee the repayment of loans. These requirements limit their ability to improve their production.

6.0 CONCLUSION AND RECOMMENDATIONS

The discussion has demonstrated that although seasonal migration has, historically, been used by people in the northern Savannah zone of Ghana to deal with environmental change, many seasonal migrants are now moving with their families to settle permanently in the transitional forest zone because the combined effects of worsening climate variability and economic change make such permanent migration a more viable option than seasonal migration. Our findings support the argument that environmental factors usually interact with political and economic factors to shape migration decisions. We also found that the decision by migrants from the north to settle more permanently in the transitional zone is influenced not only by environmental factors, such as recurrent drought and declining soil fertility, but more so by socioeconomic factors, such as the lack of economic activities in the north, rising cost of living and family pressures.

While it has already been predicted that environmental changes will bring about increased migration flows from vulnerable regions (Afifi 2011, 100–108), our findings suggest that in some cases, environmental change will also transform short-term seasonal migration flows into long-term permanent migration since seasonal migrants may be unwilling to return to areas that are facing long-term environmental stressors. Such shifts in migration patterns may help reduce pressure on vulnerable regions, but can also create pressure on resources in the destination areas, if poorly managed.

Our findings also show that although farmers who migrated from northern Ghana to settle in the forest-transitional zone face a number of challenges, including difficulty in acquiring large farm lands, lack of access to credit facilities, and shortage of farm labor, permanent relocation to the transitional zone contributes to improving the livelihoods of these migrants. Improved agricultural production and higher incomes at the transitional zone also enable the settler farmers to contribute to the food and economic security of their extended family members and friends in the origin region. In view of the positive outcomes of this population movement, we recommend that the challenges faced by the settler farmers must be addressed to ensure that they contribute meaningfully to the development of their destination and home regions. The Ministry of Food and Agriculture (MoFA) must engage traditional authorities to find ways of making the process of acquiring farm lands easier for migrant farmers. MoFA should also collaborate with financial institutions to make loans available and accessible to all farmers, including migrants. This would help improve food security and reduce household poverty in both the origin and destination regions of the migrants and in Ghana as a whole.

NOTES

1. It is a type of local drink prepared from fermented millet typically common in northern Ghana and other countries in West Africa.
2. One US dollar was equivalent to 3.90 Cedis in June 2016.

REFERENCES

Abu, Mumuni, Samuel Nii Ardey Codjoe, and Jon Sward. 2014. "Climate Change and Internal Migration Intentions in the Forest-Savannah Transition Zone of Ghana." *Population and Environment* 35: 341–64.

Adaawen, Stephen A, and Boabang Owusu. 2013. "North-South Migration and Remittances in Ghana." *African Review of Economics and Finance* 5 (1): 29–45.

Afifi, Tamer. 2011. "Economic or Environmental Migration? The Push Factors in Niger." *International Migration* 49 (S1): e95–e124.

Ajzen, Icek. 1991. "The Theory of Planned Behavior." *Organizational Behavior and Human Decision Processes* 50: 179–211.

Ajzen, Icek, and Martin Fishbein. 1980. *Understanding Attitudes and Predicting Social Behavior. Englewood Cliffs.* NJ: Prentice-Hall,

Anarfi, John, Stephen Kwankye, Ofosu-Mensah Ababio, and Richmond Tiemoko. 2003. *Migration from and to Ghana: A Background Paper*. Brighton, UK: Development Research Centre on Migration, Globalization and Poverty, 38 pp.

Awumbila, Mariama, George Owusu, and Joseph Kofi Teye. 2014. "Can Rural-Urban Migration into Slums Reduce Poverty? Evidence from Ghana." *Migrating out of Poverty Research Programme Consortium*. Accra, 41 pp.

Black, Richard, Dominic Kniveton, and Kerstin Schmidt-Verkerk. 2013. "Migration and Climate Change: Toward an Integrated Assessment of Sensitivity." In *Disentangling Migration and Climate Change: Methodologies, Political Discourses and Human Rights*, edited by Thomas Faist and Jeanette Schade, 29–53. Dordrecht: Springer.

Cleveland, David A. 1991. "Migration in West Africa: A Savanna Village Perspective." *Africa* 61 (2): 222–46.

Dun, Olivia, and François Gemenne. 2008. "Defining Environmental Migration: Why It Is Difficult, Why It Is Controversial, Why It Matters and Some Practical Processes Which May Help Move Forward." *Forced Migration Review*, 31: 10–11.

Dungumaro, Esther W. 2013. "Consequences of Female Migration for Families in Tanzania." African *Review of Economics and Finance* 5 (1): 46–59.

Fritz, Carolina. 2010. Climate Change and Migration: Sorting through Complex Issues without the Hype. Washington, DC: Migration Policy Institute. Accessed March 5, 2015. http://oppenheimer.mcgill.ca/IMG/pdf/10_03_MPI_Fritz_ClimateChangeMigration.pdf

Ghana Statistical Service. 2012. *2010 Population and Housing Census. Summary Report of Final Results*. Accra: GSS.

Henry, Sabine, Bruno Schoumaker, and Cris Beauchemin. 2004. "The Impact of Rainfall on the First Outmigration: A Multi-Level Event-History Analysis in Burkina Faso." *Population and Environment* 25 (5): 423–60.

Hunter, Lori M. 2007. *Climate Change, Rural Vulnerabilities, and Migration*. Washington D.C: Population Reference Bureau. Accessed March 18, 2015. http://www.prb.org/Publications/Articles/2007/ClimateChangeinRuralAreas.aspx

Intergovernmental Panel on Climate Change (IPCC). 2007. "Climate Change Impacts, Adaptation and Vulnerability." In *Working Group II Contribution to the Fourth Assessment Report, Climate Change* 2007. Geneva: IPCC. Accessed March 15, 2015. https://www.ipcc.ch/publications_and_data/ar4/wg2/en/ch9s9-4-4.html

Isaac, Marney E, Luke C.N. Anglaaere, Daniel S. Akoto, and Evans Dawoe. 2014. "Migrant Farmers as Information Brokers: Agroecosystem Management in the Transition Zone of Ghana." *Ecology and Society* 19 (2): 56–67.

Jülich, Sebastian. 2011. "Drought Triggered Temporary Migration in an East Indian Village." *International Migration* 49 (S1): e189–e199.

Kaur, Baljinder, Singh, J. M, Garg, B. R, Singh, Jasdev, and Singh, Satwinder. 2011. "Causes and impact of labour migration: A case study of Punjab agriculture". *Agricultural Economics Research Review* 24: 459–66.

Klutse, Nana A, Kwadwo Owusu, David Cudjoe Adukpo, Francis Nkrumah, Kwesi Quagraine, Alfred Owusu, and William J. Gutowski. 2013. "Farmer's Observation on Climate Change Impacts on Maize (Zea Mays) Production in a Selected Agro-ecological Zone in Ghana." *Research Journal of Agriculture and Environmental Management* 2 (12): 394–402.

Kniveton, Dominic R, Christopher D. Smith, and Richard Black. 2012 "Emerging Migration Flows in a Changing Climate in Dryland Africa." *Nature Climate Change* 2: 444–47.

Kniveton, Dominic, Christopher Smith, and Sharon Wood. 2011. "Agent-Based Model Simulations of Future Changes in Migration Flows for Burkina Faso." *Global Environmental Change* 21S: S34–S40.

Kwankye, Owusu S, John Kwasi Anarfi, Cynthia Addoquaye Tagoe, and Adriana Castaldo. 2009. *Independent North- South Child Migration in Ghana: The Decision Making Process.* Brighton, UK: University of Sussex.

Martin, Maxmillan, Motasim Billah, Tasneem Siddiqui, Chowdhury Abrar, Richard Black, and Dominic Kniveton. 2014. "Climate-Related Migration in Rural Bangladesh: A Behavioural Model." *Population and Environment* 36 (1): 85–110.

Mayring, Philipp. 2014. "Qualitative Content Analysis: Theoretical Foundation, Basic Procedures and Software Solution." Accessed December 12, 2015. http://nbn-resolving.de/urn:nbn:de:0168-ssoar-395173.

Meze-Hausken, Elisabeth. 2000. "Migration Caused by Climate Change: How Vulnerable Are People in Dryland Areas? A Case-Study in Northern Ethiopia." *Mitigation and Adaptation Strategies for Global Change* 5: 379–406.

Owusu, Kwadwo, Peter Waylen, and Youliang Qiu. 2008. "Changing Rainfall Inputs in the Volta Basin: Implications for Water Sharing in Ghana." *GeoJournal* 71: 201–10.

Owusu, Kwadwo, and Peter Robert Waylen. 2012. "The Changing Rainy Season Climatology of Mid-Ghana." *Theoretical and Applied Climatology* 112 (3–4): 419–30.

Pham, Bang N, and Peter S. Hill. 2009. "The Role of Temporary Migration in Rural Household Economic Strategy in a Transitional Period for the Economy of Vietnam." *Asian Population Studies* 4 (1): 57–75.

Rademacher-Schulz, Christina, Benjamin Schraven, and Edward Salifu Mahama. 2014. "Time Matters: Shifting Seasonal Migration in Northern Ghana in Response to Rainfall Variability and Food Insecurity." *Climate and Development* 6 (1): 46–52.

Sow, Papa, Stephen A. Adaawen, and Jürgen Scheffran. 2014. "Migration, Social Demands and Environmental Change Amongst the Frafra of Northern Ghana and the Biali in Northern Benin." *Sustainability* 6: 375–98.

Tanle, Augustine. 2014. "Assessing Livelihood Status of Migrants from Northern Ghana Resident in the Obuasi Municipality." *GeoJournal* 79: 577–90.

van der Geest, Kees. 2004. ''We Are Managing!'' *Climate Change and Livelihood Vulnerability in Northwest Ghana.* Afrika-Studie Centrum. Leiden: African Studies Centre, 310 pp.

van der Geest, Kees. 2011. "North-South Migration in Ghana: What Role for the Environment? ." *International Migration* 49 (S1): e69–e94.

Chapter 9

Hindered Pathways Toward Development?

West African Mobilities and European Borders in the Twenty-first Century

Joris Schapendonk

1.0 TRANSNATIONALISM, MIGRATION AND DEVELOPMENT

Since the early 1990s, the transnational migration literature has profoundly enriched our understanding of the lifeworlds of international migrants (e.g., Glick Schiller, Basch and Blanc-Szanton 1995, Portes 1999, Faist 2000). The concept of transnationalism is defined by Glick Schiller, Basch and Blanc-Szanton (1995, 48) as "the process by which immigrants forge and sustain simultaneous multi-stranded social relations that link together their societies of origin and settlement." This notion that migrants are part of both societies, "here" (in the destination countries) and "there" (in the countries of origin) has contributed to a more dynamic understanding of migration. Instead of being a rupturing departure from home communities, migration is now seen as a networked phenomenon. That is to say that migrants stay "connected" with their home communities after they have moved to other places. This connectedness, or double engagement (Grillo and Mazzucato 2008), is the basis for a renewed enthusiasm in migration and development discussions, as it acknowledges that migrants create development opportunities with the sending of money and goods (Smith 2007, Mohapatra and Rathra 2011), the exchange of ideas (Gakunzi 2006) as well as their own development projects (Grillo and Riccio 2004, Adepoju, van Naerssen and Zoomers 2008). The transnational migration discourse underlines that migrants may feel at home in two places at the same time (Manuh 2005), and that they may also act as frequent movers between these localities (Sinatti 2011). In other words, the "transnationalization" of migration has provided innovative conceptual toolsets that go beyond sedentarist thought, implying that the state of spatial fixity is the norm (Malkki 1992, Bakewell 2007, Cresswell 2010).

Although this chapter highly values the intellectual enrichment of transnationalism in migration studies, it actually aims to put in perspective the often taken-for-granted dimensions of this conceptual turn in relation to the discussions on migration and development. Especially when we focus on migration dynamics between Africa and Europe, we may come to new insights that encourage us to critically review the transnational discourse and related migration-development optimism. The main reason for this is that transnational studies and the migration and development literature tend to overlook the migration processes of individual migrants. This is particularly important in this time in which Europe is "closing" its borders toward African migrants. Those Africans with the aspiration to become trans-migrants in the near future are regularly confronted with involuntary immobility in the countries of origin (Carling 2002, Jónsson 2008). Furthermore, migrants who are actually in the process of moving toward the European Union (EU) often face harsh border policies of the North, consisting of remote border controls, externalization of asylum and "hard" borders, such as the fences between the Spanish enclaves and Moroccan territory (e.g., Andersson 2014).

Consequently, many *en route* migrants find themselves trapped in transit outside the EU (Schapendonk 2012). In addition, once in Europe, the reality for many migrants is often harsher than they had expected. Some are immobilized by lengthy asylum procedures (Mountz 2011) or in detention camps (Silverman and Massa 2012); others are trying to make a living as documented or undocumented migrants in the shadow economies of Europe (Lucht 2012). The critical question then is: How much *migration-development* dynamics and how much transnationalism do we see when we take into account the lengthy and risky migration trajectories of African migrants who are heading for Europe today?

To answer this question, this paper presents qualitative details of two empirical cases of West African migrants who are moving to the EU. These individual trajectories of migrants are written down as in-depth illustrations of contemporary migration processes that occur between Africa and Europe. In both cases it concerns a migrant who is yet to arrive in Europe. Before these empirical vignettes are provided and analyzed, however, first sub-Saharan African migration, and particularly West African migration, to Europe is contextualized. Second, I will discuss the notion of transnational migration in relation to the discussions on migration and development. Subsequently, my approach to migration trajectory research is explained further.

2.0 WEST AFRICAN MIGRATION TO EUROPE

While there exist nowadays some very helpful tools to visualize migration stocks and flows (see, for instance, the migration map initiative of Max

Planck Institute (2015)), it is still rather difficult to construct an up-to-date and straightforward overview regarding the in- and outflow of sub-Saharan Africans in Europe. The data are in general fragmented with different EU countries having their own statistical databases. In addition, different supranational institutions (e.g., EU, UN, IOM) provide different migration numbers for the same years. Furthermore, abstract data may overlap in practice as, for instance, many migrants who enter Europe through irregular channels apply for asylum soon after they have entered Europe. As a result, we cannot simply aggregate the number of asylum applications with the number of irregular entries as this would result in some double-counting. Moreover, demographics on sub-Saharan African migrants in Europe are seldom distinguished in explicit terms. With the label "African migrants," sub-Saharan Africans are often grouped together with North African migrants. The latter group has a long history of labor migration to Europe as they arrived in substantial numbers as guest workers in the 1960s and 1970s in countries like Germany, France and the Netherlands. In that sense, the statistical label "African migrants in Europe" often consist of a highly heterogeneous group of people, including former guest workers, postcolonial migrants, refugees, asylum seekers, highly skilled migrants and many other categories. In general, statistics and numbers regarding sub-Saharan African migration need to be treated with caution (Bakewell and de Haas 2007, de Haas 2008).

With these critical notes in mind, we still can, however, present some general figures on sub-Saharan African migration to the EU. In the year 2013, there were roughly 33 million non-EU nationals living in the EU (Eurostat 2014). In most countries, these third-country nationals came from other European countries that are not part of the twenty-seven EU member states.[1] When we focus on African migration, we notice that the highest numbers of Africans live in France (4.5 million, mainly from Morocco, Algeria, Cameroon, Cote d'Ivoire, Senegal and Mali; data from Insee 2015) and the United Kingdom (2.8 million, mainly from Nigeria, South Africa and Kenya; data from Official National Statistics 2015). In Table 9.1, estimations of migrant communities from six selected West African countries (Nigeria, Ghana, Cote d'Ivoire, Senegal, the Gambia and Cameroon[2]) are provided in the five most important European destinations. This table, based on data obtained from the Migration Policy Institute (2015) for the year 2013, shows that about 1 million migrants from these six different countries are residing in Europe. This figure might appear substantial; however, when we compare it with the figure for migrants from six other countries outside the West African region, this number becomes relative and not very huge (see Table 9.2). There are, for instance, twice as many Moroccan residents in the EU than migrants from the six selected West African countries.

These numbers that present the actual stocks of migrants say, of course, little about new developments. When it comes down to recent arrivals, only

Table 9.1 Estimated stocks of migrants in the EU from six selected West African countries (2013)

Country of origin	*UK*	*Germany*	*France*	*Italy*	*Spain*	*Total for 5 EU countries*
Nigeria	184,00	23,000	5,000	48,000	37,000	297,000
Senegal	9,300*	2,000	115,000	79,000	59,000	264,300
Ghana	82,000	24,000	7,000	43,000	16,000	172,000
Cote d'Ivoire	3,700*	3,000	88,000	23,000	3,000	120,700
Cameroon	6,000	11,000	77,000	10,000	6,000	110,00
The Gambia	10,000	3,000	2,000	1,000	19,000	35,000
Total	295,000	67,000	294,000	204,000	140,000	999,000

Source: Migration Policy Institute Data Hub (http://www.migrationpolicy.org/programs/data-hub/maps-immigrants-and-emigrants-around-world). Except from * as these data concern the year 2007 and originate from a different source: Max Planck Institute http://media.mmg.mpg.de/

Table 9.2 Estimated stocks of migrants in the EU from six selected outside the West African region

Country of origin	*UK*	*Germany*	*France*	*Italy*	*Spain*	*Total for 5 EU countries*
Morocco	23,000	94,000	928,000	425,000	746,000	2,216000
China	161,000	74,000	91,000	185,000	161,000	672,000
US	222,000	111,000	54,000	60,000	38,000	485,000
Philippines	127,000	41,000	14,000	130,000	39,000	351,000
Peru	600*	12,000	11,000	113,000	190,000	326,600
Iraq	74,000	94,000	6,000	3,000	2,000	179,000
Total	607,600	426,000	1,104000	916,000	1,117600	4,229600

Source: Migration Policy Institute Data Hub (http://www.migrationpolicy.org/programs/data-hub/maps-immigrants-and-emigrants-around-world). Except from * as these data concern the year 2007 and originate from a different source: Max Planck Institute http://media.mmg.mpg.de/

one sub-Saharan country—Nigeria—appears in the top ten of EU statistics. Of the estimated 1.7 million migrants who arrived in the EU through legal channels in 2012, some 21,000 came from Nigeria (counting for only 1.2 percent of the total inflow). In the same year, some 17,000 Nigerians, who did not necessarily arrive in the same year, obtained European citizenship. Evidently, this numerical overview includes, first and foremost, estimates of documented migration. Besides these recorded numbers, the EU administrates various forms of irregular migration (e.g., document fraud, irregular border crossing) through its border agency, Frontex. Again, we need to be cautious as statistics on irregular migration may easily overlap with data on documented migration and asylum 2010). Many irregular migrants, for instance, apply for asylum soon after they have entered the EU. They might also get regularized after having lived for some years as undocumented migrants. In 2013, Frontex found 9,800 cases of document fraud. In the same year, the EU detected 107,000 irregular border crossings at its external border (a number comparable with the years 2009 and 2010 and a lower number compared to 2011, the year of the Arab Spring). It is important to note that majority of these migrants registered at the external borders of the EU came from conflict states and/or oppressive regimes, such as Syria (+/- 25,000 migrants), Afghanistan (+/- 9,500 migrants) and Eritrea (+/-12,000 migrants). This underscores the fact that migrants in search of humanitarian protection can hardly enter the EU in a regular way. Interestingly, West Africans were not on the list of major countries to enter the EU irregularly in 2013. The number of entries were: Nigerians (3,386), Malians (2,887), Senegalese (1,643) and Gambians (2,817). Together, these West Africans account for roughly 10 percent of the reported irregular entries at EU's external borders in 2013 (Frontex 2015, 29).

On the basis of this discussion, we may conclude that sub-Saharan African migrants, and West African migrants in particular, form substantial communities in the EU, but in reality they are rather minorities when compared to other immigrant groups.

3.0 TRANSNATIONALISM, IM/MOBILITY AND DEVELOPMENT

3.1 Transnational Migration as a Motor for Development?

In the light of transnationalism, there has emerged a renewed enthusiasm regarding the impact of migrants on development in the countries of origin (Faist 2008, De Haas 2010). This enthusiasm has frequently been related with migrant's remittances, development of home town associations and knowledge transfer. The enthusiasm regarding remittances has been highlighted, because remittances constitute in many African countries twice as much as the official development aid. In countries such as Lesotho and Togo, it is even estimated that migrants' remittances are about 28 percent and 11 percent of their total GDP, respectively (Mohapatra and Ratha 2011). This positive perspective that sees migrants as new actors in development fits well into the shifting discourses from state- and market-led development programs to community-based development programs (Faist 2008). The argument then is that in the field of international cooperation, states have failed in bringing about structural development in the Global South, and therefore the hopes are now transferred to migrants. This, of course, creates important normative questions (see Raghuram 2009), such as: Why do we give migrants a double burden in the sense that we ask them to integrate in the host society, but at the same time to contribute to the development of the places they have left behind? We tend to speak about the development of "home communities," but what about the development of the migrants themselves?

In the light of the latter, it is interesting to remember the work of Amartya Sen who frames development as the enhancement of substantive choices people have. Sen's notion of development comes down to people's ability to lead lives that they have reason to value (Sen 1999). For many youngsters in Africa, mobility and migration, not necessarily directed to Europe (Bakewell and Jonsson 2011), are important pathways toward social and economic development but these pathways are often hampered by strict visa regulations, border controls and the lack of financial means. Overcoming barriers to one's movement can then be seen as an inherent aspect of enhanced freedom, and thus, development in the sense of Amartya Sen. This is also reflected in the 2009 Human Development Report that firmly suggested an expansion in schemes for seasonal work, increasing the numbers for low-skilled workers and lowering institutional thresholds that hamper people's mobility (UNDP 2009).

In this case, it is not only the effects of migration that are considered to impact on development, but also the migration process itself can be considered a process of development. The latter also resonates in the book edited by Akinyoade and Gewald (2015) entitled "African Roads to Prosperity. People en Route to Socio-Cultural and Economic Transformations." This volume indicates that migration is a state of being that centers around a notion of being on the way to a better future. The editors state that migration may bring social-economic development in certain zones of transition, but it is important to include a people-centered notion of the link between migration and development. This does not mean that enhancing the freedom of mobility is the same as stating that all forms of mobility are necessarily positive developments. Mobility can be very tiring, or even traumatic, as in the case of forced displacements. Tore Sager (2008, 243) claims in this framework that *freedom as mobility* is composed by the opportunities to be on the move as well as the feasibility of the choice not to travel. A trajectory approach, which is further explained in the next section, suits this notion very well, as it takes into account both mobility and immobility.

4.0 METHODOLOGY: TOWARD A MIGRATION TRAJECTORY APPROACH

Several migration scholars have paid close attention to individual migration trajectories in order to understand better the im/mobility processes that are related to migration. This notion implies that migrants' journeys, to known and sometimes unknown destinations, are seldom free from moments of rest, re-orientation and other forms of immobility. Some of these studies focus specifically on the transit situations of African migrants living near European borders (Suter 2012, Schapendonk 2012); other scholars pay attention to the *en route* experiences of these migrants (Brachet 2005), the social organization of the migration process (Belloni 2016) or the criminal activities involved when it concerns human smuggling (Van Reisen, Estefanos and Rijken 2012). These studies form together an interesting field of debate that goes beyond the notion that migration is the result of a go/no-go decision in a certain location. Migration trajectories have their own logic—a logic of process and transformation (Schapendonk and Steel 2014).

This focus on the trajectory, instead of moments of departure and moments of settlement, fits in the wider theoretical and methodological project that is called the "new mobilities turn" (Sheller and Urry 2006, Cresswell 2010, Ernste, Martens and Schapendonk 2012). As with these migration studies focusing on journeys, the general agenda of the "mobilities turn" is to gain better insights into how mobilities are practiced, what meanings are attached to mobilities and how mobilities produce difference in terms of access and speed (Adey 2010). In methodological terms, this implies that the researcher is challenged to grasp and comprehend the process of movement of people, objects and information (Marcus 1995, Merriman 2014). In terms of development thinking, this means that we see the journey of migrants as a kind of career path, with ups and downs, barriers and transgressions, investments and losses.

In my recent project (2014–2018) that centers on migration trajectories from West Africa to Europe, I attempt to follow migrant pathways from the time they arrive in Europe. In so doing, I reconstruct their journeys to Europe with in-depth interviews and I use ethnographic practices to follow the twists and turns of individual migration trajectories. These ethnographic practices include, first, the use of translocal tools (mobile telephony, internet conversations) in order to understand the daily lifeworlds of my respondents as well as their mobility in Europe. Secondly, I use these longitudinal connections to visit some of my respondents in the different places they end up in. During these visits, I use informal conversations, recorded interviews and observations to collect information about the im/mobility processes of my respondents. This process of following the migrant can best be described as "trajectory ethnography" (Schapendonk and Steel 2014).

The trajectory of two cases that are reconstructed below are based on two years of ethnographic engagements in the Netherlands and Italy. The first case presents very different migration processes of two Gambian brothers. This case also includes the risky overland route from West Africa through the Sahara desert to Libya and eventually to Europe. The second case focuses on the visa troubles that many West African citizens face when they follow the path of regular migration.

5.0 TWO GAMBIAN PATHWAYS TO EUROPE

The Gambian man, Dawda[3] has been a good friend of mine since 2008. With a tourist visa, he had reached the Netherlands by airplane for the first time in December 2007 to visit his Dutch girlfriend. In accordance with Dutch immigration regulations, he returned to the Gambia after his three months stay in the Netherlands, and there the couple started the process for obtaining a long-term visa for the Netherlands at the Dutch embassy in Senegal. Dawda finally got a visa and moved to the Netherlands for the second time (September 2008). Although the first year was rather difficult for him because he was searching for a job, he was able to reach the social status of a trans-migrant soon after. At the time of writing, he had become a citizen of the Netherlands, and is now active in a transnational space with various development initiatives. As he stated:

> You see I need to search for things now. You know my father's village, where I was born. There is a lack of water. There a lack of water. So now . . . I want to help. I want to sponsor things like that. [Conversation with Dawda, the Netherlands, February 2014]

Within a few years, he built a house for his family in Banjul and he started a gym by exporting secondhand workout machines from the Netherlands to the Gambia. But his initiatives are not only based on altruistic principles, but also to gain something out of it. He regularly sends containers to the Gambia with secondhand products he obtains in the Netherlands, as he explained in a conversation in September 2014 below:

Dawda: The container comes here. I ordered a 40feet container.
Author: You mean the container will be placed here, in this street, in front of your house?
Dawda: Haha! Yes! They come. You order it on the internet, and you pack it here, they tick it and bring it to the harbor, and then they go to Banjul.
Author: This is a complete new world for me. So you order a container on the internet?
Dawda: Yes, you rent it, it takes 3500 euro, everything included. They ship it to Africa. . . . And when it arrives in Banjul I pay another 1000 Euro commission, that is not included in the container, but everything else, the rent, the transport to the harbor, the shipping, and offloading is included. Not taxes.
Author: I see, I see . . . but that is a lot of money! Pfoe . . . 3500 euro, that is a lot of money.
Dawda: Yes, yes, it is big money. But that is why you have to be sure you make some profit in Africa. So I make a list about all the things I bring. And I travel to Banjul to see how the container arrives, then I will make a list about what I paid for

it, and at which price I can sell it. So for instance these beds [pointing at two beds stored in his living room] I paid 12euro for it, so I will sell it for maybe 20 euro. [Conversation with Dawda, the Netherlands, September 2014]

Interestingly, this business requires Dawda to be mobile as well. His physical mobility and socioeconomic development are thus closely related.

Dawda's situation is completely different from that of his younger brother, called Yahya in this paper. In mid-2013, Yahya left his home country (The Gambia) and started his move "to Europe" and to achieve this he chose the overland route. He passed through Senegal, Mali, Burkina Faso and Niger. In the city of Agadez in Niger, however, he ran out of money due to the high prices of travel services and several dubious travel taxes (see also Brachet 2005). It was only in Agadez that Yahya called his brother in the Netherlands for help for the very first time. As he told me, he had never informed his brother Dawda about his plans to leave the Gambia:

Yahya: "I did not tell him. No! I only tell him when I was in Agadez. My money was gone, so I need to inform him, and he said: You are crazy, you are crazy! He was very angry. But after some weeks he give me money . . . and I go to Libya."
Author: You did not inform your brother, why not?
Yahya: Because I knew he did not want me to take the desert road. He says you come direct, or you do not come at all.
[Conversation with Yahya, Italy, April 2014]

Dawda sent the money to his brother while he (Yahya) was transiting in Agadez, but he also knew that his junior brother might get into trouble again once he arrives in Libya. He therefore contacted a Gambian man living in Tripoli who was working as a "connection man" (recruiting potential migrants for a particular boat journey to Europe). Dawda knew him from their time together in Banjul. The two men agreed on the following: Dawda would buy a secondhand car—a Mercedez Benz—and ship the car to Banjul. There, the car would be transferred to the wife of the Gambian connection man, and this would count as the payment for Yahya's risky boat trip to Lampedusa (Italy). With this arrangement, Yahya's waiting time in Libya was reduced profoundly.

Yahya reached Lampedusa alive in the fall of 2013. From there he moved to Napoli and later to a small town in Liguria. Although Yahya had physically reached Europe, he found himself in a precarious situation for over two years. During this period, he was unable to contact his family regularly, as he stated thus:

No, I cannot call too much, I cannot call Dawda, I cannot call my parents, I cannot call my brother in Malta. I only use skype sometimes . . . but I don't have

> a good phone . . . You know, we only get 2 euro for a day. [Conversation with Yahya, Italy, April 2014]

Sometime in 2014, more than a year after he left home, Yahya started feeling guilty for not being able to contribute to the family budget in the Gambia. As I learned from Dawda (Yahya's brother), he once shared this frustration with him:

> He now wanted to sell clothes, on the streets . . . he is suffering in Italy. . . . And he asked me, should I send money home now? Because many, many people ask him for money. He asked me: should I send money home now? I said nooooo! Tell them you are searching for papers, tell them you are still suffering. Keep the money. Save it for the travel. [Conversation with Dawda, the Netherlands, September 2014]

Thus, according to Dawda, the personal trajectory of his brother is more important at this stage than the link to the family back home.

What do we learn from these Gambian trajectories in the light of transnational migration studies? Interestingly, Yayha's trajectory involves several forms of spatial friction that are often overlooked in studies on transnationalism. First, he left the Gambia in relative secrecy. This implies that some important information does not "travel" in the transnational space between the Netherlands and the Gambia. In other words, while many transnational migration studies take the facilitating role of social networks for granted as a kind of meso-structure, Yahya's departure indicates that social networks are not always "working" and people may feel in some instances disconnected from each other. This disconnectedness changed in Agadez, the moment Yahya asked Dawda for help. But again, there was spatial friction involved as Dawda waited for "some weeks" to transfer the money. This suggests that we need to pay better attention to the efforts and energy that people put in their transnational connectedness (Schapendonk 2015). In other words, transnational migration studies, as well as the migration-development literature, could be enriched when there is a clearer focus on the harsh "network work" that exists between migrants and their counterparts (Pathirage and Collyer 2011, Schapendonk 2015).

Second, we notice that Dawda's transnational mobility encountered very little resistance. Since he possesses a Netherlands passport, and is in a good socioeconomic position, he is able to travel to the Gambia frequently, and this creates some development opportunities for him. In that sense, he has passed some significant institutional as well as socioeconomic thresholds of mobility (van der Velde and van Naerssen 2011). Yayha's mobility, on the other hand, has been a very slow process. It took him roughly two months to move from West Africa to the EU. The difference in travel opportunities of the two brothers became particularly striking when their father died in October 2015. Whereas Dawda traveled to the Gambia to mourn with his family, Yahya did not have the travel documents to do so.

In this context, we must analyze Dawda's advice to his junior brother to keep investing in his migration trajectory instead of sending money back home to his family. If you are not in a privileged position yourself, the moral economy of development can be a heavy burden for the individual. It is relevant to note that in many occasions, as has also been explained by Belloni (2016), migrants are rather the receiver of family funds instead of being those who send remittances home. In the discussion of remittances, however, we focus mainly on one direction of financial flows—namely, from the developed to the developing world. However, when we look critically at the macro figures of migrants' remittances, we notice that among the top 10 remittance-receiving countries in 2010, there were four European countries (France, Germany, Belgium and Spain) and only one African country (Nigeria) (Mohapatra and Ratha 2011). This, at least, puts in perspective the issue of remittances as the motor for development (see also Smith and Schapendonk 2008).

Besides the economic component, the price Yahya paid for his journey to Europe is also high in the humanitarian sense. Yahya experienced multiple hardships on the road, and is rather lucky that he did not become part of the thousands of migrants who die crossing the Mediterranean Sea. The fact that more than 3,000 people died at the borders of Europe between January and September 2014 (IOM 2014, Ferrer-Gallardo and Van Houtum 2014) is one of the saddest and powerful illustrations that mobility has become one of the most important stratifying factors of this time of globalization (Bauman 1998). This is also reflected in the so-called passport indexes measuring the power of passports by the number of countries you can access with visa-free travel (see Passport Index 2015). This issue of blocked access will be further unpacked with the next case.

6.0 VISA TROUBLES IN A TRANSNATIONAL MARRIAGE

This case presents the story of Eugene and Caroline. Eugene originates from western Cameroon. In 2009 he met Caroline, a Dutch medical doctor in training, close to his residence. Caroline had joined a voluntary internship program in Cameroon to get medical experience in a different environment. From the moment they met, they fell in love. But they both knew that Caroline's internship would not last for ages, and that she had to return to the Netherlands three weeks after their first encounter. From the moment of her departure, they had a "transnational relationship." Through numerous telephone calls and Facebook interactions they were able to keep the "love connection" alive. However, the question was how they could live together in the physical sense. Their first two visa applications for Eugene to come to the Netherlands, in 2010 and 2011, were rejected by the Dutch embassy. Meanwhile Caroline had already traveled four times to Cameroon to spend as much time as possible with Eugene (she traveled twice in 2010 and twice in 2011).

After his visa applications were rejected, and partly to increase the chances for Eugene's residence permit in the Netherlands to be approved, they decided to marry. In 2012 they organized a marriage ceremony in Eugene's place of origin. Family and friends, from both Cameroon and the Netherlands, were present at this celebration. The married couple went to Tanzania directly after the ceremony because Caroline organized a long-term medical internship in this East African country. But again this would only be a temporary period of being together, and this time in a third country. After her Tanzanian internship, Caroline decided to move back to the Netherlands to follow the last part of her education, and Eugene had to move back to Cameroon as he had no travel documents enabling him to accompany Caroline to the Netherlands.

After their Tanzanian experience, they started Eugene's application for a Dutch residence permit. To obtain this permit, the applicant is obliged to pass a "Dutch integration test." This test can only be taken at a Dutch embassy. The fact that the Dutch embassy in Cameroon closed in 2011, made it more complicated for Eugene to take the test. Now, he had to travel to the Netherlands embassy in Cotonou, in the Republic of Benin, for the test. For this trip, he first had to obtain the right travel papers, book a flight and find a place to stay. In total, this travel to Benin cost him around 1,000 euros (US $1,100). During his stay in Cotonou, lasting from June to August, he took the test four times, all unsuccessfully. Because he had no linguistic education in his youth, he had many difficulties with the Dutch language. This turned out to be a very expensive undertaking, as a single test costs €350 (approximately $400).

After this disappointment, Eugene returned to Cameroon. The only option that was left for him was to go to the Netherlands on a tourist visa that is valid for 90 days. He went twice to the Netherlands (end of 2013 and mid-2014) and after each visit the Dutch law required him to leave the European space for at least another three months. After each visit, he complied with the European regulations and returned to Cameroon. Once back in Cameroon, Eugene traveled again to the embassy in Benin to take the integration test, and again he failed. In total, he went to Cotonou three times. From the time they started their relationship, Caroline traveled seven times to Cameroon so that they can spend as much time together as possible. During the five-year period, the couple spent at least €16,000 ($18,000) as travel costs (this excludes their stay in Tanzania). It was only early February 2015 that Caroline got the good news that Eugene had finally received a residence permit for the Netherlands. Eugene got the news a day later, as telephone links with Cameroon had been down for some time.

Whereas the example of the Gambian brothers (Dawda and Yahya) includes an irregular migration journey, Eugene and Caroline followed the strict rules of the Dutch immigration authorities. The married couple has in fact been very cautious not to violate any regulations as they believed this would reduce the chances of Eugene obtaining a residence permit in the Netherlands. On the one hand, Eugene's migration from Cameroon to the Netherlands involved moving across several borders. While Eugene wanted a long-term residence permit for the Netherlands as a regular migrant, he was unable to do so for several years. On the other hand, we notice that the processes involved various forms of mobility: Caroline's travel to Cameroon after their wedding; Eugene's journeys to and from the Netherlands and, of course, Eugene's travels to Cotonou, Benin. In a way, the spatial friction (the inability to reach the European country) *produces* new mobilities in various directions. Here, mobility cannot be considered as something entirely positive for the people experiencing it. This is fundamentally so because Eugene could not stay at the place he wanted to be. In that sense, the freedom of mobility is inherently linked to the right to stay somewhere (Sager 2008).

If we had analyzed Eugene's migration from a traditional transnational perspective, we would have depicted the interaction between Eugene and Caroline as being predominantly between "here" and "there." By following this logic, we would have paid significant attention to the diverse forms of communication and travel between the two countries. Then we would also agree on the fact that love is able to transcend national boundaries. At the same time, this transnational perspective would have easily reduced this migration process to a bi-polar phenomenon; a process in which the Dutch and Cameroonian sides matter. However, this would have wrongly reproduced the notion that migration involves a single movement from a country of origin to a certain destination: a simple process of *uprooting* and *regrounding*. The argument here is that such a narrow view on transnationalism omits so many interesting and important aspects of contemporary migration in a globalizing, yet bordering, world. It overlooks the waiting and frustration that are related to European visa regimes—a phenomenon that is shared by many Africans. It emphasizes connectedness, and bypasses feelings of isolation and disconnection. However, for the people who are on "the road to prosperity" (Akinyoade and Gewald 2015) it is exactly the ups *and* downs of their pathways that matter, as these shape their pathways to a better future so profoundly.

7.0 CONCLUSION

This chapter argues that an in-depth analysis of migration trajectories from West Africa to Europe brings valuable insights that help us to re-think the concept of transnational migration as well as a renewed enthusiasm regarding the link between migration and development. The most important shift is that this contribution moves away from the limited focus of migration and development studies that concentrates on the development effects for "the communities back home." Instead, it focuses on the normative question raised by Raghuram (2009): What about the development of the migrant?

We have seen that the barriers to people's movement result in tremendous investments, in the economic, social and humanitarian sense. These barriers are particularly high for so-called low-skilled migrants (UNDP 2009), such as Eugene. This creates another divergent factor separating the haves from the have-nots, the trans-migrant from the locally bounded persons. It is not that Eugene has been immobile in the literal sense (he has moved to various countries), but his mobility has not been based on an enhanced freedom. In this case it is important to avoid any romanticized notion of mobility (as solely positive for development) and to remember that the forced displacement of individuals and families is one of the most intense forms of livelihood destruction. But in the case of Eugene, these mobilities were actually produced by the travel restrictions he faced; these mobilities were part of a process to overcome barriers to his movement. Interestingly, Dawda's business between the Netherlands and the Gambia shows that new forms of mobile livelihoods emerge when barriers to movements are lowered.

In this context, I fundamentally support the main arguments of the 2009 UNDP Development Report that advocates for lowering the threshold to people's movement and to open up channels for international movement between the Global South and other parts of the world (UNDP 2009). If development is indeed about the expansion of people's freedom to live the lives they aspire to (Sen 1999), we need to take people's aspiration to migrate seriously. It is striking, however, that most policy initiatives in the field of migration and development are actually designed to prevent outmigration and to counter the aspiration to be mobile. Even one of the latest EU policy initiatives to manage migration—that is ironically called "mobility partnerships"—is full of conditionalities that aim at hampering the movement of people from the Global South to North. Thus, the EU's policy logic seems to be that development is indeed about people's freedom, but these freedoms are meant to flourish only in the countries and places where one is born.

NOTES

1. The EU consists of 27 member states: Belgium, France, Cyprus, Denmark, Germany, Estonia, Latvia, Finland, Greece, Bulgaria, Hungary, Ireland, Italy, Croatia, Lithuania, Luxembourg, Malta, Netherlands, Austria, Poland, Portugal, Romania, Slovenia, Czech Republic, Spain, United Kingdom, Sweden. It is important to note that the statistical overview is constructed in the period before the so-called migration crisis in Europe that started in 2015.

2. Although Cameroon is officially not part of ECOWAS, this country is considered a West African country in this paper.

3. In this paper, I do not make use of real names to protect the identity of the respondents.

REFERENCES

Adepoju, Aderanti, Ton van Naerssen, and Annelies Zoomers, eds. 2008. *International Migration and National Development in sub-Saharan Africa. Viewpoints and Policy Initiatives in the Countries of Origin*. Leiden: Brill

Adey, Peter. 2010. *Mobility*. London: Routledge.

Akinyoade, Akinyinka, and Jan-Bart Gewald, eds. 2015. *African Roads to Prosperity. People en Route to Socio-cultural and Economic Transformation*, Leiden: Brill.

Andersson, Ruben. 2014. *Illegality, Inc. Clandestine Migration and the Business of Bordering Europe*. Oakland: University of California Press.

Bakewell, Oliver. 2007. "Keeping Them in Their Place: The Ambivalent Relationship between Development and Migration in Africa" *IMI Working Papers No. 8*: International Migration Institute, University of Oxford.

Bakewell, Oliver, and Hein de Haas. 2007. "African Migrations: Continuities, Discontinuities and Recent Transformations," in *African Alternatives*, edited by Patrick Chabal, Ulf Engel and Leo de Haan, 95–118. Leiden: Brill.

Bakewell, Oliver, and Gunvor Jónsson. 2011. "Migration, Mobility and the African City." *IMI Working Paper No, 50*. Oxford University,

Bauman, Zygmunt. 1998. *Globalization. The Human Consequences*. Cambridge: Polity Press.

Belloni, Milena. 2016. "My Uncle Cannot Say "No" If I Reach Libya. Unpacking the Social Dynamics of Border-crossings Among Eritreans Heading to Europe." *Human Geography* 9: 48–56.

Brachet, Julien. 2005. "Constructions of Territoriality in the Sahara: The Transformation of Spaces of Transit." *Vienna Journal of African Studies* 5: 239–54.

Carling, Jorgen. 2002. "Migration in the Age of Involuntary Immobility: Theoretical Reflections and Cape Verdean Experiences." *Journal of Ethnic and Migration Studies* 18: 5–42.

Cresswell, Tim. 2010. "Towards a Politics of Mobility." *Environment and Planning D: Society and Space* 28: 17–31.

Ernste, Huib, Karel Martens, and Joris Schapendonk. 2012. "The Design, Experience and Justice of Mobility." *Tijdschrift voor Economische en Sociale Geografie* 103: 509–15.

Eurostat. 2014. " Immigration in the EU, 2014." Accessed February 2, 2015. http://ec.europa.eu/dgs/home-affairs/e-library/docs/infographics/immigration/migration-in-eu-infographic_en.pdf.

Faist, Thomas. 2000. *The Volume and Dynamics of International Migration and Transnational Social Spaces*. Oxford: Clarendon Press.

Faist, Thomas. 2008. "Migrants as Transnational Development Agents: An Inquiry into the Newest Round of the Migration–development Nexus." *Population, Space and Place* 14: 21–42.

Ferrer-Gallardo, Xavier, and Henk van Houtum. 2014. "The Deadly EU Border Control." *ACME: An International E-Journal for Critical Geographies* 13: 295–304.

Frontex. 2015. *Annual Risk Analysis 2014*. Accessed February 3, 2015. http://frontex.europa.eu/assets/Publications/Risk_Analysis/Annual_Risk_Analysis_2014.pdf.

Gakunzi, David. 2006. *Social Remittances of the African Diasporas in Europe. Case Studies: Netherlands and Portugal*. Migration and Co-Development–Programme. Lisbon: North-South Centre of the Council of Europe. Accessed February 4, 2015. http://www.coe.int/t/dg4/nscentre/Resources/Publications/Social_Remittances_August2006_en.pdf.

Glick Schiller, Nina, L. Basch, and C. Blanc-Szanton. 1995. "From Immigrant to Transmigrant: Theorizing Transnational Migration." *Anthropological Quarterly* 68: 48–63.

Grillo, Ralph, and Valentina Mazzucato. 2008. "Africa<> Europe: A Double Engagement." *Journal of Ethnic and Migration Studies* 34: 175–98.

Grillo, Ralph, and Bruno Riccio. 2004. "Translocal Development: Italy-Senegal." *Population , Space and Place* 10: 99–111.

de Haas, Hein. 2008. "The Myth of Invasion: The Inconvenient Realities of African migration to Europe." *Third World Quarterly* 29: 1305–22.

de Haas, Hein. 2010. "Migration and Development: A Theoretical Perspective." *International Migration Review* 44: 227–64.

INSEE. 2015. Survey Data 2011. Accessed February 2, 2015. http://www.insee.fr/fr/themes/tableau.asp?reg_id=0&ref_id=immigrespaysnais.

International Office for Migration (IOM). 2014. *Fatal Journeys. Tracking Lives Lost During Migration.* IOM: Geneva.

Jónsson, Gunvor. 2008. "Migration Aspiration and Immobility in a Malian Village." *IMI Working Papers*. Oxford: International Migration Institute.

Koser, Khalid. 2010. "Dimensions and Dynamics of Irregular Migration." *Population, Space and Place* 16: 181–93.

Lucht, Hans. 2012. *Darkness Before Daybreak. African Migrants Living on the Margins in Southern Italy Today*. Oakland: University of California Press.

Marcus, George. 1995. "Ethnography in/of the World System: The Emergence of Multi-sited Ethnography." *Annual Review of Anthropology* 24: 95–117.

Malkki, Liisa. 1992. "National Geographic: The Rooting of Peoples and the Territorialization of National Identity among Scholars and Refugees." *Cultural Anthropology* 7: 24–44.

Manuh, Takyiwaa, ed. 2005. *At Home in the World? International Migration and Development in Contemporary Ghana and West Africa.* Accra: Sub-Saharan Publishers.

Max Planck Institute. 2015. Accessed February 3, 2015. http://media.mmg.mpg.de/#

Merriman, Peter. 2014. "Rethinking Mobile Methods." *Mobilities* 9: 167–187.

Migration Policy Institute. 2015. Maps of immigrants and emigrants around the world. Accessed February 4, 2015. http://www.migrationpolicy.org/programs/data-hub/maps-immigrants-and-emigrants-around-world

Mohapatra, Sanket, and Dilip Ratha, eds. 2011. *Remittance Markets in Africa,* Washington DC: World Bank.

Mountz, Allison. 2011. "Where Asylum-seekers Wait: Feminist Counter-Topographies of Sites Between States." *Gender, Place & Culture* 18: 381–99.

Office National Statistics. 2015. Migration statistics quarterly report, November 2012. Accessed February 3, 2015. http://www.ons.gov.uk/ons/rel/migration1/migration-statistics-quarterly-report/november-2012/index.html.

Passport Index. 2015. Discover the world of passports: Where can your passport take you? Accessed February 3, 2015. https://www.passportindex.org/

Pathirage, Jagath, and Michael Collyer. 2011. "Capitalizing Social Networks: Sri Lankan Migration to Italy." *Ethnography* 12: 315–33.

Portes, Alejandro. 1999. "Conclusion: Towards a New World - The Origins and Effects of Transnational Activities." *Ethnic and Racial Studies* 22: 463–77.

Raghuram, Parvati. 2009. "Which Migration, What Development? Unsettling the Edifice of Migration and Development." *Population, Space and Place* 15: 103–17.

Sager, Tore. 2008. "Freedom as Mobility: Implications of the Distinction Between Actual and Potential Travelling," in *Spaces of Mobility: The Planning, Ethics, Engineering and Religion of Human Motion,* edited by Bergmann, S. T. Hoff and T. Sager, 243–68. London: Equinox.

Schapendonk, Joris. 2012. "Migrants' Im/mobilities on Their Way to the EU: Lost in Transit?" *Tijdschrift Voor Economische en Sociale Geografie* 103: 577–83.

Schapendonk, Joris. 2015. "What if Networks Move? Dynamic Social Networking in the Context of African Migration to Europe." *Population, Space and Place* 21: 809–19.

Schapendonk, Joris, and Lothar Smith. 2008. "Remittances Versus Migrants: Disjointed Flows in a Globalizing World," in *Tales of Development. People, Power and Space,* edited by Paul Hebinck, Sjef Slootweg and Lothar Smith, 123–34, Assen: Van Gorcum.

Schapendonk, Joris, and Griet Steel. 2014. "Following Migrant Trajectories: The Im/mobility of Sub-Saharan Africans en Route to the European Union." *Annals of the Association of American* 104: 262–70.

Sen, Amartya. 1999. *Development as Freedom.* Oxford: Oxford University Press.

Sheller, Mimi, and John Urry. 2006. "The New Mobilities Paradigm." *Environment and Planning A* 38: 207–26.

Silverman, Stephanie, and Evelyne Massa. 2012. "Why Immigration Detention is Unique." *Population, Space and Place* 18: 677–86.

Sinatti, Giulia. 2011. "Mobile Transmigrants' or 'Unsettled Returnees'? Myth of Return and Permanent Settlement Among Senegalese Migrants." *Population, Space and Place* 17: 153–66.

Smith, Lothar. 2007. *Tied to Migrants. Transnational Influences on the Economy of Accra, Ghana*. PhD. diss., Leiden: Africa Studies Centre.
Suter, Brigitte. 2012. *Tales of Transit: Sub-Saharan African Migrants' Experiences in Istanbul*. PhD. diss., Malmö: Malmö University.
United Nations Development Programme (UNDP). 2009. *Overcoming Barriers. Human Mobility and Development*, UNDP Development Report 2009, New York: UNDP.
Van der Velde, Martin, and Ton van Naerssen. 2011. "People, Borders, Trajectories: An Approach to Cross-border Mobility and Immobility in and to the European Union." *Area* 43: 218–24.
Van Reisen, Mirjam, Meron Estefanos, and Conny Rijken 2012. *Human Trafficking in the Sinai: Refugees Between Life and Death*. S. Sellars-Shrestha. Tilburg: Wolf Legal

Chapter 10

Mapping Out the Role of Labor Migrants in Ghana's Oil and Gas Economy

Sylvia Esther Gyan and Rabiu K. B. Asante

1.0 MIGRATION TO GHANA

Ghana has a long history of migration of traders and workers. The activities of labor migrants from outside Ghana and the movements of labor migrants within Ghana preceded colonization. Migrants from neighboring West African countries have moved over the years to Ghana to engage in economic activities, such as trading, mining and farming. According to Anarfi et al. (2003) from the precolonial era to the late 1960s Ghana was the destination of many migrants from neighboring West African countries. Traders from Niger, Mali and other West African countries brought ivory, kola nuts, sheep, hides of wild animals and clothes to sell at the Salaga Market in Ghana (Wolfson 1958). Aside trading, the development of gold mines and cocoa farms also attracted labor migrants to Ghana (Mabogunje 1972). Most of these labor migrants were young male adults who came to work on the cocoa farms or in the mining areas. Ghana has therefore been the destination for many migrants from other West African countries.

Largely, labor migration in Ghana (then referred to as the Gold Coast) during the colonial era was attributed to the shortage of labor in the colony. According to Anarfi et al. (2003), the shortage of labor in Ghana was because of the thriving cocoa farms and the Akans' dislike for underground work in the mining companies because of their beliefs and values. Labor migrants, both skilled and unskilled, came from West African countries such as Liberia, Sierra Leone, Burkina Faso, Togo, Ivory Coast, Mali, Benin and Nigeria (Ibid). Ghana continued to attract migrants even after its independence due to its "good" economic environment. However, by the early 1970s there was a decline in the presence and activities of labor migrants in the country because of the Aliens Compliance Order and the enactment of Ghana Business Promotion Act 334 in August 1970 (Ibid).

In the last decade, Ghana and specifically, Sekondi-Takoradi is emerging as a new destination for labor migrants following the discovery of oil and gas in the offshore areas of the Western Region of Ghana. The migration of workers to the oil and gas region in Ghana began in 2007 upon the discovery of oil and gas in commercial quantities at the Cape Three Points and has intensified since the commercial drilling of oil commenced in 2010 (Obeng-Odoom 2012, Ablo 2012, Darkwah 2013). Since 2010, there has been rapid population growth and expansion in economic activities in the Sekondi-Takoradi area. This has attracted migrants with different skills and background into various sectors, including education, construction, catering and other services. These migrants, with different skills and expertise, have moved to Sekondi-Takoradi and its environs to work. As asserted by Harris (2003), people migrate "to areas of raw material production (mines, plantations, oil), of raw material consumption, or to the places in between that connect them." Hence, the presence of oil and its noted prospects is the pull factor, attracting labor to the Sekondi-Takoradi Metropolis.

This chapter focuses on migrants working directly and indirectly in the oil and gas industry by examining both intra and international migrants in the "oil city"—Sekondi-Takoradi Metropolis. Labor migrants are discussed under two classifications; first, labor migrants working directly in the oil and gas industry (that is, on the rig) and secondly, those working in the auxiliary sector of the industry (education, catering, real estate and transport services). In this chapter, we describe the expertise and employment opportunities of migrants in Ghana's oil and gas industry by investigating the nationality or ethnicity of the people working in the industry, their specific skills/expertise, the recruitment process, the specific sectors they work in and the impact of their presence in the Sekondi-Takoradi Metropolis.

2.0 A BRIEF OVERVIEW OF SEKONDI-TAKORADI AND THE OIL AND GAS INDUSTRY

The Sekondi-Takoradi Metropolis has always been an active commercial hub from the colonial era to date. It is the most urbanized city among the 22 districts in the Western region as well as the third most urbanized city in Ghana, aside Accra and Kumasi, and serves as the administrative capital of the region with a land area of 191.7 square kilometers (Ghana Statistical Service [GSS] 2014). The metropolis is located at the south-eastern part of the Western Region. The Sekondi-Takoradi Metropolis had a population of 559,548 inhabitants in 2010, representing 23.5 percent of the region's total population (GSS 2014). The agricultural sector is a major source of employment in the Metropolis. About 75 percent of the population employed is into skilled agricultural, forestry and fishery work, 8 percent work in the service and sales sector and 5 percent are engaged as managers, professionals and technicians (GSS 2014).

Besides its importance as a major harbor city since the late 1920s, the discovery of oil offshore Cape Three Points in June 2007 has transformed the Sekondi-Takoradi Metropolis into a vibrant commercial hub in Ghana and West Africa. The discovery of oil in commercial quantities in the Western region was seen by many as a new dawn of hope for the creation of employment opportunities in the area. Since the discovery of oil in Ghana, the expectations of large sections of the Ghanaian population for the newly found resource to stimulate economic development in the Western Region have been high. Others are also optimistic that the development of the oil industry will create more employment avenues and improve the country's economy. Thus, the oil and gas industry in Ghana is attracting both skilled and unskilled labor from within and outside the country into the various sectors of the economy, including education, construction, catering and other services. Since the oil fields are in the Western Region, specifically offshore Cape Three Points, the Sekondi-Takoradi Metropolis has been the main destination point of most migrants to the Western region. These include persons who migrate to the area with the sole aim of working directly in the oil and gas industry as well as those who move in with the intention of benefiting from the emerging oil economy. Thus, migrants come to the Sekondi-Takoradi Metropolis with different skills and expertise for direct employment in the oil and gas industry or engage in other auxiliary economic activities. The result of the oil find can thus be said to have contributed to the rapid growth of the population of the Western region.

3.0 METHODOLOGICAL APPROACH

Data for the study come mainly from secondary sources. They derive from research results and publications that have a bearing on labor migration issues in Ghana's oil and gas industry in the Sekondi-Takoradi Metropolis. Because we are interested in mapping out the role of labor migrants in Sekondi-Takoradi since the commencement of the drilling of oil in commercial quantities in the Western region, we explored the types of migrants, their expertise and the type of employment they undertake in Ghana's oil and gas industry. In addition, we also examined the sectors of the oil and gas industry the migrants work in, the recruitment processes for labor migrants working directly on the oil rig as well as the impact of their presence in the development of the Sekondi-Takoradi. To achieve this, we analyze the structure of labor migrants working in Ghana's oil and gas industry in the metropolis. Migrant workers working in the oil and gas industry were assessed on the selected indicators (the nationalities of the workers in the industry, their specific skills/expertise and their experiences with the recruitment process) by looking for data from relevant publications and other documents from institutions that deal with labor migration issues. Since the oil industry does not thrive on its own, auxiliary works that have emerged in Sekondi-Takoradi because of the oil industry are also discussed and analyzed. Understanding the changes in the various sectors of the economy because of the oil and gas industry will bring to the fore how Sekondi-Takoradi Metropolis is serving as a destination for various actors in the economy and how these other actors in their bid to tap into the "oil money" are accelerating the economic growth of the metropolis. These data are analyzed based on contextual evidence obtained from Ghana.

4.0 GHANA'S LOCAL CONTENT REGULATION AND LABOR IN THE OIL AND GAS INDUSTRY

Ghana's local content policy was passed into law in 2013 and is largely aimed at Ghana progressively taking control of the work force and materials used in the oil and gas sector (Panford 2014). However, because of the unavailability of skilled Ghanaians as well as the low capacity of Ghanaians to take up both middle- and low-level jobs in the oil and gas industry, the Ghana government with the assistance of a number of oil companies, particularly Tullow Oil and the Ghana National Petroleum Corporation (GNPC) set up various training centers to increase the capacity of Ghanaians (Ablo 2012, Darkwah 2012). For example, an aspect of the legal Instrument states that:

> First consideration is given to services provided within the country and goods manufactured in the country where the goods meet the specifications of the petroleum industry as established by the Standards Authority by other internationally acceptable standards; (ii) qualified Ghanaians are given first consideration with respect to employment; and (iii) adequate provision is made for the training of Ghanaians on the job . . . (5) Where Ghanaians are not employed because of lack of expertise, the contractor, subcontractor, licensee or other allied entity shall ensure, to the satisfaction of the Commission that every reasonable effort is made to provide training to Ghanaians in that field locally or elsewhere (Ministry of Energy and Petroleum 2013, 9–15).

This legislature does not restrict access to jobs to residents of the region. Consequently, the recruitment of labor is open to all Ghanaians with the requisite expertise and training. In this regard, there are no restrictions to the citing of training facilities by the oil companies. Some of the notable training facilities are located in Tema and Accra, that is, outside the Sekondi-Takoradi Metropolis. This gives opportunity for Ghanaians residing outside the Sekondi-Takoradi Metropolis to participate in the oil and gas industry. The siting of such training institutions in other parts of the country frustrates many indigenes of the Western Region, as it limits their ability to acquire the skills needed to secure high-end jobs in the oil and gas industry. As a result, many indigenes tend to partake more in the provision of auxiliary services to persons working directly in the oil and gas industry as well as meeting the needs of residents of the Sekondi-Takoradi area. Indigenes of the region, particularly chiefs, landlords and wealthy individuals have also benefited from the boom in the property and construction sector. Generally, despite a legal framework that provides that locals benefit from the oil find in the region, the dearth of persons with specialized skills in the region makes this harder to achieve. The subsequent sections discuss the role of migrant labor in the oil industry and the various auxiliary jobs within the Sekondi-Takoradi Metropolis with particular focus on the structure of labor.

5.0 THE ROLE OF MIGRANT LABOR ON THE OIL RIG

This section focuses on tracing the country of origin as well as the ethnic composition of workers in Ghana's offshore oil sector. It further explores the factors that aid jobseekers to find jobs and the various roles migrants play on the oil rig to provide a picture of offshore employment opportunities, challenges and outcomes for Ghanaians.

Studies on the labor structure of Ghana's offshore oil sector suggest that employment on the oil rig is largely driven by factors such as education, skills, past experience, good health as well as gender (Obeng-Odoom 2014, Darkwah 2013, Ablo 2012). The types of job on the oil rig can be broadly categorized into two: the high end and low-end jobs. The high-end jobs include managerial positions, rig engineers, legal teams, medical officers, rig manager, and all other managerial positions across technical and financial operations (Panford 2014, Ablo 2012, Obeng-Odoom 2014). Because the requisite training and experience needed to take up the high-end jobs are not readily available in Ghana, expatriates, especially persons from the United States, Japan, Norway, Sweden, and until recently China, tend to occupy these positions (Ablo 2012, Panford 2014). Although expatriates dominate in this sector, a few Ghanaians can be found playing managerial roles. These are mainly individuals with a high level of education, specialized training and long years of experience (usually between 10 and 40 years).

The low-end jobs, on the other hand, consist of jobs such as roughnecks, roustabout, utility personnel (housekeeping), painters, electricians, welders, scaffolders, radio operators, motorman and chefs, among others. These jobs are often manned by people with lower educational levels and are mainly male dominated. These jobs do not require high educational attainments, instead, having some experience and being in a good physical condition often suffice. Labor migrants from other regions of Ghana other than the Western region as well as those from neighboring oil-producing African countries take up most of the low-end jobs (Ablo 2012, Darkwah 2013, Panford 2014). Similarly, most Ghanaians working on the oil rigs are in low-end jobs. Panford (2014) in evaluating the manifest of drill ships from 2010 to 2012 identified 30 to 35 percent of the personnel on board oil vessels and rigs as Ghanaians with almost all of them employed in the low-end jobs. Similarly, Ablo (2012) indicated that 62 (i.e., 37.6 percent) of the 165 personnel who were employed on a particular rig were Ghanaians. As at 2012 close to 4,000 Ghanaians have been employed on the rig (Ibid). Both Ablo (2012) and Panford (2014) pointed out that the majority of the locals were employed as either roughnecks, roustabout or deckhands, mainly positions that require little or no skills. For instance, a roughneck works with the drilling crew under the supervision of the driller and is responsible for making or breaking the connections as the drill pipe is tripped in or out of the hole (Ablo 2012). An additional duty of the roughneck is the maintenance and restoration of some of the equipment on the drill floor and rig. A roustabout, on the other hand, is a manual laborer on the rig site who packs and unpacks equipment, cleans, scrapes and paints rig components where necessary (Ibid). The job descriptions of these low-end jobs are in line with the skills and experience of the personnel required at this level. In most cases, locals who are employed as either roughnecks or roustabouts have some experience working as such in other countries in West Africa or in Saudi Arabia (Ablo 2012, Obeng-Odoom 2014, Panford 2014). Ablo (2012) further adds that the locals were often from ethnic communities along the coast of Ghana, particularly, Ga-Dangme, Fanti and Ewe, with few, if any, hailing from the middle and northern parts of the country. Almost none of the workers on the oil rig came from the Sekondi-Takoradi area.

The mode of recruitment to the oil rig contributes to the large numbers of migrants working on the rig. The oil rig companies in Ghana often do not directly recruit their personnel; instead, they outsource these services to local recruitment agencies. This is partly in compliance with Ghana's local context policy requirement. Most of the recruiting agencies are headed by people who have worked on oil rigs elsewhere. Some of them have even worked with the same rig companies in the past. Due to their past relations, trust is built in the process so they are the first to know if a rig company needs to recruit. Once they are informed, they proceed to recruit for the rigs. People who get jobs on the oil rig are mainly persons who have experience from other oil-producing countries. They get these jobs because of their networks. Returnee rig workers have formed the Rig Workers Association, with a primary purpose of pushing for Ghanaian domination in offshore employment. Aside getting jobs on the rig through one's social network and previous experience, some rig workers also assist their friends to get jobs in the sector.

In terms of recruiting labor for the rigs, it is also interesting to note how getting a job is driven by ethnicity, gender and experience (Ablo 2012, Darkwah 2013, Obeng-Odoom 2014, Panford 2014). Obtaining a job is heavily influenced by ethnic familial connections to onshore recruitment agencies. The decision by some employers to recruit particular ethnic/regional groups has resulted in the regionalization of the recruitment process, where recruiting companies employ workers only from their own ethnic background. Closely linked to this is the fact that most companies prefer to recruit people with experience in working at sea. This policy tends to favor migrants emanating from the coastal areas of Ghana and those with previous experience in working at seas, such as the Ewes, Ga-Dangmes and the Fantes who dominate the fishing industry in Ghana (Odotei 2002). These persons tend to have the experience or benefit of having worked at sea and thus stand a better chance of being employed to work on the oil rigs.

6.0 LABOR MIGRANTS IN AUXILIARY SERVICES

The oil and gas industry in Sekondi-Takoradi has not only attracted labor migrants in search of jobs on the oil rigs, but also pulled other service providers and workers with diverse interests and skills to the metropolis. The economy of Sekondi-Takoradi has boomed and attracted numerous private and public service providers to extend their services to the oil city. The oil city has witnessed a surge in educational institutions, catering services, real estate and transport services. It can be said that the oil and gas industry has affected the livelihood of the people of Western region, specifically Sekondi-Takoradi. In this section, we focus on the new service providers and their role in the economic development of Sekondi-Takoradi.

6.1 Educational Services

The service providers in the education sector play two major roles. First, the educational sector provides avenues for people to create jobs in the Sekondi-Takoradi Metropolis. Secondly, the educational sector provides training for people who want to be employed directly in the oil and gas industry. In effect, setting up a training institution and enrolling on a training program provides an avenue for migrants to move to Sekondi-Takoradi. To find employment in the oil and gas industry, one requires some skills, training and/or experience. Most people who aim at participating in the industry lack the skills and training needed, particularly those living closest to the find. Consequently, various training institutions that specialize in equipping people with the requisite skills for working in the oil and gas industry have emerged. The emergence of these institutions was largely through public-private partnership. For instance, the government of Ghana in partnership with the Jubilee Partners, the owners of the rigs, set up an enterprise development agency with the aim of enhancing the capacity of local companies to take advantage of the oil find (Ablo 2012). The Takoradi Polytechnic Jubilee Training Centre has also developed a program to train technicians for the oil and gas industry.

Aside the public institutions, several training centers with a special focus on training people to work in the oil and gas industry have also sprung up in the Sekondi-Takoradi Metropolis. The data show that Ghanaians and sometimes migrants from Nigeria and other countries own some of these training institutions. These institutions focus on improving the capacity of both skilled and unskilled labor in the industry. However, due to the cost of training and the location of these training centers, the majority of the trained workers are largely from the Tema-Accra area with only a few coming from the Western region. Further investigations show that because of the high cost of training in the sector, many indigenes are unable to utilize their services (Ablo 2012, Darkwah 2013). An analysis of the various training centers show that majority of the private training centers are off-shoots of other training centers in other countries (Obeng-Odoom 2014, Panford 2014). Consequently, apart from those who managed the publicly run training centers, most of the privately run training centers are managed by foreigners from the West African Region.

6.2 Real Estate Services

The oil and gas industry in the Western region has also attracted real estate services to the Sekondi-Takoradi Metropolis. Because most of the direct and auxiliary workers in the oil and gas industry are expatriates and migrants from neighboring African countries, the demand for accommodation in the metropolis has shot up. This has brought about the emergence of a new real estate industry with the sole aim of meeting the accommodation needs of the migrant workers. The expatriates are the main targets of the emerging real estate industry. The industry has taken on a new form, whereby wealthy individuals collaborate with persons from the property-owning class, particularly the local chiefs and foreign investors mainly from Western Europe to acquire lands and build houses or apartments for rent or sale to expatriates and wealthy individuals. The increasing demand for land and investments in the metropolis has resulted in an increase in the prices of property in general and rent in particular. Commenting on this phenomenon, Obeng-Odoom (2014, 101) reiterates CHF International's 2010 annual report that:

> Rents range from US$1,000 to US$4,000, depending on the types of accommodation in the village, in a city where the median household income is $4.91 per day and most of the households (74%) earn between $60 and $150 per month.

Labor migrants in the oil and gas industry have made the real estate sector more lucrative because of the increasing demand for rented accommodation, office space and housing for staff or workers in the industry. These developments have resulted in a high rent for traditional housing and a general increase in the cost of living in the Sekondi-Takoradi Metropolis.

6.3 Transport Services

Urban transportation services in the metropolis have also improved to meet the demands of a growing population. Unlike the real estate sector which is dominated by foreigners, the transportation sector has witnessed an increased participation by local residents. Indeed, the sector is dominated by indigenes. More commercial vehicles are running on the streets of Sekondi-Takoradi providing transportation services to the numerous labor migrants working in various sectors of the economy. The financial institutions are providing support in the form of car loans to transport owners to expand their businesses and cash in on the vibrant local economy.

7.0 THE OIL AND GAS INDUSTRY AND LABOR MIGRANTS IN THE SEKONDI-TAKORADI METROPOLIS

The emergence of the oil and gas industry and the accompanying migration of labor to the Sekondi-Takoradi Metropolis have both positive and negative aspects. Some of the benefits include an expansion in job creation in the metropolis and improved standard of living for families with members working on the oil rig. According to Obeng-Odoom (2014), employees on the rig indicated an improvement in their financial situation.

On the other hand, some of the negative impacts include a lack of job security for workers in the oil and gas sector. Workers in low-end jobs are laid-off easily as there is no job security for low-end workers on the oil rig. This has been attributed to the fact that Ghana has no employment policy and salary structure for the offshore sector. No law regulates salaries paid to low-end workers on the oil rig, thus, workers are left at the dictates of their employers and the recruiting agencies. Generally, both the well-educated and the not so educated workers are casualized and experience poor labor conditions and rights at different levels.

There is also the issue of growing unemployment of indigenes in the Sekondi-Takoradi Metropolis. Darkwah (2013) asserts that young men and women living in communities near the oil reserves remain unemployed due to the lack of appropriate policies and the non-enforcement of the local content act. Migrants from the larger cities such as Accra and Tema are benefiting more in terms of employment opportunities on the oil rig. As noted earlier, the nature of the employment requires some training and medical screening, which is usually undertaken in Accra.

The injection of capital into the local economy of Sekondi-Takoradi has also seen an increase in the involvement of migrants in the nightlife in the twin-city. According to Darkwah (2010), the influx of foreign workers who are often paid large sums of money as expatriates makes commercial sex work potentially lucrative in such communities. Some migrants are also working as sex workers (Turner and Brownhill 2005). In Obeng-Odoom's (2014) *Vienna City and Migrants*, it was established that with the production of oil in large quantities comes an influx of sex workers into the Sekondi-Takoradi township. The town has seen a heavy investment in places noted for nightlife activities with some likely to rival entertainment centers in the West. Some of the notable places for sex work in the twin-city include Vienna City, Old Zenith Area and Paradise. The sex work is largely dominated by indigenes and nationals from the ECOWAS region, specifically, Nigeria, Benin, Cote d'Ivoire, Liberia, Togo, and other Ghanaians.

8.0 CONCLUSION

The study has outlined the role of labor migrants in Ghana's offshore oil and gas industry, specifically on the rig, as well as labor migrants in the provision of auxiliary services in the Sekondi-Takoradi Metropolis. We examined the skills and expertise that labor migrants bring to the oil industry, the process of getting employment on the rig as well as the impact of their employment on the oil and gas industry in Ghana. In addition, the role of other labor migrants providing auxiliary services onshore in Sekondi-Takoradi was also mapped out. The study revealed that there were two groups of labor migrants working on the rig. One group is made up of mostly expatriates and a few Ghanaians working in high-end jobs and the other group consists of Ghanaians from regions other than the Western Region working in low-end jobs on the rig. Most of the workers in the low-end jobs were Ghanaian migrants and were entangled in a web of improving their living conditions and job insecurity. To ensure job security for labor migrants in the low-end jobs, it is important for the duty bearers to come out with clear policies outlining rules and regulations governing work on the oil rigs. On the other hand, auxiliary service providers have become indispensable in the economy of Sekondi-Takoradi.

Their services such as in the real estate sector, the transport and educational services are providing jobs for the numerous migrants trooping to the Sekondi-Takoradi Metropolis. Furthermore, these auxiliary services are providing the training and skills needed by people to secure jobs on the rigs. Overall, labor migrants, whether from other regions in Ghana, West Africa, Europe, Japan, United States or China have a role to play in the emerging oil industry until Ghanaians have acquired the requisite training and skills needed to secure work on the rig and also invest in the provision of auxiliary services in Sekondi-Takoradi.

REFERENCES

Ablo, Austin D. 2012. *Manning the Rigs: A Study of Offshore Employment in Ghana's Oil Industry* MPhil thes., University of Bergen.

Anarfi, John K, Stephen Kwankye, Ofosu-Mensah Ababio, and Richmond Tiemoko. 2003. *Migration from and to Ghana: A Background Paper*.

Darkwah, Akosua. 2010. *The Impact of Oil and Gas Discovery and Exploration on Communities with Emphasis on Women*. Accessed May 15, 2015. *http://www.grap.org/docs/oil_and_gas/netright-akosua_darkwah-2010.pdf*

Darkwah, Akosua K. 2013. "Keeping Hope Alive: An Analysis of Training Opportunities for Ghanaian Youth in the Emerging Oil and Gas Industry". *International Development Planning Review* 35 (2): 119–134.

Ghana Statistical Service (GSS). 2014. *2010 Population and Housing Census of Ghana: District Analytical Report – Sekondi Takoradi Metropolitan Area*. Accra: Ghana.

Harris, Nigel. 2003. "Migration of Labour: Constructing Transitional Arrangements". *Economic and Political Weekly* 38 (42): 4464–4470.

Mabogunje, Akinlawon L. 1972. *Regional Mobility and Research Development in West Africa*. Montreal and London: Queen's University Press.

Ministry of Energy and Petroleum. 2013. *Petroleum (Local Content and Local Participation) Regulation, L.I. 2204*. Accra: Ghana

Obeng-Odoom, Franklin. 2012. "Problematising the Resource Curse Thesis." *Development and Society* 41 (1): 1–29.

Obeng-Odoom, Franklin. 2014. *Oiling the Urban Economy: Land, Labour, Capital, and the State in Sekondi-Takoradi, Ghana*. New York: Routledge.

Obeng-Odoom, Franklin. 2014b. "Oil, sex and temporary migration: The case of Vienna City, Sekondi-Takoradi, Ghana". *The Extractive Industries and Society* 1 (1): 69–74.

Odotei, Irene K. 2002. *The Artisanal Marine Fishing Industry: A Historical Overview*. Institute of African studies, University of Ghana, Legon.

Panford, Kwamina. 2014. "The Academy and the Successful Management of Ghana's Petroleum Resources." *Africa Today* 61 (2): 79–107.

Turner, Terisa E, and Leigh S.Brownhill. 2005. "The Curse of Nakedness: Nigerian Women in the Oil War," in *Feminist Politics, Activism and Vision: Local and Global Challenges*, edited by Luciana Ricciutelli, Angela Miles and Margaret H. McFadden, 69–191. London: Zed Books.

Wolfson, Freda. 1958. *Peasants of Ghana*. London: Oxford University Press.

Index

Aliens Compliance Order (Ghana), 184
asylum seekers, 167–68

brain circulation, 107–9, 119
brain drain/gain, 23, 30, 84, 107–9, 119
brain waste, 107

colonial authorities (government), 131–32, 134, 137–39
Cameroon, 57–58, 60–65
Cameroonian associations, 57, 60–61
chain migration, 76
Chiefs (traditional leaders), 77, 79, 81, 84
Children left behind, 90–91, 93–97, 99–100, 102–3
climate change/variability, 147–49, 157
cognition theory, 149
colonial and precolonial migration, 2, 3
colonial Ghana, 125–27, 132
Common Market for Eastern and Southern Africa (COMESA), 4, 26, 110

destitution, 126, 128–30, 132, 134–37, 140–41
development chiefs, 81
diaspora, 28, 49–50, 70–109, 119–120

East African Community (EAC), 110
emigration of skilled labor, 107, 112, 119

family labor, 153
female migration, 6–7, 92, 152, 154–55
forced migration, 72, 147
forest-transition zone, 147, 155, 158–59, 161–62

Ghanaian migrants in the United Kingdom, 82
globalization, 69, 89, 120
Gold Coast colony, 126–28, 130–32, 135, 137, 140

highly-skilled professionals, 107–8, 111–12, 119–120
hired labor, 153
hometown associations, 42, 69, 70–83
human trafficking, 16–17, 111, 129, 132, 171

Intergovernmental Authority for Development (IGAD), 110
international (transnational) migration, 57, 69, 73–74, 89, 94, 165, 178, 183
International Monetary Fund (IMF), 30, 84, 107
International Organization for Migration (IOM), 110–111
intra-African migration, 6–10, 126
investments, 110, 116–17, 119–120

involuntary migration, 134, 166
irregular migration, 72, 74, 94, 168, 177

Kassena-Nankana Development League (KNDL), 70, 74, 77–78, 81, 83
Kenya, 119
Kwahuman association, 70, 7 4, 77, 79, 83

labor migration/mobility, 147, 154
labor migrants, 89, 147–48, 152, 158, 183–84, 192–196, 188–89
livelihood strategy, 148–49, 153, 159
local content policy/act, 185, 192
long-distance migration, 125

migrant and non-migrant parents, 90, 94–98, 100, 103
migrant associations, 25, 58, 72
migrant children, 93–94
migrant households, 89, 93, 96, 97, 99, 102
migrants in Germany, 57–60, 62
migrants in The Netherlands, 43–51
migration and development nexus, 18–20, 60, 64, 100, 102, 166, 169–70, 174, 178
migration policies, 28, 90

National Democratic Congress (NDC), 30, 43, 45–51
network theory, 73–74
new economics of labor theory, 149
New Patriotic Party (NPP), 30, 43, 45–51, 72
Nigerians, 126–31

Organization of Economic Cooperation and Development (OECD), 4, 89, 107
oil and gas industry (Ghana), 183–93
out of Africa migration, 10–14

permanent migration, 147, 149, 152, 154, 157–160
parental migration, 92, 94, 99

refugees, 17–18, 28, 167, 178
remittances, 20–23, 29–30, 51, 60–61, 64, 70, 82, 84, 94–95, 108–9, 110, 116–17, 119–20, 165, 169, 175
repatriation of destitute Nigerians, 129, 134–38
return migration, 110, 119
return visits, 110

seasonal migration, 147–48, 153–54, 159–61
Sen, Amartya, 73–74, 170, 178
social capital, 73, 107, 109
social exclusion theory, 130, 140
social vulnerability theory, 129–30
single father family, 91–92
single mother family, 91–92
skilled migrants, 107, 111
skilled and unskilled labor, 185
stranger communities, 125–26

theory of marginalization, see social exclusion theory
trans-border migration, 126
transnational activities, 45–51, 109, 110, 119
transnational marriage/relationship, 175–76
transnational social space, 76, 172
trust, 81–84
transnationalism, 30, 41–46, 57–59, 109, 165–66, 169, 174, 177

undesirable immigrants, 125–26
UNICEF, 93

voluntary migration, 72, 147

World Bank, 30, 84, 107

Yoruba traders, 125, 128

About the Contributors

Theophilus Kwabena Abutima is currently a PhD candidate at the Centre for Migration Studies, University of Ghana, Legon. He holds a BA degree in Social work and an MPhil degree in Migration Studies from the University of Ghana. His research interests are in migration, family, livelihood, education, and child welfare. He has research experience in migration studies as well as other disciplines in the social sciences. He also teaches at the Centre for Gender Studies and Advocacy and is involved in research projects at the Centre for Migration Studies, University of Ghana, Legon.

Rabiu K. B. Asante is a lecturer with the Department of Sociology at the University of Ghana. He received his PhD in Sociology from the University of Ghana in 2014. He is currently examining the role of smartphones in conducting fieldwork and enhancing research reliability and validity. His research interest spans across the field of technology and society.

Sylvia Esther Gyan is a lecturer at the Department of Sociology, University of Ghana where she obtained her PhD in Sociology. Gyan's research interest focuses on the vulnerable in society, specifically women and children. She has a research proposal exploring the effects of the oil and gas industry on the social structure of the Western region, Ghana. Her areas of teaching include Culture and Development, Culture and Reproductive health, and Social Research Methods.

Danielle Minteu Kadje has a BA degree in Law and Political Science from the University of Yaounde 2, Cameroon and a PhD degree in Political Sciences from the University of Bordeaux, France. She has been a fellow of GARNET, at the Kassel University in Germany. Parallel to her appointment as the Dean of the Faculty of Law and Political Science of the Bertoua Catholic University in Cameroon, she was serving as an associate lecturer at the University of Yaounde 2 and the Catholic University of Central Africa. She has written extensively on Migration, Development, and Security issues.

Leander Kandilige holds a DPhil in Migration Studies from the University of Oxford. He also has an MSt in Forced Migration (University of Oxford); MA in International Affairs (University of Ghana); Postgraduate Certificate in Managing Voluntary Organizations (University of Southampton), and BA in Political Science and Philosophy (University of Ghana). He has published several book chapters and journal articles. His areas of academic research include Global South-North migratory movements; migration, development and population dynamics; migration, globalization, and development; labor migrations in Africa; and immigrant transnationalism and conceptualizations of the state.

Justice Richard Kwabena Owusu Kyei holds a BA degree in Theology from the Holy Cross Pontifical University, Rome and an MA degree in Immigration, Migration and Social Transformation from Ca Foscari University, Venice. He also holds a second MA degree in Economy and Society from Lancaster University, United Kingdom. Currently, he is a PhD candidate at the Institute of Philosophy and Sociology of the Polish Academy of Sciences, Warsaw. His PhD dissertation investigates the religiosity of second-generation Ghanaians and African Christian churches in Amsterdam. He has published in peer-reviewed journals on religiosity and sociocultural integration of second generations and transnational religious and political practices of West African immigrants in Europe.

Jane Mwangi holds a PhD in Migration Studies from the University of Ghana (2013). She also has two master's degrees; one in Economic Policy Management (EPM) from the University of Ghana (2006), and the other in International Studies from the University of Nairobi (2000). She also has a BA Anthropology degree from the University of Nairobi (1997). Jane is the founder and director of Diaspora Interlink, an organization that focuses on migration and diaspora issues in Africa. She was a visiting scholar at the African Population and Health Research Center (July 2015–May 2016) and a lecturer at the University of Ghana (2007 to 2014). Her research interest is migration and diaspora issues.

Peter Bilson Obour holds an MPhil in Environmental Science from the University of Complutense, Madrid and an MSc in Agro-Environmental Management from Aarhus University. He is currently a PhD Candidate in the

Department of Agroecology, Aarhus University. His research areas are soil workability and fragmentation, soil compaction, soil structural evaluation and management, environmental change, and impacts of development-induced projects on population and environment.

Omon Merry Osiki teaches international history in the Department of History and Strategic Studies of the University of Lagos. He holds a BA in History (Lagos), MSc in International Relations and Political Science (Benin), PhD in Specialized History (Nanjing, China), and PhD in History and Strategic Studies (Lagos). His area of research includes International Relations, Social History, and Gender Studies. He has published widely in both local and international journals.

Kwadwo Owusu is a senior lecturer at the Department of Geography and Resource Development, University of Ghana, Legon. He holds an MSc and a PhD degree in Geography from the University of Florida, Gainesville. His research interests are in the areas of climatology, climate change, and variability impacts on agriculture and climate change adaptation. He is currently the coordinator of the University of Ghana's Graduate program in Climate Change and Sustainable Development.

Joris Schapendonk is assistant professor at the Department of Geography, Environment and Spatial Planning at Radboud University Nijmegen (the Netherlands). His current research is on sub-Saharan African migration and mobility, the border politics of the European Union, and the geography of grassroots welcoming acts toward undocumented migrants. He has been published in journals including *Annals of the Association of American Geographers* (2014), *Migration Studies* (2015), and *Population, Space and Place* (2015). His current research project follows the intra-EU im/mobility of African migrants across time and space.

Mary Boatemaa Setrana is a lecturer at the Centre for Migration Studies, University of Ghana, Legon. She holds a PhD in Migration Studies from the University of Ghana, Legon. Her research interest includes transnational migration and diaspora; migration, social change and development; migration and gender, return migration, and reintegration of international migrants into sub-Saharan Africa. She has published in both local and international journals.

Joseph Kofi Teye is a senior lecturer at the Department of Geography and Resource Development, and the coordinator of Postgraduate Studies at the Centre for Migration Studies, both of the University of Ghana. He holds a

PhD in Human Geography from the University of Leeds and an MPhil in Social Change from the Norwegian University of Science and Technology. His current research interests include environmental change and migration, reproductive health of migrants, natural resource policy analysis, and poverty alleviation programs.

Steve Tonah is currently professor at the Department of Sociology, University of Ghana, Legon. He obtained a Dip. Ed. and BA in Economics and Sociology from the University of Cape Coast, Ghana, and a PhD degree from the University of Bielefeld, Germany. Between 1993 and 1998 he was a research coordinator of the Christian Council of Ghana and managed the Ecumenical Church Loan Fund (Ghana ECLOF). Tonah has published over 100 journal articles, book chapters, and workshop/consultancy reports. His main book publications include *The Development of Agropastoral Households in Northern Ghana* (1993); *Fulani in Ghana* (2006); *Ethnicity, Conflicts and Consensus in Ghana* (2007); *Contemporary Social Problems in Ghana* (2009), and *The Management of Chieftaincy and Ethnic Conflicts in Ghana* (2016).

www.ingramcontent.com/pod-product-compliance
Ingram Content Group UK Ltd.
Pitfield, Milton Keynes, MK11 3LW, UK
UKHW012039150926
475560UK00001B/95

9 781498 516839